Grampa's Log House
by Gordon Beer 1949
First US house of Ann & Charles Dowell

Bible Christian Chapels of the Canadian Conference

by
Sherrell Branton Leetooze

Lynn Michael-John Associates

Bible Christian Chapels of the Canadian Conference

The History of the chapels and circuits in North America.

by
Sherrell Branton Leetooze

Acknowledgements:
    So many people helped to make this leg of **The Bible Christian
Project** possible. Throughout the text credit is given to those people and
organizations who assisted. Without their help this book would not have
been possible.

Frontispiece: Grampa's Log Cabin, from a painting by Gordon Beer, in
the family collection of Sherry Lynn Gertz, Detroit.

Library and Archives Canada Cataloguing in Publication Data:

Leetooze, Sherrell Branton, 1946 -
Bible Christian Chapels of the Canadian Conference/ by
Sherrell Branton Leetooze

Includes Bibliographical references
ISBN   **0-9737330-1-2**

1. Church buildings – Ontario – History – 19th Century
2. Church buildings – Lake States – History – 19th Century
3. Bible Christian Church – History
I. Title

BX6510.B55L44 2005 246'.95'0971309041 C2005-902179-9

Published by:
Lynn Michael-John Associates,
80 Roser Cres.,
Bowmanville, Ontario, Canada
L1C 3N9

Printed by:
Mothersill Printing (1988) Inc.,
182 Wellington St.,
Bowmanville, Ontario, Canada
L1C 1W3

Contents

The Built Heritage of the Bible Christians

The many small chapels that dotted the countryside, primarily in Devon and Cornwall, saw their congregations leaving for new homes in Canada, the United States, Australia and New Zealand. With each successive decade, 1840's, 1850's, 1860's, the remaining congregations in most of these chapels found it extremely difficult to support their chosen faith. Some closed, some struggled for years before union with the Methodists finally eased their financial burdens.

We leave these struggling congregations and take a look at the new homes and lives of those who left. They had come from primarily agricultural areas such as Bradworthy, in north Devon, and Morwenstow in North Cornwall, and most of the parishes along the Tamar River that separates the County and the Duchy. Among their number were a few miners. The people who practiced these occupations were hard pressed to feed their families and for them there were few options open - emigration was the one most people chose.

But they did not leave their chapels behind. As soon as they were established in their new homes they built new chapels and the Bible Christians flourished in these far away places. This was due in no small part to the efforts of the Missionaries sent out by the English conference, to 'gather in the lost sheep' as one missionary called it.

As Frances Metherall at Prince Edward Island, and John Hicks Eynon in Ontario developed their new congregations, they had from them promises to build a chapel within a certain time. Not coercion! Here is an example of the reception awaiting them most often, as they came across desolate cabins in the bush.....

Mrs Smith had been sitting by the window of her cabin, looking at her 4 children, all born in Canada, playing on the floor. She was happy, but she missed home. She missed her friends, her family, but most of all she missed gathering for Sabbath prayer. She looked out the tiny window of the cabin, into the wall of trees that surrounded their rude home, and her memory took her back to those days in Cornwall, as people gathered from the farms for miles around to hear the Bible Christian preacher. It was nearly 10 o'clock. The preacher was late. They talked among themselves, hoping nothing had befallen him in his journey. But then over the hill he came, his broad-brimmed hat and long drab coat making his silhouette unmistakable.

Mrs. Smith wiped the tears from her eyes as she rose to go back to her tasks, but a movement among the trees made her go back to the window and look carefully. There among the pines she saw the broad-brimmed hat and drab coat that was so familiar to her.

"It's one of our parsons!!" She exclaimed as she ran to open the door, startling her children as she did so. And presently, who should step into the cabin to a tearful, happy greeting - none other than John Hicks Eynon, the missionary from England.

This comes from Mrs. Smith's obituary, as written by her son, Rev.George Smith.

Many people were so glad to see that they had not been forgotten by their church that they were eager to construct their chapels in the bush. Some donated logs, a commodity that glutted the countryside in those days! Some donated labour. Some, who could work with wood, made the interior fittings. Within Eynon's first 12 months in Canada, he had 14 promises for chapels. And they were all built!!

The first Bible Christian chapels, built between 1832 and 1845, were likely log structures and have not survived. The next building erected to replace the log structure was usually a frame chapel. These lasted the congregation about 20 years, by which time they had set aside enough money to either apply brick veneer to their chapel, or build chapel number three. Most of the surviving Bible Christian Chapels are brick, though there are a few frame ones still in use. The extant frame chapels are found mostly on Prince Edward Island, with the very few found in Ontario.

We move now through time to those brick chapels I mentioned, constructed from about 1860 onward. The people who constructed them had been in Canada for 20 years or more, many never having seen the chapel that had been built, finally, in their home parishes in Devon and Cornwall. The younger members of the congregations had been born in Canada, never having seen their ancestral homeland let alone the chapels. But, despite these things, a Bible Christian Chapel was a Bible Christian Chapel, no matter on what side of the Atlantic it was located.

Here is a photo of Lake Chapel featuring the basic, plain, *country* design, and we can built on that. It always had a plain front with a plain door. Usually, each side had 3 *Gothic style* windows with the back wall, behind the pulpit, being blank. This design was found all across Devon and Cornwall, Prince Edward Island and Ontario and can best be described as the basic "Lake Chapel" look. In Devon and Cornwall most chapels of this design were finished in stucco or exterior plaster, reinforcing the "plain living" doctrine held by the

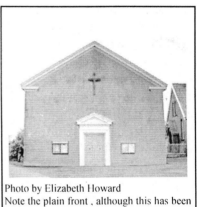

Photo by Elizabeth Howard
Note the plain front , although this has been altered since it was constructed in 1847, with the front windows removed and plastered over.

Bible Christians. In Canada the first of these were frame construction with clapboard exterior (I have a feeling this is purely a North American term). I have yet to find a Bible Christian Chapel in Canada finished with a plaster or stucco exterior.

The next most popular design was constructed in either brick or stone no matter where you find a sample. However, the front facade was just a little fancier. For those of you familiar with some of the West Country chapels, and can access photos of these, I would draw your attention to Burrington Chapel in Devon and

Bugle Chapel in Cornwall. Because this design was of a later date than the early plain chapels, we begin to see the Bible Christians straying a little, putting bold cornices on their chapels, and in many cases, the window jamb stones or bricks stood proud of the surrounding wall, as did the coynes or corner stones and bricks. These fancier chapels in Devon and Cornwall seated about 200 to 250 people, while their counterparts in Canada, especially Ontario, seated 300 to 400. Why I don't know. Bible Christian Congregations in Ontario rarely exceeded one hundred. I suppose they were hopeful in building subscription and membership. This larger, fancier design was found in the villages and prosperous small towns.

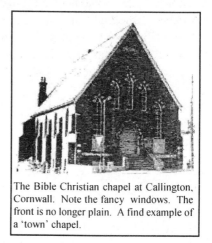

The Bible Christian chapel at Callington, Cornwall. Note the fancy windows. The front is no longer plain. A find example of a 'town' chapel.

The last style to which I would draw your attention was the final style to be used by the Bible Christians, and this was definitely a *town* chapel, and by far the most ostentatious of any previously built. The cornices, window jambs and corners were now presented in a paler brick, or a different type of stone. The roof-line was now arrayed with gables, as was becoming the custom with large dwelling places. On rare occasions these *town* chapels even had a steeple built onto it, or at least some sort of eaves decorations that suggested steeples. At this time there was a great deal of rivalry between the Bible Christians and the Methodists for their "piece of the pie", as they say today. There were only so many members to go around, and everybody wanted them. In order to entice people to come to the Bible Christian Chapel instead of the Methodist Chapel, I do believe the Bible Christians often "borrowed" from the Methodist design book, for some of the later *town* style chapels were a far cry from "the plain life" upon which James Thorne and William O'Bryan built the basis of the denomination.

But how did the people of Canada, most of whom had never seen the chapels being built in Devon and Cornwall, know to build their chapels on these designs? We can only assume that the Bible Christian Conference supplied something like *a book of designs* for local congregations to choose from. I know the trustees of many chapels sat down with local builders to work out costing on the new chapel, as has been recorded in **The Observer**, the newspaper of the Bible Christians in Canada. Did they cost out standard elevations? This was likely more or less what happened.

I was asked one time if there was a Bible Christian style. I think I would say YES! But I'm afraid I must qualify my answer. In the early days of the denomination Lake Chapel and its contemporaries reflected a Bible Christian style. However, as the

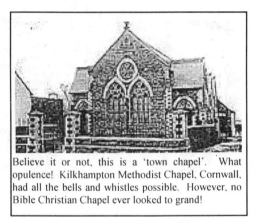

Believe it or not, this is a 'town chapel'. What opulence! Kilkhampton Methodist Chapel, Cornwall, had all the bells and whistles possible. However, no Bible Christian Chapel ever looked to grand!

years wore on and congregations (and the movement as a whole) became more affluent, this style was "improved" until it resembled more and more the Methodist model. Kilkhampton Methodist Chapel is a prime example of what I mean.

The Bible Christians barely had enough time to develop their chapels and their style before union with Methodists ended their individuality (1884 in Canada, 1907 in UK, 1925 in Australia), and so we can only guess what a present-day Bible Christian Chapel might have looked like had the denomination continued and flourished. Provided the doctrine of "plain, simple living" did not change, Lake Chapel at Shebbear, as we see it today, would likely be the design that stands the test of time.

As you learn about the chapels in Ontario and Prince Edward Island you will see that photos were found of some of them. Compare them to the chapels pictured here in 'the old country' and see the similarity of pattern.

Lake Chapel, Shebbear, c1900, before the face of the building was altered.

Hastings County

Hastings County Circuits

Hastings County was settled fairly early in the scheme of things in Ontario, but only those townships closest to the lakeshore - Tyendinaga, Thurlow and Sidney. Huntingdon, Hungerford and Rawdon came next. Later came the mining areas of Marmora, Madoc and Elzevir and these are the townships in which we are interested for the account of the Bible Christians.

Of these nine named townships only four had chapels, though there were meeting places in Rawdon Township, probably in the schoolhouse at Springbrook. There was also a meeting place at Elzevir and

From a sketch by George Ackermann c1870
The Bible Christian Chapel at Tweed, on the right side of the picture, built in 1852.

another in Lot 3, Concession 10 of Hungerford in the Orange Hall.

Hungerford:
Tweed - in the village
Bethel - Lot 8, Concession 7 - Chapman P.O.
Bethesda - Lot 10, Concession 4 - Duff's Corners

Tyendinaga:
(Part of the Hungerford Circuit)
Ebenezer - Lot 34, Concession 5
Zion - Lot 5, Concession 7 - also called Halstead's

Huntingdon:
Salem - Lot 12, Concession 6 - also known as Fuller's Chapel
Zion - Lot 7, Concession 8 - at Ivanhoe (n.w. corner of Wm. Collins' farm)

Madoc:
(part of Huntingdon Circuit)
Madoc - in the village
Ebenezer - Lot 20, Concession 1 - also known as English Chapel
Best's Chapel - Lot 19, Concession 5 - at Upper Eldorado Mine
McCoy's Chapel - was located at Joseph Hazzard's farm Lot 11, Concession 8 - moved a few miles north to unknown location
Bethel - Lot 20, Concession 9 - also known as the Allen Settlement.

It is believed that the preacher who was incumbent on this circuit in 1850 was Rev. John Williams, even though the Douglas Walkington Directory of Canadian Bible Christian Preachers says his service at Huntingdon did not begin until 1851.
Besides the Rev. Williams, assistant preachers on the circuit in 1851 included Arthur Doble and Joseph Dix.

Belleville:
A circuit of one located on Rear Street.

Hungerford Circuit

Hungerford Circuit in Hastings County had five chapels - Tweed, Bethel, Bethesda, Ebenezer and Zion.

Tweed:
Tweed Bible Christian Chapel was located at 320 Metcalfe St., W. It was constructed in 1852, and was the earliest chapel to

be built on the circuit.

Of frame construction it measured 34 feet by 40 feet, a substantial size for an early chapel, indicating a large and loyal congregation. The chapel stood on half an acre of land, and the frame parsonage was likely on the same parcel. This chapel is now a private home.

Notes from the Tweed and Area Heritage Centre say that stewards for 1879 were Robert Gordon and John Farnsworth.

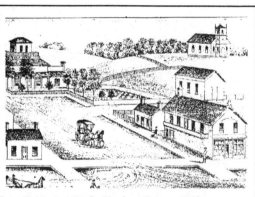

From Belden's Atlas for Hastings County, 1879. Another drawing of Tweed, showing the Bible Christian Chapel, the middle building in the row of three on the right side of the picture.

Bethel:

Located at Chapman P.O., Lot 8, Concession 7 of Hungerford Township, Bethel was a very small frame chapel, measuring only 22 feet by 25 feet. It served a rural congregation. No date has been found for it's construction.

Bethesda:

Located on Lot 10 of the 4th Concession, Bethesda was constructed in 1871. It was a frame chapel 26 feet by 30 feet located on half an acre of land in the corner of Henry Ostrum's farm, according to the 1878 Belden's Atlas of Hastings County.

Ebenezer:

Ebenezer Chapel was in the southern portion of Hastings County, in Tyendinega Township, Lot 34, Concession 5. It rivalled its town cousin, Tweed Chapel in size, being 26 feet by 36 feet, and served a broad rural congregation. Ebenezer was a frame chapel constructed in 1869 on a small lot 56 feet by 90 feet.

Zion:

Although no exact location in Tyendinega Township has been found for Zion Chapel, we do know, from the Bible Christian Property Book, that it was of frame construction, 26 feet by 30 feet, built in 1871 on half an acre of land. This could very well be Halstead's Chapel in Concession 7, Lot 5, on land given by Stephen Halstead, January 27, 1868.

Other meeting places not listed in the Bible Christian Property Book, but found in the research of Anne Rowe, include:

The Lodge Rooms in the upper level of the Orange Hall, Concession 10, Lot 3.

Elzevir (possibly a chapel) at Mr. McConkey's (though a search of the 1878 Atlas for Hastings County does not reveal a person by that name)

The 4th Line Chapel at Duff's Corners - Lot 10, Concession 4, Hungerford

When the early ministers started preaching in Hungerford, the whole of Ontario was made up of just one district - the Canada West District. In later years many more Districts would be formed as the population grew. By 1852, Hungerford was part of the Cobourg District. Ministers to serve down through the years in Hungerford Circuit were:
1850 - John Williams (with Huntingdon)
1851-53 - (with Huntingdon) Joseph Dix and Arthur Doble
1853-55 - Thomas Green and Henry Stevens [Stevens was assistant]
1856-58 - Garrance Tink Colwell
1859-60 - John Williams
1861 - Isaac Ashley

1862-64 - Jesse Whitlock
1865-66 - George Bodle and Mark Browning
1867 - Richard Thomas Courtice
1868-69 - Andrew Gordon and James Collins
1870-71 - Andrew Gordon
1872 - Henry A. Newcombe and Moses Metherall
1873 - Henry A. Newcombe and John Pooley
1874 - Henry A. Newcombe
1875 - Robert Baker
1876 - John Kinsey
1877-79 - Thomas J. Sabine
1880-81 - John M. Tredrea
1882-84 - Unknown

In 1870, William Hooper made "A Missionary Tour" as he called it, and wrote about it for the Observer. It was published in November of that year. Rev. Hooper made a tour of Hastings County and visited every meeting place and chapel along the highways and byways of that county, and this included both Hungerford and Huntingdon Circuits. Here is his report, including his comments of this area ....

"*Mr. Editor, -*

I left Cobourg by train for Belleville the morning of October 15th. Two men on board were something of a grievance to me, as well as affording me an opportunity to expound my opinions on such matters. The one, a drunk, behaved in a very unseemly manner and I was pleased when it came time for him to get off; the other, a religious man, who was quite sure his way was the only way .... A little way from the station we met Brother Gordon with a cheerful smile on his face. He conducted us to a tavern where dinner was being made ready, for which our journey had rightly prepared us ....

After dinner we started for Ebenezer, in Hungerford Mission, a distance of about 12 miles, weather very pleasant .... Went with Brother Kinsey to Huntingdon. there is no need of drawing gravel to make roads in these parts - the stones are already on the road, only need breaking, and you have an everlasting road, no fear of sinking in the mire! Found Mr. Kinsey's family well; but the old parsonage looked ready to fall on their heads; the church, too, never painted, looks but little better!

Sabbath, 16th. Preached here 10:30, good congregation, good feeling. At 2:30 Bro. Gordon came for me and drove me to Lodge Room.

17th. Back to Tweed, joined Bro. Kinsey in Elzevir. We all meet and find a very warm reception at Mr. McConkey's. Dark, wet evening but we get a good, very good meeting, notwithstanding.

18th. Off to Madoc, to the region of gold. Called on a family and had a good season in prayer. Passed a place called "Hazzards". Here we have a frame church which is not occupied and our friends talk of moving it to another place where we have a small society. It was a sad blunder to build it where it is. The Wesleyans and the Methodist Episcopal preach here, - one body is all that is needed. Took dinner at McCoy's where Brother Kinsey preaches once a month as he does in other places; little better than nothing.

Held a meeting at Best's Schoolhouse this evening. House full, meeting pretty good, collection in advance. This schoolhouse is about a half mile north of Upper Eldorado. Mr. Wm. Allen, formerly of Newcastle, is living here with his daughter and son-in-law, Mr. Scott. I went with him to spend the night. Mr. and Mrs. Scott were very kind.

19th. Ice for the first time this year. After breakfast, I started alone to Lower Eldorado to the far-famed Richardson Mine. Here I found some 4 or 5 men sinking a shaft several rods north of where the gold had been found. Had a tour of the Anglo Saxon mine and crusher about a half mile distant ....

7

I now returned from the village of about 26 frame houses to the Upper City of about seven houses, two of which are taverns, one for sale at $25.00

Brothers Kinsey and Gordon met me at Scott's where we all dined, then left this remarkable gold field for Robinson's. Pretty good meeting in a poor little schoolhouse. Glad to find that our friends are preparing to build a church.
20th. Off to Huntingdon, 16 miles through Madoc Village, which as grown to quite a town - 4 churches, 2 Methodist, 1 Presbyterian, and 1 Episcopalian; quite a good number of buildings. Preached at 3 p.m. in a schoolhouse; very good season. Collection and subscriptions $16.00 - first rate that!

21st. Quarterly meeting at 2 p.m. Our last meeting was at Calvert's a good schoolhouse lit up with two "farthing candles"; dull time, but we made the best of it. Back to old friend King's; found him and his wife near Heaven, with a bright prospect...... Huntingdon must give up a place or two so as to work the rest to advantage, then with a new parsonage and God's blessing she may prosper."
"signed. W. Hooper"

Many thanks to Marg Rosen for transcribing this article and making it available to this project. This addition certainly adds a descriptive element to the matter-of-fact material found in the Bible Christian Property Book.

Huntingdon Circuit

There were seven chapels on the Huntingdon Circuit in Hastings County - Ebenezer, Bethel, McCoy's, Best's, Madoc village, Salem and Zion. There were also some meeting places which included at the home of the Robinson's (location unknown), and probably the schoolhouse at Springbrook in Rawdon Township.

Ebenezer Chapel:
This chapel was located on Lot 20, Concession 1 of Madoc Township, Hastings County. On Belden's 1878 Atlas Map of the township, this chapel is on the corner of Charles English's farm and the small rural community that grew at this place was called English Settlement, the name sometimes given to the chapel. It commemorated Charles English who was an early settler and who gave the land for the chapel.

After meeting in the local schoolhouse and in private homes for many years, the congregation was finally in a position to build their chapel in 1873. It was a frame building, 24 feet by 34 feet on one quarter of an acre.

Bethel Chapel:
This chapel was located in Lot 20, Concession 9 of Madoc Township. It was erected in 1872 and should have appeared on the 1878 Atlas of the County. This chapel was of frame construction, 24 feet by 36 feet and was located on one half acre of land. There was a small but growing settlement here known as the Allen Settlement.

Best's Chapel:
This chapel was built at Upper Eldorado in 1857. Located in Lot 19 of the 5th Concession. It was likely a log church, seeing as it was built so early. In the report of the Canadian Conference of that year, Best's was listed as having contributed to the Mission Fund £1, 5s, 2 ½ d. It has been recorded in local history that it was closed at time of Union in 1884, however, it does not appear in the Bible Christian Property Book, which was compiled in about 1874. But then, the Bible Christian, though wonderful record keepers when it came to Baptism, marriage and burial records, did not keep a very complete property book.

Another reference to Best's Chapel, collected by Marg Rosen while researching her Hastings County roots, says the congregation at Best's met in the schoolhouse until their church was dedicated in 1881. Could it be that the old log chapel was taken down and a new chapel erected? Very possibly.

Because the chapel was no longer needed after Union, the Methodists advertised it for sale in the *Madoc Review*, September, 1885. A later edition carried the story of the Township purchasing the property

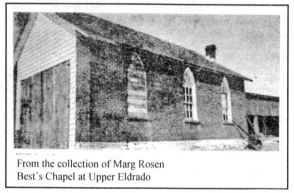

From the collection of Marg Rosen
Best's Chapel at Upper Eldrado

for use as a community hall, or some similar use ...

"At the meeting of the Township Council a proposition was made to that body by the trustees of the Methodist church at Eldorado, offering for sale to the township for use as a Hall, the Bible Christian church, lately erected in that place and for which they had no further use since the union. The price asked for the church and lot, including shed, chandeliers, lamps and stoves, etc. was $700.00, although the property cost a good deal more. The members of the council had the matter under consideration and visited the place on Monday, the 21st to inspect the property. Although the price asked was $700, the deal went through for $600, scarcely half the real value of the property."

This area was of great mining importance. The first gold discovery at Ontario was at Eldorado found in the 6th Concession. On the 1878 map we can find a number of mining companies owning land in the vicinity, including :

Toronto Mining Company L.15, Conc. 6;

the A.S. Mining Company L17, Conc. 6;

the Toledo Mining Company L.22, Conc. 7

A list of the mines in the county number 81, and a number

of these were found in Madoc Township, including the Eldorado Mine. Is it any wonder we find a very large Cornish population in this area? Many Cornish mining families settled here for there was certainly no shortage of work in times gone by.

Madoc Village:
Information on this chapel is by word of mouth. It was not listed in the Bible Christian Property Book, and I believe it may be one in the same with Ebenezer chapel, in Lot 20 of the 1st Concession, which would put it just down the road from Madoc Village. There was never a cemetery associated with either one, so it is difficult to place this one now.

McCoy's Chapel:
This chapel was also known as Hazzard's Chapel, because it had once sat on the Hazzard farm. It was probably a frame chapel, for it was moved from Hazzard's a few miles further north. No date has been given for it's construction or its subsequent move. It was torn down in 1871, and this is why it does not appear in the Bible Christian Property Book.

Records say that the original site was Lot 12, Concession 7, however the Hazzard's were elsewhere - John on Lot 21, Concession 8 and Joseph on Lot 11, Concession 8. I would suggest that the chapel used to sit on Joseph's farm, Lot 11, Conc. 8.

Salem Chapel:
This chapel was located on the 6th Concession, in Lot 12 of Huntingdon Township, at a little community called Fuller. It was sometimes called Fuller Chapel. It was the only stone church in the county, built in 1872. It wasn't very large, just 26 feet by 36 feet, and the lot it sat on was very small as well, just 45 feet by 85 feet. This chapel was constructed on land from William and Margaret Hollinger, the date of transfer being May, 1873. Many times people simply delayed transferring the land legally and differences in dates of beginning use and actual ownership will vary, sometimes by as much as five years.

Zion Chapel:
This was the first chapel to be built on this circuit. Built in 1850 it was only 24 feet by 34 feet of frame construction on 1 acre of land in the 8th Concession of Huntingdon. The parsonage for the circuit was also located here on the church lot, likely built much later. It was a brick house 24 feet by 30 feet with a frame kitchen wing.

Zion was located at the village of Ivanhoe, Concession 8, Lot 7 on land transferred from George Carscallen, March 20, 1848.

Old Fuller Schoolhouse at Huntingdon where Bible Christian services were held prior to the construction of Salem chapel.

It is believed that the preacher who was incumbent on this circuit in 1850 was Rev. John Williams, even though the Douglas Walkington Directory of Canadian Bible Christian Preachers says his service at Huntingdon did not begin until 1851.

Besides the Rev. Williams, assistant preachers on the circuit in 1851 included Arthur Doble and Joseph Dix.

Other preachers on this circuit included:

1852 - John Williams with Joseph Dix and Arthur Doble
1853 - Arthur Doble and Thomas Green
1854-55 - Thomas Green and possibly Thomas Raynor Hull who was received on trial in 1855.
1856-58 - Thomas Raynor Hull (still a probationer)
1859-60 - Garrance Tink Colwell
1861-63 - Jacob Gale
1864-66 - William Woodman

1867-68 - George Bodle
1869-71 - John Kinsey
1872 - William Kinley
1873 - George Smith
1874-75 - Richard E. Mallett
1876-79 - Robert Baker
1880-82 - George Dunkley
1883 - Thomas Brown

Belleville Circuit

The chapel on Rear St, Belleville, was the only one on the *circuit*. Some records say the chapel was located on Grier St., but the Belden's Atlas for 1878 shows the street name as Rear St.

Belleville was early settled by the French and once the American Revolution had caused so many Loyalist families to come north, the settlement was named for Capt. John Waldenmeyer who built the first mill at *Meyer's Creek*.

Meyers Mill at Meyers Creek, now known as Belleville.

Gold was discovered near Madoc in 1866 and so Belleville came to be known as the Gateway to the Golden North, the place to stop for supplies before heading out to mine for gold. And so Belleville grew, and because it was on the Grand Trunk railway line, that growth was nearly doubled.

The Bible Christian congregation at Belleville was a large one, and by the time the minister held his regular meetings and

13

classes, and visited his sick and elderly parishioners, the hours of the day were used. It was a busy place indeed once the growth from *gold fever* began.

From 1845 up until that time the congregation at Belleville met either in private homes or in rented premises, but by 1873 the congregation had enough funds to put a substantial down-payment on the construction of a chapel.

The chapel was 34 feet by 48 feet and of brick construction. It was located on one fifth acre of land on Rear St. In 1876 a parsonage was built, also a brick structure, 30 feet by 24 feet with a 16 foot by 18 foot kitchen wing. The parsonage was on a quarter acre of land, listed at town lot #15 - likely Rear St. The Bible Christian Property Book says Grier St., but no example of Grier

East Hill, Belleville, c1875

St. can be found on the 1878 Belleville plan. In the Bible Christian Property Book, the Chapel and the Parsonage were listed separately, indicating they were not on the same piece of land, but could have been adjacent. Where the chapel was located in comparison to Lot 15 is not known at this time. The preacher to oversee the building of the new chapel was Andrew Gordon.

From the 1849 Bible Christian Magazine, comes the following article describing circumstances in those early formative years on this circuit.....

"August 16th, 1848... I am almost ashamed to send the accounts for the past quarter; money is a very scarce article in this neighbourhood, and the harvest is not quite saved, so that the people have no chance of getting any money. And what has added

to our difficulties is the afflictions of Brother Ebbott and myself also. During the first twenty years of my itinerancy, I do not recollect having omitted one Sabbath appointment through affliction until three weeks ago. I was taken ill have not been able to attend my appointments since. I am better at this time, but I fear I shall not be able to take my appointments next Sabbath. Brother Ebbott has also been very unwell, so that several plans have been disappointed; and his horse has also been ill. These things took place just at the time our collections were to be made which, in part, has caused our receipts to be so low. In addition to the above, my wife took a violent cold by attending the Sabbath School Anniversary which was held in the open air last Sabbath. She is quite laid up, and I have been obliged to nurse her instead of being nursed.

September 4th .... I had purposed sending this two or three weeks ago, but not getting it finished by post time I deferred sending it till now. I remained home for four weeks, and when I left last Thursday I was in a very weak state. During the last quarter we have bought an acre of land for thirty dollars and have built a frame house, twenty four feet by eighteen, and on the fifth of November [?] we took possession of it. It will answer for a summer house, and we hope to make it fit for the winter also. I was under the absolute necessity of doing the greater part of the work with my own hands, besides disposing of my old house for lumber and for three months past have done without a horse. Notwithstanding these seeming disadvantages, I think the Lord is working and good is doing. And I understand that some of the friends are talking about building a chapel in the central part of the east of our mission.... Brother Abraham Morris, Belleville."

Ministers who served at Belleville down through the years include:
1845-47 - John Edwards
1848 - Abraham Morris, Henry Ebbott
1849 - Abraham Morris, Richard Lyle Tucker
1850 - Joseph Dix and John Williams

There is a break in the records here of 22 years ....
1872-74 - Andrew Gordon
1875-77 - Lewis W. Wickett
1878 - Alexander Richard
1879-80 - Anselm Schuster
1881-83 - Daniel Williams

During his pastorate Rev. Anselm Schuster started 'The City Mission' at Belleville. From the book, *Life and Labours of Rev. Anselm Schuster*, by Rev. David Mitchell, 1886, we find this information....

"*Mr. Schuster had long pondered the problem, 'How to reach the poor and minister to those who wee outside the church'. Looking on Belleville, he saw a city 'white unto the harvest'. He opened his mind on this subject to several brethren, and I well remember how he used to come into my study and talk over the subject of City Mission work. There was one point on which he was very clear, viz: that he should not accept any salary, but should cast himself upon the Lord, and depend upon Him to put it into the hearts of the people to send money or gifts according to his requirements.... Brother Schuster had estimated the cost and was prepared for any suffering..... Look at 'Our Mission' now, according to the last report, and see how well Brother Schuster had calculated....*"

Many thanks are extended to Gerry Boyce and the Hastings County Historical Society for furnishing the story of Brother Schuster's Mission.

Northumberland
County

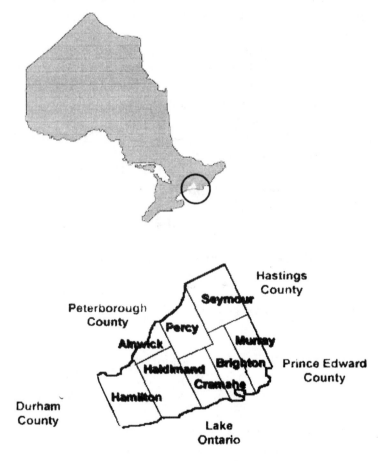

Peterborough County

Hastings County

Durham County

Prince Edward County

Lake Ontario

Seymour

Percy

Alnwick

Murray

Haldimand

Brighton

Hamilton

Cramahe

Northumberland County Circuits

Northumberland County had only two circuits, Seymour Township including Campbellford, and Hamilton Township, including Cobourg. Both were agricultural areas, however, Campbellford was known for it's mills at one time, and it was the waterways of the Trent River system which drew people to that spot in the beginning.

Of all the chapels erected in Seymour Township, Campbellford chapel was the last, even though the town was well populated for many years prior to its construction in 1870.

In Hamilton Township on the other side of the county there were four chapels, however, it seems there may have been a meeting place at Cold Springs and another at Baltimore, though records still have to be found to prove this.

Seymour Circuit aka Campbellford Circuit:
Campbellford - in the town
English Line - Lot 15, Concession 3 - later known as the Tabernacle
Zion - Lot 8, Concession 12 - at Petherick's Corners
Bethel - Lot 8, Concession 11 - often called Clark's Chapel locally
Salem - Lot 3 Concession 5
Stanwood - in the village - also known as The White Chapel

Cobourg Circuit: (Hamilton Township)
Cobourg - on James Street in the town
Precious Corners - Lot 21, Concession 4 - just north of Cobourg on
        the Rice Lake Road
Camborne - in the village - Lot 20, Concession 4
Plainville - in the village - Lot 20, Concession 7

It should be noted that Cobourg was the "home base" of John Hicks Eynon and his wife Elizabeth Dart, as they began their missionary work in Upper Canada in 1833. Many of the congregations in this township were formed in the first few years the Bible Christians were in Canada, their members being among the pioneer families of the township.

Campbellford Circuit

Campbellford Circuit was made up of seven chapels in Seymour Township, Northumberland, with only one town chapel, the rest being rural chapels.

Campbellford:
In about 1854 the Bible Christians began preaching at Campbellford. The first minister appointed to the itinerancy in this area was Arthur Doble. The congregation at Campbellford met in private homes and in rented premises until 1870 when they built their chapel. It was not a grand structure, only 27 feet by 37 feet, built of frame, but after waiting sixteen years, they were glad to have it. It was erected on a quarter acre on Doxsee St.

At the Quarterly meeting of the circuit in 1875, the members authorized the purchase of town Lot 13 in Block 11 (consisting of a quarter acre), Campbellford, which was on Rear St., and in 1876 a brick parsonage was built. This house was 24 feet by 30 feet with a 16 foot by 16 foot kitchen wing. Until this time a house had been rented for the circuit preacher and his family. The trustees for the parsonage were, at that time Joseph Temple, John Clark, Edward Stephens, and incumbent pastor, Joseph Archer.

1st Tabernacle: (there were two)
This church was found on Lot 15 of the 3rd Concession of Seymour Township. This was also called *The English Line* Chapel.

This was the first church erected on the circuit, built in 1856. It, like the others in the circuit, was of frame construction,

19

and for its day was fairly large, 30 feet by 47 feet, indicating the large rural congregation it housed each Sabbath. The 1861 census says "with seating for 150."

About a quarter acre of land was purchased on August 2nd, 1855 from Grace and Thomas Grills upon which the church was constructed the following year. In 1859, the Grills donated a further parcel of land for a cemetery making one parcel of half an acre housing both the chapel and cemetery.

The trustees for this church (in 1856) were: William Heard, George Stollery, James Finch, John Martin, Richard Sloggett, Joseph Grills, Nathan Grills, George Potts and Robert Davidson, all of Seymour.

Zion:

This chapel was built in 1869 on Lot 8 in the 12th Concession of Seymour. It was a frame chapel, 24 feet by 36 feet, built on a quarter acre of land. This quarter acre also contained a small cemetery. It is possible that this chapel was short-lived and ceased to be used when another *Zion* chapel was built at Petherick's Corners (see below) in 1878.

Bethel:

Located in Concession 11, Lot 8, this chapel was also known as Clark's Chapel. The cemetery across the road from this chapel was also known as Clark's Cemetery (C.12, L8). The land was acquired through a Crown Patent dated July 8, 1869, however the Bible Christians were using the land much earlier than that because it is recorded in the Bible Christian Land Book that the chapel, built in 1857, was 24 feet by 36 feet, and ... "was capable of holding 100 persons". It was located on the corner of what would later be Henry Dunham's farm. The cemetery was in operation before 1863, and may have been used from the time the chapel was constructed.

Trustees of the land in 1869 included:
Archibald Thompson, Neil McCulloch, John Clark, Archibald Clark, and Neil McNaughton.

Salem:

The only log church on this circuit mentioned in old records was Salem Chapel. Located on the 5th Concession in Lot 3 it was on the Turner property. It was also the tiniest chapel on the circuit, measuring only 20 feet by 24 feet, and likely started out life as a settler's first log house. The entry in the Bible Christian Property Book says this chapel was built in 1869 on a quarter acre of land.

The church disappeared many decades ago, and this land is now the site of the Northumberland Dump.

Stanwood:

Also known as *The White Church*, this chapel was located on the 13th concession in Lot 20, on a parcel of land donated by James Jacobs Very little has been recorded about this chapel, but we know there was a cemetery on the same parcel of land. Even though the chapel was taken down many years ago (probably just over 100 years ago now) the old cemetery remains to remind us where the Bible Christians of the area worshipped.

Courtesy: Retired Teachers of Ontario, from their book
School Days in Northumberland
Petherick's Corners school where Rev. Archibald Clark taught school and preached Sabbath services 1867-68

Zion:

This chapel was found at Petherick's Corners, in Lot 20 Concession 8. The land was donated by Daniel Petherick for the purpose of constructing a chapel thereon. Built in 1878, this chapel does not appear in the

21

Bible Christian Property Book

Until this chapel was built, the local people walked to the White Church at Stanwood or attended services, when they were available, in the school house. When a preacher was not available, Amos Barnum and other laymen lead the services.

Ministers to serve this circuit were:
1854 - Arthur Doble
1855-56 - Abraham Morris
1857 - Henry Stevens
1858 - Joseph Dix
1859-61 - Thomas Raynor Hull
1862-64 - George Bodle
1865-66 - John Harris
1867 - Archibald Clarke
1868-70 - Charles James Pearce
1871 - Anselm Schuster
1872-73 -Richard E. Mallett and Robert Davidson
1874 - George Smith and John Gilson
1875 - Henry Ebbott and Joshua Elliott
1876 - Joseph Archer
1877-78 - Joseph Archer and James Hoskin
1879-80 - J.G. Yelland and John Pooley
1881 - James D. Kestle and Samuel W. Muxworthy
1882 - James D. Kestle and John Oke
1883-84 - George Dunkley

Cobourg Circuit

In 1832 when John Hicks Eynon was assigned to the Canadian wilderness as a missionary, Cobourg was chosen as his destination, to which he arrived in 1833, with his wife, Elizabeth Dart.

After finding lodgings, they began their circuit work. I say *they* because Elizabeth Dart had been known across Devon and

22

Cornwall as the foremost woman preacher in the Bible Christian denomination. She preached along side her husband throughout the bush of Ontario. Their circuit was about 200 miles in length and covered Northumberland and Durham Counties. Within their first year they had the promise of 14 chapels to be built, and all 14 congregations worked diligently to make sure that happened. Eventually, the Cobourg Circuit had four charges, all in Hamilton township. Other places where Bible Christians were found (along Eynon's early trails) were separated off into other circuits.

Cobourg consisted of Cobourg Village, Camborne Village, Precious Corners, and Plainville Village.

Cobourg:

From the time of the arrival of John Hicks Eynon and his wife, there was 21 years until a chapel was built. To understand the area a little better, here is a brief history .....

The first store was opened in 1819. The first plan of subdivision was issued in 1824 consisting of about 30 lots along the beachfront. In 1825 Peter Robinson arrived with his boat loads of Irish immigrants, all of whom were camped along the beach at Cobourg until they could be taken out to the bush north of Rice Lake (they would start the future town of Peterborough). In 1828 a group of local businessmen and yeoman farmers formed a harbour company and applied to the government for permission to build a wharf, and in 1829 an act was passed to enable them to form a stock company for the purpose of raising funds to construct their harbour and wharf.

So even though the population may have been fairly sparse in those days, the people were certainly getting the village and the township at large in good order by the time John Hicks Eynon and his wife arrived to begin the Bible Christian Mission.

They made their home at Cobourg, but the location of their house has been lost to memory. Cobourg's 1st Bible Christian Chapel may have been a log building, but the first one we know

23

about today was built at the corner of James and Bond Streets in 1854. You may be wondering why it took 21 years to raise a chapel at Cobourg. It does not appear that the lack of money was the reason when we read of Harbour Companies rasing funds, and steam-ship building companies raising funds locally. However, the monied people were either Church of England, Presbyterian or Methodist. Each of these denominations being well established by the time the Eynons arrived. The citizens in those formative years were mostly Americans (United Empire Loyalists) with only a smattering of English among them.

The influx of immigrants from Great Britain did not begin until about 1832 when the lake boats were kept busy carrying thousands each year to various destinations, Cobourg and vicinity being a popular one.

It was these immigrants, many from Devon and Cornwall, to whom Eynon directed his missionary work, for it was these immigrants who had largely espoused the Bible Christian faith in their homeland.

So, in a way, it was a lack of funds on the one hand that slowed the progress toward their chapel. A settler's first duty was to his family, to build a dwelling house for them, then to clear the land and get a crop in. It was often many years before a settler family could turn its attention toward Godly matters. On the other hand, had Eynon had a few more preachers to take some of the early work in the bush, he may have had the time to put more attention toward the Cobourg congregation.

The 1854 chapel was built of brick. And for a small community it was almost cathedral-like in its proportions - 42 feet by 60 feet. It was also an expensive chapel to erect. The quarter acre of land upon which it was built cost $300 and the building itself cost $4200 to erect. In those days, a small fortune.

By 1869 the circuit had extended enough funds to build a parsonage at Cobourg on the same lot as the church. This was a brick house, 32 feet by 28 feet and cost a whopping $1500.

Camborne:

Camborne is a small village in Lot 20, Concession 4 of Hamilton Township. From an account written in August 1932 by the late Albert J. Lacey, we find that the first Bible Christian chapel at Camborne was built in 1851, though the Bible Christian Property Book says 1855. Anniversary celebrations were held to celebrate 1851, so that date seems correct. This was a frame church erected on three-eighths of an acre, the carpenters being Thomas Gage and William Hore Sr. Mr. Lacey goes on to say .....

"Previous to a church being built, services were held in the old schoolhouse, which used to stand facing the gravel road. It used to be crowded at Sunday service and was lighted by tallow candles. And before there was a schoolhouse the residents often attended services at Precious Corners in a small Bible Christian Chapel close to Joe Precious's property."

"The first church had box pews, the pew had a door the full height of the front and back and fastened with a metal button. The pulpit was octagonal, built close to the west wall, and rested on a cutaway base. The pulpit floor was three feet above the church floor and was reached by steps and entered through a swinging door. The choir enclosure was at the back, close to the church lobby and remained until about 1885....... A string of pipes up either side [of the pulpit] stretched from box stoves at the back to the chimneys near the front and rested at intervals on supports which came down to the end of the pew making anything but an ornamental interior. Coal Oil lamps hanging by cords from the ceiling completed the inside furnishing of the church...."

This frame building with clapboard exterior cost $1200 and measured 28 feet by 50 feet, a good sized country chapel! There was also a cemetery attached to this piece of property.

This church was enlarged in 1871 and the interior completely renovated. The box pews were taken out and nice pews with carved ends replaced them. The big octagonal pulpit was replaced with a modern desk. The Rev. Moses Metherall was invited to officiate at the re-opening of the church and solicit subscriptions to defray the expenses incurred, which he succeeded

25

in doing, ..." *for he was adept at begging. He told the people that if they would give liberally in support of God's cause, their hens would lay basketfuls of eggs and their cows would give slathers of milk.*"

The land for this wonderful chapel was sold to the Bible Christians by William and Esther Hoar for one shilling. On the deed of transfer the trustees for the land and future chapel were: John Cullis, George Ward, Herman McEvers, Richard Cullis, Walter McEvers, William Hill and Nicholas Cullis. Witnessing the purchase was Bible Christian minister, George Webber. The odd thing about this transaction is that it was not made until 1869, the chapel having been erected 18 years beforehand!

Precious Corners:

As we saw in the Camborne information, before that chapel was erected people came south to Precious Corners to the small chapel there. Even though no year is known for its construction, I would suggest that this chapel was built about 1845 and was possibly a log chapel, measuring 22 feet by 26 feet, just about the size of a settler's log cabin. Some old records say it was of frame construction, so it may have been put up on the big square-hewn foundation logs of the original log building.

From the pen of Albert Lacey, we also hear about Precious Corners ..... " *Mother told us that sometime before her marriage in 1849, she walked down to Precious Corners to church where there was a small Bible Christian Chapel just west of Mr. Manley's blacksmith shop ....*"

A small cemetery was also located on this quarter acre parcel, and in recent years descendants of the pioneers buried therein have gathered the crumbling stones together into a cairn to commemorate their life.

Plainville:

This was the most northerly of the chapels on the Cobourg Circuit. The small village is located in the seventh concession and the chapel on the west half of Lot 20. In 1854 a frame chapel was erected on this half acre parcel at a cost of $400. In 1874 the Bible Christians figured that parcel of land was worth $45 - not a bad rate of increase on their investment, as this parcel was sold to them for one shilling.

Like Camborne, it was many years before there was an official transfer of the property to the Bible Christian Church, taking place for Plainville Chapel 5th December, 1868, witnessed by John Hicks Eynon. The trustees for this

From the family album of John Bray
The 'gate' at the Plainville Cemetery. The Precious Corners gate is nearly identical indicating a very dedicated Bible Christian metal worker.

chapel at the time of transfer were: Samuel Williams, Thomas Doidge, James Grose, James Parkins, James Benson, Thomas Cole and George Ward. The land was sold to the Bible Christians by Peter Wellington.

The cemetery, apparently across the road, was known as the Cole Cemetery, as well as the Plainville Cemetery, mainly because of all the Cole families in the area, and the number of them who are buried there. The other families, though not with the Cole name are all closely related through marriage, so says John Bray whose ancestors were from Plainville. Whether or not Peter Wellington gave this parcel to the Bible Christians or whether it came from the Cole family is not known.

Preachers serving this circuit over the years were:
1833-39 - John Hicks Eynon
1840 - J.H. Eynon and John Edwards
1841 - J.H. Eynon and Philip James

1842 - Robert Hurley
1843-45 - J.H. Eynon and Philip James
1846-47 - Thomas Green and Abraham Morris
1848 - Robert Hurley
1849-51 - Henry Ebbott and Paul Robbins
1852-54 - John Edwards
1855-56 - John Pinch and J.H. Eynon
1857 - William Hooper and John Hooper
1858 - William Hooper and William Robert Roach
1859 - Henry Stevens and W.R. Roach
1860 - Henry Stevens and John Chapple
1861-62 - Archibald Clark and John Chapple
1863 - Andrew Gordon and John Chapple
1864 - Andrew Gordon and Henry James Nott
1865 - Cephus Barker and J.T. Sencebaugh
1866-67 - Cephus Barker
1868-69 - George Webber
1870-72 - William Hooper
1873-74 - William Jolliffe and James Pollard Rice
1875 - John Kenner and Samuel James Allen
1876 - John Kenner and John M. Tredrea
1877-78 - John Kenner and William Rollins
1879-80 - William C. Beer
1881-82 - Richard T. Courtice
1883-84 - James Joseph Rice

In 1879 the Camborne congregation withdrew from the circuit and had its own incumbent preachers who were:
1879 - James A. Dafoe
1880 - Andrew Cory Courtice
1881 - Thomas W. Blatchford
1882 - Samuel W. Muxworthy
1883 - William Coombe
1884 - Unknown.

Durham County

Durham
County

Victoria County

Fleetwood✗ ✗Franklin

✗Velverton

✗Caesarea

✗Blackstock

Cartwright Twp

Cavan Township

Manvers Township

✗ Enfield

Tyrone ✗

✗Leskard

Hope Township

✗Eden

Hampton ✗

Perrytown✗

Darlington Twp

✗Orono

✗Courtice

Bowmanville ✗

Clarke Township

✗Zion ✗anton

✗Welcome

Port Hope ✗

Ontario Cty.

Northumberland Cty.

Lake Ontario

W E

Durham County Circuits

The three 'front' townships of Durham County were settled by Loyalist families in the beginning. These townships included Darlington, Clarke and Hope. Each township had its principal town - Darlington had Bowmanville, Clarke had Newcastle and Hope had Port Hope. Each developed its own bustling harbour and became important to the early families as a place to bring their produce to be sold to the world at large.

Of the 'back' townships - Cartwright, Manvers and Cavan, these began to see serious settlement in the 1830's and within 20 years were as developed as their sister townships to the south. The principal towns included: Blackstock at Cartwright, Janetville (and later Bethany) at Manvers and Millbrook at Cavan.

From the lakeshore there were four main roads that went to the north, one in each of the 'front' townships except at Hope where there were two. At Darlington the road went up through Hampton and on to Blackstock and Caesarea in Cartwright (Caesarea being on Lake Scugog). At Clarke, the road left the harbour at Bond Head, up through Newcastle, Orono and on through Ballyduff and Janetville in Manvers and thusly on to Lindsay in Victoria County. At Hope Township we find the Rice Lake Road which ran from the harbour at Port Hope, out through many small villages, passed Rice Lake and on to Peterborough. The second road at Hope also left Port Hope, but went north through Welcome, Canton, Perrytown, Elizabethville and on to Cavan Township and Millbrook. From there it went north through Cavanville, Ida and Mount Pleasant then over toward Omemee in Victoria County.

It was along these four roads that the Bible Christians built their circuits, reaching a little to the left of the road, or the right of the road to develop congregations in the small nearby villages. The circuits were:

Port Hope:
A single chapel circuit in the town.

Welcome Circuit: (Hope Township)
Welcome - at the village
Zion - Concession 3, Lot 31
Mount Pleasant - Concession 4, Lot 22
Port Britain - on the lakeshore west of Port Hope
Elim - at Trelawney later known as Port Granby (this was actually
    in Clarke Township.
    All of these chapels were at one time part of the old
Cobourg circuit, but in 1871 these Hope chapels were formed into
the Welcome Circuit.

Perrytown Circuit: (Hope Township)
Canton - north of Welcome
Ebenezer - at Perrytown
Elizabethville - on the Ganaraska Road
Providence - on the 6th Conc. at Rice Lake Road (now Hwy 28)
Eden - Lot 27, Concession 6
Forest Union - Lot 19, Concession 5
East Zion - also known as Moon's - Lot 4, Concession 7
Osaca - Lot 34, Concession 5
Perrytown - in the village
Note: this large circuit was eventually split into two: the new
Canton Circuit taking Canton, Osaca, Moon's and Providence.

Bowmanville Circuit: (primarily Darlington Township)
Bowmanville - in the town at Division and Queen Streets.
Salem - northwest of the town on Concession 3, Lot 11
Providence - northeast of the town on Concession 3, Lot 3
Bethesda - south of Tyrone (Lot 8, Concession 6)
Tyrone - in the village (Lot 9, Concession 7)
Haydon - in the village Lot 14, Concession 8 - also known as
    Peniel
Orono - on Mill Street in the village (Clarke Township)
Leskard - in the village (Clarke Township - Lot 31, Concession 7)
    These chapels were all east of the Gravel Road (aka The

Old Scugog Road).

Hampton Circuit:
Ebenezer - south of Shortt's Corners later known as Courtice
    (named for the early settlers there)
Eldad - at the village of Solina
Hampton - in the village at Mill St. and Scugog Road.
Enfield - in the village - also known as Cardiphonia Lot 29,
    Concession 8
Rehoboth - in the village of Taunton on the townline between
    Durham Cty and Ontario Cty just north of the 5th
    Concession Road.
Providence - s.e. of Enfield - no exact location known
    These chapels were all west of the gravel road.

Port Hope Circuit

Port Hope Circuit came into being in 1866 when it was
separated from the Cobourg Circuit. This was a circuit of one
station.
        Even though the congregation at Port Hope had been
formed for many years, they did not have a place of worship of
their own. They held meetings in private homes, in the school
house and in other rented premises until 1853 when they built their
own chapel on Hagerman St. It was a brick chapel measuring 33
feet by 62 feet, and was of substantial size for a town chapel. An
advertisement in The Port Hope Guide, Saturday April 2, 1853
announced a bazaar to be held at the chapel April 8th and 9th for the
purpose of raising funds to help defray the cost of its erection.
Admission would be seven shillings, ha'penny and refreshments
the same. A rather expensive event, for those days.

But Port Hope was growing. The harbour afforded much business to develop there and mills flourished along the Ganaraska River. The Molson Brewery/Flouring Mills employed a great many people, lawyers and physicians offices lined Ward St. and manufacturing grew along the back streets. It was a town with a well-to-do population.

And the congregation of the Bible Christian chapel reflected this. By 1872 a new chapel had to be constructed, and so the old chapel was rebuilt under the guidance of Rev. Lewis Wickett, doubling its size to 66 feet by 120 feet - an impressive building indeed.

In 1875 a building lot of one eighth acre at Charles and Julia St. was purchased and in 1876 a brick parsonage was erected. This too was a substantial building, 22 feet by 30 feet with a brick kitchen wing of 16 feet by 16 feet. It fitted in nicely with the myriad of large exclusive homes of the Port Hope merchants and businessmen.

The sort of house being built in Port Hope in 1865, giving the town its aire of prosperity that came with the railroad in 1858.

Ministers who laboured at Port Hope included:

1866-67 - Henry Ebbott
1868-69 - E. Price (might be Edward Price)
1870 - Robert Hurley
1871-73 - Lewis W. Wickett
1874-75 - William H. Quance
1876-77 - James Kestle
1878-81 - William Henry Butt
1882-83 - George H. Copeland

Welcome Circuit

Welcome circuit was located north of Port Hope and consisted of six stations - Welcome, Zion, Osaca, Mount Pleasant, Port Britain and Trelawney.

Welcome:

Welcome chapel was located at the village of Welcome, once known as Guideboard, for it was at this corner that a post had been raised with arrows attached showing which way to go for the various villages in the area.

The area had been settled in about 1810 by second generation Loyalists whose parents had settled at Port Hope. The first chapel built by the congregation was in about 1848, however, the Rev. John Hicks Eynon began a congregation there as early as 1839. Records of the exact location of that first chapel seem to conflict, as two people have been sited as giving or selling the land upon which it stood. Thomas Oke is listed in one old record as having given land, as well as Samuel Naylor. Samuel

From the album of Mabel Clemence Goode
Welcome Bible Christian Chapel, c1880

Naylor donated the land where the present church stands, but Thomas Oake's land was farther south along the road. Perhaps it was on Oke land that the first chapel existed, or perhaps it was on Oke land that the parsonage was built in later years.

In 1856 the original chapel was replaced by a brick chapel, 33 feet by 48 feet, a rather modest, country chapel. It was located on the present site of one quarter acre.

In 1873 a parsonage was purchased further south along the Toronto Road, and this may indeed have been the Oke property mentioned in old records. The house was of frame construction and measured 23 feet by 36 feet.

In 1880 the chapel was replaced by a 33 foot by 54 foot brick chapel, but unfortunately it burned down nine years later. It was replace that same year, but by this time was a Methodist church, which is still in use today.

Land for the cemetery was purchased from Jeremiah Parker, Lot 11 Concession 2, about a mile south of the church. It consisted of a parcel of two acres. Before his death, Mr. Parker made arrangements that an additional five acres of land be made available to the congregation and his executors saw that this was done. The cemetery is still seven acres in size.

Zion:

Again, we see Samuel Naylor's name in connection with a Bible Christian Chapel. In 1839 he donated one quarter acre of land for the building of a church on Lot 31, Concession 3, but it seems there was a congregation of Bible Christians there before that date. From the diary of the Rev. John Hicks Eynon, who arrived in Upper Canada in 1833, we learn .... *"Early in the winter of 1833 I was invited to preach at what was called* The Log School House *in the western part of the Township of Hope. This was the commencement of the society now known as Zion. The first protracted service that I held in Canada was at the log school. At the close of the meeting it was agreed to build a chapel ... "*

That first chapel was of log or squared timber construction. Some old documents refer to it as a frame chapel. From a little booklet written for the diamond jubilee of the chapel is this ...." *In 1858 it was replaced by a brick chapel, 35 feet by 44 feet. Mr. Rowson helped to tear down the wooden church which was then converted into a private dwelling. The bricks for the new church were brought from Cobourg, two of the masons being Messrs. James Britton [from Port Hope] and Fishley. Mrs. Job Dickinson*

35

boarded the carpenters, while among those who helped to dig out the basement were Messrs. C. Crossley, R. Tabb, William Runnalls, J. Sleeman, William Tamblyn and others."

However, later on this new chapel had to be moved for they found that it was built partially onto the road allowance (there was no roadway in use at that time). There

Courtesy: Port Hope and District Historical Society
Zion Chapel and cemetery in later years.

was a cemetery on the same lot, and it too had to be moved, but there is speculation that part of the old cemetery still remains under the road. The new chapel cost £500.0.0 and was the fifth substantial brick chapel in the circuit.

In later years Zion became part of the Canton Circuit which was made up of chapels from both Welcome and Perrytown Circuits.

(The Diamond Jubilee Booklet for Zion Chapel sited above was likely written by Lucy McCullough in 1933, a copy of which was donated to the Bible Christian Project by Ed Walker of Ottawa, whose ancestors resided in the Welcome Circuit.)

Osaca:

At Osaca there was a Bible Christian Chapel. It appears on the 1861 Tremaine's map on Lot 34, Concession 5 of Hope Township, and may have been there about 20 years at that time. It does not appear in the Bible Christian Property Book, nor does it appear on Belden's 1878 map of the township.

We do know that it was still being used, at least

occasionally, because of an ad in an old newspaper announcing a Sunday School Soiree to be held there in 1876.

It was likely not taken up by the Methodists after the union of 1884 and in 1901 it was sold and moved to the Brimacombe farm in Lot 30, Concession 6.

Mount Pleasant:

Anytime the name Mount Pleasant is found you know the Cornish had something to do with it.

Mount Pleasant Chapel in Hope Township was situated on Lot 22, Conc. 4, in the south part of the lot. In 1870 this parcel was sold to James Elliott by Justin Johnston, and some old records say that the small frame chapel was constructed that year. The Bible Christian Property Book has it recorded that the chapel was erected in 1872.

The parcel in question was a quarter acre in size, and was likely sold to the Bible Christians by James Elliott who was perhaps the first settler in the area, arriving on his land about 1830.

This chapel was used by the Methodists after Union, until about 1906 when the building was taken down.

Port Britain:

Port Britain is found on the lakeshore, about 2 miles west of Port Hope. The first Bible Christian Chapel to be erected here was on the east side of the mill pond on land granted to the church by Reuben Grant in 1851, or so local history says. This is difficult to believe because Reuben Grant's land was over near Zion Chapel.

The bricks to build this chapel were made on the site during construction. These were likely not seasoned very well prior to construction, for a new brick chapel was constructed in 1869, with the old one being sold. The new chapel was located at the cross-roads in the centre of the community, on the south-west corner on land donated by someone named Crocker. It does not appear that he or she was a landowner of any size, for the name does not appear on either Tremaine's (1861) or Belden's (1878) maps. This second church lasted the community until about 1902, serving the Methodists after union.

Trelawney/Port Granby:

In the early days of settlement, Port Granby was known as Trelawney (again, very much a Cornish name). This community on the lakeshore is nestled up against the township line between Clarke Township and Hope Township, but on the Clarke side.

The chapel here, called Elim, was an early chapel and may have been one of the earliest on the circuit, and perhaps was of log construction. The next chapel which has no date attached, was frame and measured only 18 feet by 24 feet.

It was rebuilt in 1875, again in frame construction. This time the size was 24 feet by 38 feet, showing how much the population of the village had grown in the intervening years.

After union the chapel sat unused for many years, the congregation being divided between Newtonville Methodist Chapel and Wesleyville to the west. The building was moved in 1917 to Port Hope to be used as a residence, but sadly, no record of it's new address can be found.

All of these chapels were at one time part of the old Cobourg circuit, but in 1871 these Hope chapels were formed into the Welcome Circuit. Ministers who served this large rural circuit included:
1871-72 - Robert Hurley
1873-75 - R. Hall
1876-79 - William Kinley
1880-82 - Archibald Clarke
1883 - Richard T. Courtice

Perrytown Circuit

In the beginning, Perrytown Circuit was made up of only 3 chapels, Perrytown, possibly known as Ebenezer,

Elizabethville/Eden and Providence. As the number of chapels expanded the circuits of Hope Township were re-aligned and Canton Circuit was formed, taking some of Perrytown Circuit (Providence, Moon's and Osaca) and some of Welcome Circuit.

Perrytown, by this time, had expanded to include Forest Union and Mount Pleasant Chapels.

Perrytown:

This was a very early chapel in the township, built in about 1840 in the centre of the growing village. This frame chapel was fairly small, measuring only 20 feet by 24 feet. Located on the 5th Concession, in Lot 15, this small chapel served its

From the family album of John Bray
The Bible Christian cemetery at Perrytown - the stones have been gathered together into a commemorative grouping.

congregation for 35 years. James Rutledge gave the land in 1843, but it was in use by the denomination before that time.

In 1875 a new brick chapel was erected on the same one acre parcel. It was nearly twice the size, measuring 30 feet by 40 feet - an indication of the growth of the congregation.

Providence Chapel:(also known as Brown's)

Providence Chapel and cemetery were located at the corner of Concession Road 6 and what is now Highway 28, in Lot 1. The land was given to the congregation by Anthony Brown in 1843, but it was in use by the Bible Christians long before that. The earliest stone in the cemetery is dated 1837. The cemetery sits atop a small knoll and surveys the surrounding countryside. The chapel was

39

constructed in 1841, a frame building measuring 25 feet by 30 feet. The congregation was drawn from two counties - Durham and Northumberland - the people of the immediate area of Hope Township in Durham and Hamilton Township in Northumberland.

This is a very small cemetery as it had to share only half an acre with the chapel. How long this chapel stood is unknown, but it may have been there only until about 1850. At this time it seems that it was replaced by another frame

From the author's collection
Although Providence Chapel (aka Brown's) has been long gone from the site, the cemetery remains to remind us of our Bible Christian Heritage.

chapel which served the congregation until after union when it was taken down in 1890.

Though small, the cemetery is still in use and cared for by a board of directors.

Elizabethville:

It is sometimes difficult to now place chapels mentioned in old records. Terms of reference have changed. So it is with the chapel listed in the Bible Christian Property Book.

The church at Elizabethville was always a Wesleyan Chapel, so it is likely that this refers to Eden Chapel which was located directly south of the village of Elizabethville, at the far end of the concession in the same lot. As well, Eden chapel is not listed in the Property Book, so this seems to be a fair conclusion.

The land for Eden Chapel was given by John Elliott to Ethan Allen on March 21, 1851. Mr. Allen was likely a prominent

40

member of the congregation and a trustee for any property they were likely to acquire. It can be assumed that the chapel was erected shortly after this, for it appears on Tremaine's 1861 map of the township

The Bible Christian Property book says the date of construction for a brick chapel was 1872, but this may be a replacement for what was likely a frame chapel, or a log chapel seeing as that first chapel was fairly early. The dimensions of the brick chapel were 28 feet by 36 feet, just about right for the time period.

In his book, '*The History of the Township of Hope*', Harold Reeve recounts this tale from Eden Chapel at the time when the chapel had undergone redecorating (no date given) or it could have been when the brick chapel was erected.

"*The re-opening day was hot, the varnish had not set hard enough, the clothes stick, the clothes gave - disaster!!*".

Moon's Chapel: (also known as East Zion)

Moon's Chapel took its name from the family who gave the land upon which the chapel was built. It was given the name Moon's so as to distinguish it from Zion Chapel elsewhere in the township. Located in Lot 4 of the 7th Concession it was not likely of an early construction. However, it is shown on Tremaine's 1861 map. It is not listed as part of the Bible Christian holdings in their property book , but was likely in use right up to Union in 1884. After that time it was used for community meetings and Sunday School only. The building was finally sold at auction in 1930. Though not in constant use, the cemetery continued to be used up until about 1923.

Forest Union Chapel:

This chapel was not listed in the Bible Christian Property Book, but was located at Lot 19, Concession 5. It was taken down in the 1920's and was the last of the township's log structures. It appears that this was one of the last of the early churches to be built, and why it was constructed of logs is a mystery, for it seems to have been built at a time when frame and brick churches were in vogue. It does not appear on either the 1861 or the 1878 map, so it must be assumed that it was built after 1878. It is also possible that the land for the chapel was donated by Robert Finney, for he owned the east portion in the south half of Lot 19, and he was also one of the lay preachers that filled the pulpit at this chapel.

It has been recorded in many places that Forest Union Chapel served its community for over 50 years, however, it was probably more like 40 years.

Canton Chapel:

It is likely that this congregation did not start out as Bible Christian, but as a congregation of people without a minister, who gathered together to pray and worship. According to the Port Hope Guide, March 20, 1877, Hope Chapel, as it was called, was built in response to the needs of the local congregation who had been

From, *The History of the Township of Hope*, by Harold Reeve. Hope Chapel at Canton, north of Port Hope, c. 1930

meeting in an unfinished house in Lot 11, Concession 4, since about 1819. At this time the congregation was not attached to any religion, they simply met to read their bibles, be reminded of the virtuous life they ought to lead, and this was presided over by a lay preacher - most likely Methodist in his leanings. It would not be

42

long, however before William Peters came among them and they were connected with the Bible Christians. The land for the chapel was donated by a very early settler to Hope Township, James Hawkins, and the chapel was most likely built shortly after the arrival of John Hicks Eynon in 1833. By 1843, Mr. Hawkins had also given land for a cemetery directly across the road from the chapel.

In 1876 a beautiful new church was built to replace Hope Chapel, and the chapel was then used as a church hall for all social events, as well as by the Orange Lodge, the sons of England, and gave a place for the Canton band to practice. In 1927, the Right Honourable Vincent Massey, then a resident of the village, donated $5000.[00] for the upgrading of the hall, and Mrs. Massey donated the window curtains.

This chapel is still in use today.

Ministers who served the Perrytown Circuit included:
Prior to 1857 - J.H. Eynon and likely people like Paul Robins, Robert Hurley and other early itinerant preachers.
1857 - J. Hughes
1858 - J. Langdon
1859 - A Morris
1860 - Arthur Doble
1861 - a supply minister when available
1862 - John Brown Tapp
1863 - Henry Ham
1864 - John Brown Tapp
1865-67 - Andrew Gordon
1868 - Jacob Gale
1869-70 - J. Archer
1871-73 - Roger Allen
1874 - James Collins
1875-76 - Moses Metherall
1877 - John Tredrea
1878-79 - George Bodle
1880-81 - George Smith

1882 - T.R. Hull
1883 - S.J. Thompson

Bowmanville Circuit

Bowmanville Circuit, located in Darlington Township and Clarke Township in the former County of Durham, had eight or nine chapels and a number of preaching places. This was the centre of Bible Christian activity in Ontario, despite the fact that the Missionary, John Hicks Eynon, had made his headquarters at Cobourg.

It was at Darlington and Clarke where the most interest in the Bible Christian movement was shown. The majority of the population were from Devon and Cornwall and many of them had been Bible Christians back in England before they had emigrated. Conference was held here in 1865 and again in 1870, and it was from Bowmanville that *The Observer* was published from 1865 until union in 1884.

Bowmanville:

The chapel at Bowmanville was the largest on the circuit, being 45 feet by 75 feet. The entry in the Bible Christian Property Book says this brick chapel was built in 1857, and it is the only one listed. It can safely be assumed that it replaced an earlier chapel, possibly frame or perhaps even an old log chapel.

This brick chapel was erected on ½ acre at the corner of Queen and Division Sts. A parsonage was built on the same lot in 1870. It was a large brick house about 35 feet by 40 feet and was likely two storeys tall.

This chapel was no longer used after union, the congregation joining with two Wesleyan congregations to form the single congregation known as Trinity and who now met on Church St, at Bowmanville Methodist Church, now known as Trinity United.

After union this building was used as a meeting hall, for it was large enough to hold a sizeable crowd. It was also used, at one time, for a dance hall. In fact, in 1894 when the celebrations for the centennial of the arrival of the first settlers was held, this building was the only one in town large enough to hold the crowd who came out for the celebrations and ceremonies. It was taken down in about 1959 or 1960.

From *The Townships of Darlington and Clarke* by Prof. John Squair, we have a list of people who donated to the Mission Fund in 1878 from Bowmanville. I would imagine they were all members in good standing in that congregation ....
G. Foster, W. Allin, John Pinch, Christopher Minns, Robert

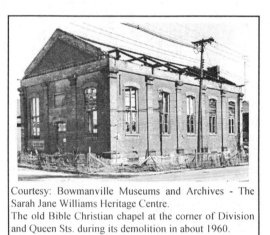

Courtesy: Bowmanville Museums and Archives - The Sarah Jane Williams Heritage Centre.
The old Bible Christian chapel at the corner of Division and Queen Sts. during its demolition in about 1960.

Strutt, T. Woodley, P. Robins, T. Bowden, Jacob Neads, S. Mason Sr., C. Coombe, W. Jolliffe, R. Jennings, J. Perkins, Richard Hambly, W. White, Levi Morris Jr., W. Osborne, J. Slute, J. Gale, Levi Morris Sr., W. Thickson, W. Deacon, George Haines, J. Knight, J. Meader, W.W. Mason, P. Trebilcock, P. Martin, T. Trewin, G. Sanders, W. Coombe, J. Westcott, E. Westcott, S. Allin, J. Stacey, W. Pinch, H. Meader, D. Stott, Mrs. McFeeters, Mrs. G. Ball, Mrs. B. Puley, Mrs. J. Jacobs, Miss M. Hambly, Miss A. Hicks, Miss M. Cleverdon, Miss E. A. Knight, Miss M.J. Knight, Miss H. Williams.

Salem:

Located at Lot 12, Concession 3 of Darlington Township, this chapel was built in 1868 or 69. From the history of the congregation, written in 1968 for the centennial of the chapel, it is thought that the original chapel was built about 1850. It was a

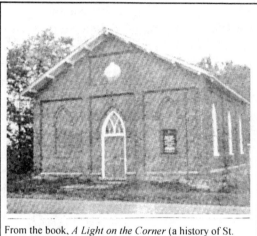

From the book, *A Light on the Corner* (a history of St. Pauls United Church)
Salem Chapel joined with St. Pauls at Union.

white frame chapel, and stood on the parcel of land along with the newer brick chapel until 1899, being used for social functions and Sunday School. It was sold to John Trull at Hampton and removed to his farm.

The 1869 brick chapel measured 32 feet by 42 feet. The parcel of ½ acre plus 16 rods also housed a cemetery. Unfortunately there are only three stones left in this old cemetery and they have been mounted on a concrete slab with a little fence surrounding it, a memorial to the early Bible Christians who worshipped here.

The chapel and cemetery were built on the corner of Joseph Clemens farm. This family came from Cornwall and gave the land for the use of the Church.

Again, from Squair's history, is a list of people who donated to the Mission fund from Salem in 1878 ....
W. Windatt, James Heal, J. Pipe, J. Stephens, H. Hocking, B. Werry, Edmund Prout, W. Deacon, G. Stevens, C. Honey, Joseph Clemens, A. McFeeters, Mrs. M.A. McLean, Mrs. E. Rutledge,

Mrs. M.A. Clemens, Mrs. E. Pollard, Miss E.F. Rutledge, Miss J. Plummer.

Providence:

Though no longer standing, Providence Chapel sat at Lot 3 Concession 3 of Darlington Township. It was a brick chapel built in 1865 on ½ acre of land on the corner of Richard Smale's farm. The Smale's were another Cornish family from the parish of Whitstone. Richard Smale and his wife, were lay preachers in some of the Bible Christian chapels in the vicinity.

From the Squair history there is also a list of those who donated to the Mission Fund from Providence congregation 1878-79 .... R. Souch, T. Crago, W. Crago, J. Elford, S. Allin, J. Wight, W. Blackburn, E. Prout, W. Mann, S. Allen Sr., J. Elford, C. Walk, R. Wight, W.J. Bragg, A. Allin, F. Allin, G. Wight, Mrs. R. Allin, Miss N. Allin, Miss C. Elford, Miss S.J. Johns.

Bethesda:

From, *Historical Sketch of Tyrone*, by Robert and Nancy Lambert, comes this information ....

"The deed for the Bible Christian church at Bethesda was signed on February 6, 1856. The description of the land being : *three quarters of an acre, the north-west corner, part of lot 6 in the fifth concession, Darlington Township.* This land was acquired from William Werry for a token sum of five shillings.

Indications are that the first church erected was of frame construction ..... (from the Hoar family history) .... "March 5, 1849, Mr. and Mrs. Hoar and children, including Silas Hoar, worshipped in a little frame church in the neighbourhood with Rev. J.H. Eynon."

The second church was built of red brick and boasted a choir loft and good basement which accommodated the Sunday School and a fine kitchen. The church was used as Bible Christian until Union in 1884 and remained in use [by the Methodists] until approximately 1932. The church was sold in 1937 to the Trustees of Scugog Island United Church, the building was torn down moved to Scugog Island and there rebuilt as a church."

According to the Bible Christian Property Book, this brick chapel was constructed in 1857, its size being 32 feet by 42 feet.

Information about the cemetery located here also comes from the same booklet by the Lamberts .....

"The deed for Bethesda Cemetery, adjacent to the church, was signed by John H. and Agnes W. Werry on July 18, 1881 and turned over to the trustees of the Bible Christian Church. The trustees were - Roger Cole, Robert Collacott, William Deacon, John Roger Cole, Henry C. Hoar, John Hoskin and Silas V. Hoar. The cost was $30.^{00}.

There still remains a lovely cemetery at Bethesda as well as a fine red brick chapel which was built in 1963. A donation of $5,000 was made by Miss Alice Creeper, Toronto and the balance of the $13,000 cost was met with donations and subscriptions. The beautiful stained glass window, *The Reaper*, was donated by Mr. C. Ewart McLaughlin, Oshawa."

It appears then, that the holdings of the Bible Christians was added onto by the son of William Werry, though this account of it does not say by how much. By the date of the deed, we can see that this must be an addition to the cemetery and chapel grounds, as the cemetery was in use since the little frame chapel was in existence.

Tyrone :

The first church on this site was likely of frame construction, built about 1850 when the land *for use by the Bible Christians* was donated by the McClung family. Located in the centre of the village of Tyrone, this little chapel served the people until 1868, when Robert Hodgson donated additional land [more than doubling the size of the property] so that a larger chapel could be constructed.

This second chapel was brick and measured 35 ½ feet by 52 feet. The entry in the Bible Christian Property book puts the total land occupied at one sixth acre.

From Prof. John Squair's history, *The Townships of*

Darlington and Clarke, comes this list of members for 1882-83, just prior to Union ....
R. Callicott, G. Emmerson, Jabez Vanstone, J. Hellyar, P. Werry, J. Creeper, T. Williams, James Curtis, W. Wight, S. Pollard, R. Woodley, T. Hardy, C. Cailor, R. Callicott Sr., John Doney, Matthew Cole, ... Woodley Sr., W. Brent, H. Werry, Mrs. Reed, Miss P. Cole, Miss M. Hodge, Miss C. Curtis.

Haydon:

The original chapel on this site, in the small hamlet of Hayden, Lot 14, concession 8 of Darlington Township, was likely built about 1851. The entry in the Bible Christian Property Book describes the chapel as frame, measuring 24 feet by 45 feet - a small country chapel indeed! It may have been called *Peneil*, for, according to author Helen Schmid, an 1858 edition of "The Day Dawn" (a Bible Christian Newspaper) embedded in the plaster in the attic of the former Gamsby House in Orono, has a list of the itinerancy preaching plan for the circuit, and it calls Haydon *Peneil*.

The present brick church was constructed in 1868 to accommodate a steadily growing congregation . It is now used as an auction hall.

At the time of the centennial celebrations, the people put together a short history of the settlement, and this is what they found out about their church ....

"In 1868 a great many of the Haydon people belonged to the Bible Christian Church which was on the north end of the back street. Rev. J.H. Eynon was the minister of the Tyrone Circuit. Mr. William Cowling gave the land where the church is now built."

We can see, then, that the original frame church was on a side street in the village and the new brick church was built on the 8th Concession Road (the main street of the village).

Orono:

The first Bible Christian Chapel to be erected in Clarke township was at Orono. It was dedicated October 26, 1845, and so it is likely that it was constructed the previous year. The speakers at the dedication of this little frame chapel were Rev. John Hicks Eynon and Rev. John Brown Tapp.

Charles Barrett had given the land upon which this chapel was built. Prior to this the congregation met in a schoolhouse near the old cemetery.

Photo by Helen Schmid
The two Bible Christian chapels, the first one (frame) added to the back of the second one (brick) as a church hall.

Helen Schmid, author of *Out of the Mists, A History of Clarke Township*, tells us ......

"In this schoolhouse the Millerites (or Second Adventists), Mormons and Universalists also held services. These sects would pack the schoolhouse in sweltering weather and carry on religious debate for three hours at a stretch. It is little wonder the Bible Christians wanted a church building of their own."

At the time of it's dedication, the Rev. John Brown Tapp wrote a report about the chapel at Orono .....

"The chapel is a good frame one. It is 20 feet by 32, covered with shingles and painted white. There will be a few pews put in next spring, if the Lord please. It would have been done before, if we had purchased the lumber in the winter, but it will now be given us. The cost of the building is about £60."

Eventually the little frame church became too small for the

growing congregation and a new brick chapel was constructed on the site, more than double the size of the old chapel at 32 feet by 50 feet. James Eddy was hired to do the brick work and plastering, and John martin of Orono did the joinery work. William Warren of Newcastle was hired to do the painting.

The old chapel was kept and added to the back of the new chapel to be used as a church hall and Sunday School room. Both structures still stand on Mill St in Orono.

After union, the church was sold to the Anglicans who were in need of a building of their own, and it remains an Anglican church today.

Members of the congregation at Orono in the early days included the families of Tamblyn, Dobson, Walkey, Allin, Cobbledick, Reed, Moon, McCombe, Berry, Best, Vickers, Watts, Billings, Hill, Odger, and Hicks.

At the time of the first chapel, families in the congregation included Hooper, Barrett, Connell and Miller.

Leskard

Leskard chapel was located in the milling community of Leskard in the north end of Clarke Township, Lot 31, Concession 7. It was not a very large chapel, for it has been said that it housed only about 90 people. The entry in the Bible Christian Property Book states it's size as 24 feet by 32 feet, not much larger than an early settler's log cabin.

This was a frame chapel, built about 1855 on 40 square rods of land. Samuel Way and his son laid out the town lots in a plan in the early 1850's, and James Bawkes was also selling off his land as town lots, but it is not known just who gave or sold the land to the Bible Christians. The erection of the chapel in 1855 was part of the early history of the village, as was the awarding of their own post office in 1856.

Starkville:

This chapel was short lived. Helen Schmid, in her book,

Out of the Mists, said there was a Bible Christian Chapel at the foot of the hill west of the Starkville School, but when it was built and when it was no longer used we do not know. It does not appear in the Bible Christian Property Book, so it was likely closed and sold prior to 1874.

Preachers to serve these chapels, all east of the Gravel Road (aka The Old Scugog Road), included:

1833- 45 - John Hicks Eynon
1845-55 - John Hicks Eynon, J.B. Tapp, Robert Hurley
1856 - Paul Robins, William Hooper
1857 - John Chapple
1858 - John Chapple and Henry Newcombe
1859 - John Chapple and George Bodle
1860-61 - Robert Hurley and Edward Roberts
1863 - Henry Kenner, Archibald Clarke, Paul Robins
1864 - Henry Kenner and Archibald Clarke
1865 - William Jolliffe and Thomas W. Glover
1866-67 - William Jolliffe and Richard Hicks
1868 - William Jolliffe and James Joseph Rice
1869 - Cephas Barker and J.J. Rice
1870 - W.S. Pascoe and Cephas Barker
1871-72 - W.S. Pascoe and Robert Baker
1873-74 - W.S. Pascoe and W.R. Roach
1875 - William Jolliffe and Edwin A. Tonkin
1876-77 - William Jolliffe and Henry Ebbott
1878 - William Jolliffe and William Limbert
1879 - John Kenner and William Limbert
1880-81 - John Kenner and Richard Mallett
1882 - John Kenner and Samuel T. Bartlett
1883 - John Harris, Alexander Richard(s) and Samuel T. Bartlett

Hampton Circuit

The Bowmanville Circuit covered those chapels that were east of the Gravel Road, or Old Scugog Road, that went right out to Lake Scugog, through Cartwright Township to the north. Now, with the Hampton Circuit we take a look at the Bible Christian Chapels that were found west of the Gravel Road in the Township of Darlington.

Ebenezer:

This chapel was one of the very early chapels in Darlington Township. It was built by one of the area's early settlers, Christopher Courtice, after whom the settlement was

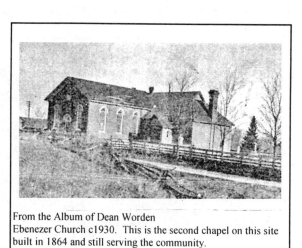

From the Album of Dean Worden
Ebenezer Church c1930. This is the second chapel on this site built in 1864 and still serving the community.

eventually named, and who gave the land upon which it sits.

The oldest part of this brick chapel dates to 1864, though it has had at least two additions since that time, possibly more if one counts the *new* basement, itself many years old! It no doubt replaced an early chapel, for Christopher Courtice arrived in Darlington in 1832 and he constructed a chapel in about the 1845-48 time period. The original may have been a log chapel.

In the early days when the Bible Christians were in their hey-day, Ebenezer Chapel was the foremost chapel in the Bay of Quinte Conference, due to a large degree to the active part members of the congregation played in the day to day affairs, especially Christopher Courtice and other members of his family.

Rehoboth:

Rehoboth was a small frame country chapel measuring 20 feet by 30 feet, built in about 1853 in the 5th Concession, just north of the village of Taunton on the county line between Durham County and Ontario County. Old records simply say „..."north of the village", none say which side of the road. The chapel was likely on the Ontario County side of the road, the west side, and was erected on the farm, owned in 1878 by John Gronk. The chapel has long since disappeared.

From the book, Heritage Buildings of Darlington Township, by the Local Architectural Conservation Advisory Committee
Hampton Bible Christian Chapel, built 1874 in the centre of the village at Mill and Scugog Sts.

Hampton:

Located in the village of Hampton, the first chapel was built of frame in about 1847. Whether it was on the west side or the east side of the mill pond I do not know, but the *Pioneer Bible Christian Cemetery* is on the west side of the mill pond.

In 1874 the Bible Christians erected a 30 foot by 59 foot brick chapel, this one is on the east side of the mill pond. Both chapels were located on a half acre parcel.

A frame parsonage was constructed in the village in 1865

on a half acre parcel, and just about the same time the "new" cemetery was being started on the north edge of the village.

From Prof. John Squair's, *The Townships of Darlington and Clarke*, we have a list of subscribers to the Mission Fund from Hampton for 1882-83 ..... Henry Elliott Sr., William Elford Sr., R.B. Rowe, J.R. Lavis, John Rundle, Thomas Ward, Henry Elliott Jr., William Allin, R.H. Bunt, Thomas Burrows, Mrs. Hoidge (widow of the Rev. Joseph Hoidge), Joseph Ward, Thomas Elliott, Edward Cann, Joseph Clatworthy, John Elliott, William Elford Jr., Richard Katerson (undertaker), John Elford, John Ruse, Mrs. Thomas Ward, Mrs. H. Elliott Jr., Mrs Hamblyn, Miss Ella Motley, Miss Lavina Gully, Miss T. Burrows..

Eldad:

Eldad Chapel is located in Lot 25, Concession 6, in the village of Solina. Built on land donated by Peter Werry, this brick chapel was erected in 1855. It was originally

Photo by Roger Leetooze
Eldad Chapel, built on a gift of land from Peter Werry at Solina.

without a basement and measured 30 feet by 40 feet. Enough land for a cemetery was included in the donation of ½ acre.

The Werry's and most of the people in the village of Solina were from Cornwall, most having been Bible Christians before their emigration to Canada. Peter Werry was a lay preacher, and strict in his Sabbath discipline. He kept the Sabbath Holy and never did any work on the Sabbath day. He even hitched the horse to the buggy Saturday night so as not to soil the Sabbath. It is said that he even refused to shave on the Sabbath. However, he never refused the bounteous meals prepared by his wife on the Sabbath, especially on the days when it was their turn to host the itinerant preacher.

Prior to the erection of the chapel on the Werry land, the local congregation met, as did the Methodists, in the local schoolhouse, possibly as early as 1840 or 1841. Located in Lot 21 it was 4 lots east of the village on E.B. Cryderman's farm. Because this log building was used as a church as well as a school it was called Mount Pleasant, and was located on a hill above Michael Cryderman's mill.

Beside the church there was a small burying ground, and as late as 1939 several stones from this graveyard were known to be still tucked away in the grass along the fenceline. However, now all traces of the church location and cemetery have disappeared, sad, too, because one of the earliest settlers in this part of the township, Michael Cryderman (from Loyalist stock) and all his family are buried there.

Enfield:

Located in Lot 29, Concession 9, Enfield is a small hamlet in the north end of the township. It had been fairly early settled, even though it was a long distance back from the 'front', but the Bible Christians took quite a while to find their way out to Enfield.

The Ontario Gazette of 1870 lists T.R. Hull as the Bible Christian Preacher at Enfield, however, Brother Hull had not been there for two years. The Gazettes of those days were likely compiled over a two year period and were out of date long before they went to press.

Where the Bible Christians were meeting at that time is uncertain, possibly, like many places, the schoolhouse did double duty. This chapel was also known as Cardiphonia.

The Bible Christian Property Book states that the frame chapel was constructed in 1877 on one eighth acre. It was a very small chapel, measuring only 24 feet by 34 feet.

As far as other meeting places, there were likely a number of them over the years. There was either a meeting place or a chapel at Millville, also spelled Melville in an old record I found, north of Hampton where Michael Cryderman and others had erected mills along the creek. The old cemetery is still in the memories of some of the very oldest citizens, but the stones of the old cemetery that maked the place have all been removed to the hedgerows and lost and the 'field' plowed for crops.

Preachers who served the Hampton Circuit (all those chapels west of the Gravel Road):
1842-43 (included Whitby) Philip James, John Edward and
      R.Hurley(1843)
1844 - John Hicks Eynon and Philip James
1845 - John Brown Tapp, Thomas Ford
1846-47 - Henry Ebbott
1848-49 - Thomas Green
1850-51 - John Edward(s), Abraham Morris
1852 - John Hodgson and Abraham Morris
      (1853-55 with Bowmanville)
1853 - George Haycraft, John Hooper
1854 - Henry Ebbott, James Hughes
1855 - Paul Robins and J.H. Eynon
1856 - John Hooper
1857 - John Brown Tapp, Richard Mallett
1858 - John Brown Tapp, Isaac Ashley
1859 - William Hooper, Isaac Ashley
1860 - William Hooper, Adam Curry
1861 - William Hooper, Henry Kenner
1862-63 - W.R. Roach, David Cantlon
1864 - W.R.Roach, Jesse Whitlock
1865-66 - Joseph Hoidge

1867 - Joseph Hoidge, James Collins
1868 - T.R.Hull and Richard T. Courtice
1869 - Edward Roberts
1870-71 - Edward Roberts, William Hodnett
1872 - Edward Roberts, Mark Hardy
1873 - Henry Kenner, Alexander Richard(s)
1874 - Henry Kenner and W. Rollins
1875 - William Wade and M. Nichols
1876 - Stephen H. Rice and William Limbert
1877 - S.H. Rice and John Gilson
1878 - S.H. Rice and S.J. Cunnings
1879 - R.B. Rowe and Thomas Brown
1880-81 - R.B. Rowe and J.W. Cannom
1882 - W. Down
1883 - Jesse Whitlock and J.H. Oke

Peterborough County

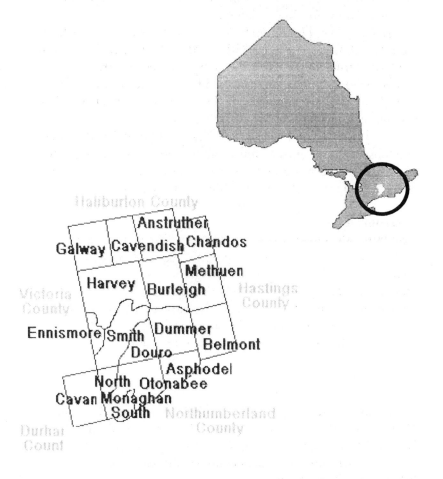

Peterborough County Circuits

Peterborough County saw it's first major settlement with the coming of the *Peter Robinson Irish* in 1825. Though most of the townships were slow to settle in the years that followed, small settlements, like *The English Settlement* in Dummer Township were found as early as the 1830's. Many of the people in these scattered farms and small settlements, outside the original Irish settlers who were now spreading out from Peterborough Town, were from England's south-west, Devon and Cornwall, and they brought with them the Bible Christian faith.

It wasn't long before the Missionary, John Hicks Eynon, and those who followed within a couple of years, found these little congregations and log chapels were constructed. Most of the chapels on these circuits started life as log chapels.

Peterborough:
Peterborough - In the town at 217 Murray Street - first chapel was likely log, replaced with frame about 1853.
Ashburnham - Built 1872 in the village.
Salem - Lot 26, Concession 10, Otonabee Township
Providence - acquired by Bible Christians in 1858 - may be a former schoolhouse. Location unknown.
Bethel - Built 1863, frame, square, location unknown.

Lakefield:

Lakefield - in the village, sold to Catholic congregation in 1884.
Douro - Lot 20, Concession 2, Douro Township, built c1870
English Line - aka Warsaw Chapel, Lot 16, Concession 1, Dummer Township - first chapel built of logs early 1830's.
Northey's - likely at Lakehurst.
Smith's - location unknown
Payne's Schoolhouse - Lot 12, Concession 3, Dummer Township

Peterborough Circuit

Peterborough Circuit had at least five chapels : Peterborough, Ashburnham, Bethel, Providence and Salem. It has been said that John Glass, the missionary that was sent to Ontario before John Hicks Eynon, made his way to Peterborough, and that by the time Eynon arrived there about 1834-35, there was a congregation meeting in homes under the guidance of lay preachers.

Peterborough:

There was likely an early log chapel built at Peterborough in the time of John Hicks Eynon, and this may have served the local congregation for ten or twelve years. From the Bible Christian Property Book we know that a frame chapel was constructed there in 1853, 30 feet by 42 feet, which was likely the second chapel on the site.

Who donated or sold the land for a chapel we do not know at this time, but it was ½ acre in size. Also on this lot was constructed a Parsonage for the circuit. This too was a frame building, 24 feet by 36 feet.

From *The Peterborough Story*, by G. Wilson Craw, we find out that the Bible Christian Chapel stood where the Legion Branch is now located, at 217 Murray St.

Ashburnham:

Ashburnham, on the east side of the Otonabee River, used to be called *Scotch Village*. In 1858 it had grown large enough to attain village status and changed its name at that time to Ashburnham.

We do not know when the first congregation of Bible Christians started meeting at Ashburnham, but we do know that a brick chapel was built there in 1872, and was called Mark Street Chapel. A good portion of the inhabitants of Ashburnham must have belonged to this congregation for it was a fair sized chapel, 36 feet by 48 feet, slightly larger than its Peterborough counterpart,

61

and was located on a town lot of 1/3 acre.

The first mention of it in the list of preachers for the circuit by Douglas Walkington is 1873

Salem:

Salem Chapel was located on Lot 26, Concession 10, Otonabee Township. According to staff at the Trent Valley Archives on Carnegie St., Peterborough, the Concession Road is now Highway 7, and the chapel may have sat just about where the Harley Davidson Dealership is today (2005) as close as local experts can figure..... Highway 7, when constructed, meandered all over the place and lining up the concessions now is a little tricky.

At that time the chapel was located out in a rural setting, and its size, 26 feet by 36 feet, tells us this brick chapel was a country chapel, as most were much smaller

Courtesy: Trent Valley Archives
Signatures on the deed for the land upon which Salem Chapel was built.

than their town counterparts. This chapel was built in 1875, but it may have replaced an earlier chapel.

The deed transferring the land to the Bible Christians is dated 15th of January, 1876, so we know the property was in use by the Bible Christians prior to its ownership by them.

The land, consisting of 1/8 acre, was deeded to the Bible Christians by Thomas Sloman, for the princely sum of $1. The Trustees to whom the property was sold were:
John Sargent, Samuel Sargent, James Armstrong and Thomas

Johnston. All were farmers of the Township of Otonabee.

As part of the agreement, Sloman added a paragraph that said if the land should cease to be used by the Bible Christians, and remains that way for one year, it will revert back to Sloman or his heirs. If this was to happen the Bible Christians would be given enough notice to remove their property, such as buildings, from the land.

Providence:

Providence chapel was the second chapel to be constructed in the circuit about 1858. It was of log construction, but may not have been constructed as a chapel. It may have been a former school house taken over by the Bible Christians at that time. It was in existence until at least 1874, because it is listed in the Bible Christian Property Book. Location unknown.

Bethel:

This was a square chapel, 36 feet by 36 feet, of frame construction built in 1863 on 1 acre of land. The location of this chapel is unknown, but it was no doubt in Harvery Township.

From the history of Lakehurst United Church, we find that Bethel was on this circuit after the Union of 1884. The Lakehurst Methodist Church was built in 1887, and to help raise funds for the circuit the Bethel Chapel was sold in 1899. Members of the Bethel Chapel in those days were Matthew Waram and family (they also appear as Bible Christians on the 1871 census), Miss E. Walroth and Miss L. Barcroft, and so we can safely assume that Bethel Chapel existed prior to 1884 as a Bible Christian chapel. Many of the people associated with Bethel Chapel are listed as living in Smith Township, but in those days Harvey had not yet been separated off into a township of it's own, and so in theory, Bethel Chapel was founded in Smith Township.

Because we have, for the most part, lost touch with our history, and are now only just reclaiming it as best we can, there is a great deal of confusion about the location of some of these chapels, who their members were, and whether they were indeed

Bible Christian chapels. The confusion in this case comes from having found another Bethel chapel in the pages of Peterborough County's history...... and this one was indeed a Bible Christian chapel with J.W. Butcher mentioned as the minister on the circuit in 1871, and he was, in fact, the minister that year. But why was there two Bethel Chapels on one circuit? Here is what was found....

This second Bethel Chapel was located at Stewart Hall in Otonabee Township. From the book, *Forest and Farm*, we have this information about Bethel ....

"In the Stewart Hall community there were two of the Matchett homes at which the 'Saddle Bag Preachers' could be sure of a welcome, a night's shelter and feed for their horse. There were Alexander and Robert Matchett. In the evening not only the neighbours but also the Indians that camped along the Otonabee River would come to hear the Saddle Bag Preachers preach and all would join in the singing of hymns. The people attending these services were called the Bible Christians.

Both homes were thought to have been log houses. Robert's home was built further back from the road from where the Matchett Brothers' home stands today.

As time went on it was decided a church had to be built as the log houses could no longer accommodate this growing congregation. On October 13, 1862, Mr. Joe and Mont Nethercott deeded a piece of their land, which was directly across the road from the Hanbidge and Hutchison farms, for a church, shed and cemetery. On this property was to be built the first church for Stewart Hall, to be known as Bethel Church. It was a rough-cast buiilding 50 to 60 feet long. There were 3 windows at each side. A porch was at the entrance with two doors. As you entered the church there was a large box stove, almost in the centre with a row of pipes the length of the building. The aisle was in the middle and pews at each side which were good substantial ones, with the high straight back. There was a step up to the pulpit and choir loft, and pews were at the north side of the pulpit for the members of the choir.

To keep the expense of building at a minimum it is thought it was built by the men of the congregation, supervised by Mr. Robert Matchett who was a good carpenter. Even now a few folk can recall pieces of furniture he made such as a bed for his tall neighbour because the boughten beds were too short for him to be comfortable.

Mr. and Mrs. Robert Hanbidge's home was not far from the church; the family always lit the fire and kept the church clean. The ministers were always welcome at the Hanbidge home and often left with a loaf of fresh home-made bread, a jar of buttermilk or some other treat. Their horses enjoyed the Hanbidge hospitality too.

Service was held at Bethel in the afternoon. As soon as it was over, the children and young people would walk up to the red brick school house where Sunday School was held. The red brick school was across from Stewart Hall United Church. Mr. George Stewart was the first superintendent. The others were Sandy Savigny, and for many years Sandy Matchett, then Melville Stewart, Ormie Stewart, Will Dawson.

The majority of the congregation had quite a distance to come. Some walked while others came by horse and buggy or double rigs and there were those who crossed the river. During the winter they came in cutters and sleighs. Mr. Robert Deyell's family whose home was not far from Bensfort Bridge have walked and also the John Deyell family. Once Mr. and Mrs. John Deyell, carrying their baby, walked all the way to attend a special service at Bethel Church."

The writer went on to say that the congregation joined with the Methodists in 1871, though I doubt this because she went on to add that they became part of the Circuit with Mark St. Methodist where Rev. Butcher preached. Rev. Butcher did indeed preach at Mark St. chapel at Ashburnham, but not until 1872 when the chapel was built. Besides, this was not a Methodist church until Union in 1884.

A quick check of the 1871 census confirms that all these people were indeed Bible Christians at Otonabee Township, and so we can accept this information.

But what about the other Bethel? A small mystery indeed!

Bible Christian Ministers serving this circuit were:
Prior to 1840 - John Hicks Eynon
1840 - John Kemeys
1841-42 - John Edwards
1843 - John Brown Tapp
1844 - John Brown Tapp, Philip James
1845 - Thomas Green
1846-48 - Paul Robins
1849-50 - Robert Hurley
1851-54 - William Hooper
1855 - Joseph Hoidge
1856-57 - Thomas Green
1858 - Edward Roberts and Thomas Rice
1859 - Edward Roberts and Henry James Colwell
1860 - John Edward and Isaac Ashley
1861 - Garrance Tink Colwell
1862-63 - Garrance T. Colwell and Adam Curry
1864 - John Chapple
1865-67 - David Cantlon
1868-71 - John Watson Butcher
1872 - Joseph Hoidge
1873 - William Hooper
1874 - William Hooper and William Davies
1875 - Andrew Gordon and James Pollard Rice
1876-77 - Edward Roberts and Moses Metherall
1878 - Edward Roberts and Francis Metherall Whitlock
1879 - Edward Roberts and John Wesley Cannom
1880 - Edward Roberts and Thomas W. Blatchford
1881 - William Jolliffe and Thomas Brown
1882-83 William Jolliffe

Lakefield Circuit

There were at least five chapels on the Lakefield Circuit and these included the Village of Lakefield, Douro Chapel, English Line Chapel, Northey's and Smith's. There was also a meeting place on the Dummer Township 3rd Concession and one on the Dummer 4th Concession.

Lakefield:

Preaching by the Bible Christians began at Lakefield Village long before a chapel was erected. Local historian, Gord Young, says that the Bible Christians opened their first chapel for business on Reid Street in the village July 12, 1864. But then he adds .... *"It seems everything in Lakefield was only officially launched on the 12th of July, the day the Orangemen celebrated their day."*

Who preached there in those days I do not know, but it may have been Jacob Gale who looked after the English Line Congregation. By 1869 Richard T. Courtice, from Devon, England, began preaching there.

In 1871 a frame chapel was erected, 32 ½ feet by 45 feet, a good size for a country chapel, so it looks as if there were many in the village who joined with the Bible Christians at that time. This was likely the second chapel in

Courtesy:Christ Church Community Museum, Lakefield
The old manse/parsonage, photo taken from the Tanner yard across the street.

the village. The earlier chapel was likely now too small to hold the growing numbers of adherents.

67

That same year a parsonage was built at Lakefield, a 24 foot by 24 foot frame house on 3/8 acre.

"*At Union in 1884, this congregation refused to join the Methodists, whom they thought had become far too liberal and centerist in their doctrine.*" So reports Gord Young. According to Bill Twist, Chairperson for the Christ Church Community Museum at Lakefield, the church was used as a meeting place for the local Foresters and the Lakefield branch of the Salvation Army. In 1888 the we portion of the property and parsonage were sold privately . In 1892 they eventually gave up and went with the Methodists and sold their remaining property to the Catholic Church. They were a practical lot and soon found out how difficult it was to keep their church going. The present Catholic Church at Lakefield sits on the Bible Christian property.

Though the Bible Christians have been noted for their piety down through the years, it seems that many of the Lakefield congregation also belonged to

Courtesy: Christ Church Community Museum, Lakefield
Moving the old parsonage across the Otonabee on a barge in 1931.

the Orange Lodge, who in those days were in bitter conflict with the Catholics. After selling their property to the Catholic Church, the Orangemen would parade every July 12th right across the front of the Catholic Church and made sure that King Billy's horse dropped a big plop on cue on the front walk.

Douro:

Located on Lot 30 of the 2nd Concession of Douro

Township, was a chapel built in 1871 on 1/16th acre of land. It was a small country chapel, frame construction, 24 feet by 34 feet. This was the second location for this congregation who started out in a chapel erected at Broad's Corner (Dummer and Douro Corner on Stoney Lake Road) two concessions away. Among the trustees of the first chapel were Silas

From the collection of Roberta Thompson, Peterborough, Ontario - A sketch of Douro Chapel by M. Knox, after it was moved to Clarina.

Cox and Henry Downs. At the second location were Isaac Garbutt, Levi Payne, Lazarus Dunford, George Singleton and Richard Dawkins.

In 1888 this second chapel was taken down and carted to Clarina where it became Carmel Church on the Methodist Warsaw Circuit.

English Line:

Also known as Warsaw Chapel, it was located in Dummer Township on Concession 1, between lots 16 and 17. One of the first settlers in the area was William Bullock, who arrived in 1831 from St. Wenn in Cornwall, England. Bullock himself was from the parish of St. Stephens, where he had been a member of the Bible Christian Society in that place since 1816. It was William Bullock who began the first congregation of Bible Christians in this area, among the early settlers whom he found as neighbours. From his obituary in the Bible Christian Magazine we find that ...."*His house was a home for the preachers on both sides of the Atlantic.*"

69

Peterborough County

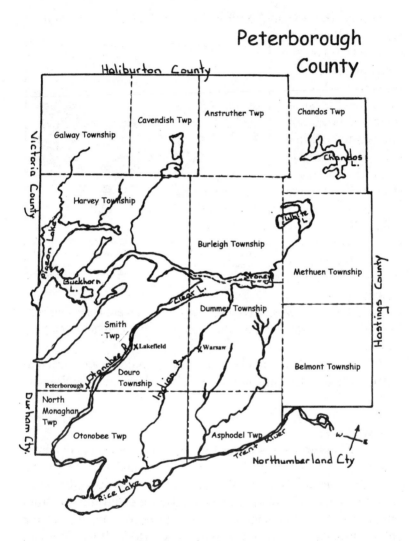

Haliburton County

Galway Township

Cavendish Twp

Anstruther Twp

Chandos Twp

Chandos L.

Victoria County

Harvey Township

Burleigh Township

Lily Pt

Methuen Township

Pigeon Lake

Buckhorn L.

Clear L.

Stoney

Dummer Township

Hastings County

Smith Twp

Otonabee

X Lakefield

Indian River

X Warsaw

Belmont Township

Peterborough X

Douro Township

Durham Cty.

North Monaghan Twp

Otonobee Twp

Asphodel Twp

Trent River

Northumberland Cty

Rice Lake

From the booklet, *The Heat and the Soul, A History of the Warsaw United Church,* comes the information that the land was contributed by William Bullock and Lazarus Payne, one parcel for the chapel, the other for the cemetery beside the chapel.

From the Bible Christian Property Book we find that the chapel here was frame construction, but no date was given for its erection. However, Rev. Herrington, who preached on the Methodist Circuit between 1925 and 1930, collected some local history, and wrote it up. He had in his possession at that time 'Dr. Poole's notes from 1867' which contained this information ......

"Methodist Churches were erected in 1850 and 1853 and the opinion among the older people is that the Bible Christian Chapel was built before the Methodist churches. The Bible Christian parsonage was built on Lot 17 Concession 2, on the farm of Gerald Donaldson. Later a parsonage was built across from the church on the farm of William Crowe. This was destroyed by fire in 1895."

This would have been the second chapel on the site, the first being a log chapel likely built in the early 1830's by Mr. Bullock and that early congregation. From Rev. Herrington's writing we have this paragraph as well ...... *"Later, a larger church was built of squared timbers. This was built larger than the former building and built around it so that the second church enclosed the first. The older building continued as a place of worship during the erection of the new building. Mrs. J.J. Crowe told of looking out the window during the service at the walls of the new building."*

Jeanette Cooper, from the Douro-Dummer Historical Society tells us that there are only one or two stones remaining in the cemetery and a few small pieces of the others. The Society is planning on placing a memorial marker at the cemetery and try to find out who is buried there.

Much of the history of the individual chapels on this circuit was also "dug out" by Jeanette for use in this book.

Northey's:

No doubt located at the Northey farm, or near it, at Northey's Bay, but no definite location has yet been found.

This chapel started out as a 25 foot by 30 foot log building, perhaps a settler's log house. It was located on 1/16 acre.

In 1881 it was replaced by a brick chapel, 24 feet by 36 feet, and it seems that the land was also increased to 1/4 acre. No further details are available.

Smiths's:

No location for this chapel has been found - there were many Smith's in the area upon whose land this chapel may have been built. It was built about 1878, was of frame construction and measured 20 feet by 34 feet.

The Schoolhouse at Payne's Cemetery:

Located on Lot 22 of the 3rd Concession of Dummer, this school house was on the property of David Payne, at the top of the hill at Payne's Cemetery, also known as Batten's Cemetery. The other school house where Bible Christian meetings were held was located at Lot 15, on the 4th Concession.

The old Dummer Schoolhouse, possibly Payne's, where Bible Christian services were held for so many years.

From the book, *Origins - The History of Dummer Township*, by Jean Murray Cole and the Township of Dummer (1993), comes this information ..... *"When the forerunner of Bethel*

Chapel was built at Batten's Hill in 1850 it was with assistance from the congregation of Bible Christians from the little log schoolhouse on Lot 22, Concession 3. For a time the new church was shared by the two groups, the Wesleyan Methodists meeting in the morning and the Bible Christians in the afternoon. Friction arose over doctrine (the Wesleyans followed conservative practices, separating men and women on opposite sides of the church, among other differences) and the Bible Christians returned to their former quarters [at the schoolhouse]."

The Rev. Herrington also tells us .... " Mrs. J.J. Crowe, who died at the age of 90 attended services at this school as a little girl, (Mrs. Crowe passed away in 1930) and her father, William Taylor attended service there. Mr. Taylor had been brought up in the Church of England in the old country but there being no Anglican services here at the time he threw in his lot with the Bible Christians and continued with them even after Anglican service was held in Warsaw."

It is also from the "Origins" book that we read .... " [Rev.] Eynon was an enthusiastic converter of men, and was known to join potential followers at logging bees, doffing his coat and helping

From: *Valley of the Trent*, Edwin C. Guillet
Levi Payne's log house on the banks of the Indian River, where Missionary John Hicks Eynon often stayed while out riding the circuit. Photo by Guillet c1930

with the work. 'When they paused to rest he would stand upon a stump and preach to them', wrote Rev. Herrington. 'By nightfall, though his conscience was clean, his shirt was soiled.' Eynon's host on these occasions was often George Payne Sr., son of Levi, and Herrington asserted that '*Mrs. Payne would put him to bed and wash his shirt.* "'

We know that John Hicks Eynon visited this area between 1833 and 1845, and was likely delighted to find the Bullocks, the Paynes, and the others continuing their Bible Christian teachings and Bible Classes so far from home.

Preachers to serve on the Lakefield Circuit included:
1855-56 - Henry Stevens
1857-58 - Abraham Morris
1859-60 - John Brown Tapp
1861-62 - Arthur Doble
1863-65 - Jacob Gale
1866 - Archibald Clarke
1867-68 - William Woodman
1869 - Richard T. Courtice
1870 - Thomas W. Glover
1871-73 - Stephen H. Rice
1874 - Alexander Richard(s)
1875 - Henry A. Newcombe and John Gilson
1876 - Alexander Richard(s)
1877-78 - R.B. Rowe
1879 - John Guard
1880 - Samuel W. Muxworthy
1881-83 - Roger Allin

Victoria County

Victoria County Circuits

Although Victoria County eventually had 12 townships in the 19th century, only two townships, Fenelon and Mariposa, plus the town of Lindsay feature in our story of the Bible Christians.

Some members of these congregations lived outside the two townships, and likely only came to chapel when the roads were passable, and that was in the winter with a sleigh, weather permitting. Once the townships and counties started to *macadamize* the roads in the late 1870's and early 1880's it was much easier to travel all year long.

Fenelon Township:
There were five chapels on the Fenelon Circuit:
Fenelon Falls - in the town
Ebenezer -
Bethel -
Zion - at Cameron
Cambray - in the village
Powles Corners - Lot 14, Conc. 7

Note: Fenelon Falls had the only parsonage in the township and Zion at Cameron had the only Bible Christian cemetery in the township.

Mariposa:
This was a very large circuit, the largest in Ontario, and possibly the largest in Canada. It had 11 chapels:
Little Britain - in the village
Manilla - in the village
Oakwood - Lot 18, Concession 7
Zion - Lot 11, Concession 3
Bethesda - Concession 2
Shiloh - in the broken Concession on the lakeshore, Lot 19 (Lake Scugog)
Providence -

Bethel -
Salem - Lot 5, Concession 6
Finger Board - also known as Port Hoover
Ebenezer -

Lindsay Town:
The chapel at Lindsay was located on the east side of Cambridge Street, between Wellington and Peel Streets.
The Preachers who served this congregation were:

Manvers and Cartwright:
Although these townships were in Durham County, they were under the jurisdiction of Victoria District. To make things even more confusing, they were originally part of the Prince Albert Circuit of Ontario County. No matter what jurisdiction these townships fell under, there were eight chapels on the circuit.

Blackstock - in the village aka Williamsburg or Cartwright
Caesarea - on the shore of Lake Scugog at the north edge of
Cartwright Township
Bethel - on the township/county line between Durham and Ontario
Counties, Lot 1, Concession 3, Cartwright Township
Carmel - at Burtonville on the township line between Cartwright
and Manvers Townships, Lot 24, Concession 5
Janetville - in the village - Manvers Township
Fleetwood - in the village - Lot 19, Concession 12, Manvers
Franklin - in the village, Lot 25, Concession 12, Manvers
Newry/Yelverton - rented space in the New Connexions chapel

Fenelon Circuit

There were six chapels on the Fenelon Circuit. Of these six, Cambray appears to be the oldest of the congregations.

The congregations of Fenelon Township were attached to various circuits and missions at various times. In 1852 it was part of the Mariposa Mission which in turn was attached to the Bowmanville Circuit. By 1857 Mariposa was separated into a circuit by itself with Fenelon still attached to it.

In 1871 Fenelon was attached to the Victoria and Peterborough District and likely became a circuit in it's own right at that time, though I would think it was a full-fledged circuit before then, but the old records are unclear on this point.

Fenelon Falls with its first mill, a sketch by Anna Robinson

Fenelon Falls:

From the book, *County of Victoria Centennial History*, by Watson Kirkconnell, is this passage .....

"At the south-east corner of Cameron Lake its waters issued in a considerable river, thundered down 23 feet over a limestone cliff, and then boiled and spumed through a rocky gorge to Sturgeon Lake, half a mile distant. The conditions of the day made the banks of this cataract an inevitable mill site and ultimately a village site, known first as Cameron's Falls, and later as Fenelon Falls."

And so, with this very descriptive passage we travel from the view of the early settler to the day when a village formed and the Bible Christians arrived.

After meeting in private homes and perhaps the schoolhouse, the congregation at Fenelon Falls erected their first chapel in 1866 on a half acre parcel of land in the village. This was a frame chapel measuring 32 feet by 40 feet. A parsonage was built on the same lot in 1872, measuring 25 feet by 30.

Powles Corners:
This chapel is not listed in the Bible Christian Property book. It was a short-lived chapel, of unpainted frame construction. It was built in about 1865 in an effort to expand the Fenelon Falls congregation. It was located on the east half of Lot 14 in the 7th Concession, just four miles from Fenelon Falls on the road to Lindsay. A deed for the property, dated 24th May, 1869, and registered the 11th August, 1870, shows the property sold to the Bible Christian trustees, by John Gillis for the *"consideration"* of $600.[00]. The trustees at that time were William Marshall, Emanuel Smitheram, William Powles, Mark Saunders and William Brokenshire.

Services were discontinued in this little chapel a few years after the Victoria Methodist Church was constructed in 1865-66 across the road. Some of the congregation stayed with the Bible Christians and transferred to Ebenezer Chapel about 4 miles north on Cameron Road, now Highway 35.

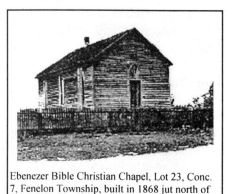

Ebenezer Bible Christian Chapel, Lot 23, Conc. 7, Fenelon Township, built in 1868 jut north of McCormick's Corners.

Ebenezer Chapel:
A congregation started in the vicinity in about 1866, first meeting in private homes, then meeting most likely in the school house. In 1868 they constructed their chapel, and on October 2, 1870 it was dedicated. It was a small chapel, 24 feet by 34 feet, and was of frame construction. There was nothing fancy about it,

and indeed, when comparing it with the fine brick structures found in the towns, it was positively a poor country cousin. But congregations tended to put up the sort of chapels they could afford, and rich or poor, their chapel was cherished. Measuring only 24 feet by 36 feet, this chapel was located in the East half of Lot 23 in the 7th concession, on land sold to the Bible Christians by William Isaac for $1.^{00}. William Isaac came out to Canada about 1861, a few years after his brother John arrived, John taking up land in Middlesex County. The trustees on the deed were William Marshal, Joseph Pearn, George H. Imrie and William Brokenshire. This little chapel continued to serve the Methodists after Union, but disappears from their records in 1904. The building stood unused until about 1918 when it was dismantled and moved to the property of Mrs. Harold Pearn across the highway, to be used as a shed. The pulpit was stored in the barn of George Isaac, a descendant of William.

Bethel Chapel:
No information is available about the location of this chapel. It resembled Ebenezer and Powles Corners chapels in that it was frame and small, measuring only 24 feet by 34 feet. It was located on 8 rods of land.

Zion Chapel:
This chapel was built north of Cameron in 1864 on a half acre parcel of John Moynes land, Lot 18, Concession 4. At a very early date there was a meeting conducted at Moyne's farm and is recorded as part of the Mariposa Circuit.

Sometime in the mid 1950's, a student by the name of Fay Webster, a pupil at S.S. #5, Fenelon, wrote an essay about this chapel. It came to this project from David Kemlo, via Jim Hobbs, people with a vested interest in the history of this section of the country. Here, in part, is that essay .....

"I have chosen as my topic one of the oldest landmarks in the vicinity, the Zion Bible Christian church.

It was a sturdy, hand-hewn, timber building about 32 feet

long and 24 feet wide, with clapboard siding and six beautiful frosted windows set on a hill overlooking the Zion-Fenelon countryside.

An architectural achievement for those early days of hand labour, it has stood the test of time and weather for 90 years and today is still doing duty, although no longer as a church.

In those days everyone worked together in 'Bees' to get a job done. They raised the church with reverence and care. To this day the shingles on the church are good and the original floor is still in it. The seats are used now in the basement of the new church.

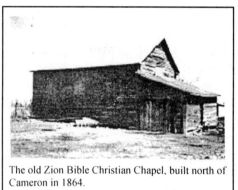

The old Zion Bible Christian Chapel, built north of Cameron in 1864.

On the weather-beaten tombstones in the church-yard can be read the names of these early pioneers. When ministers weren't available two or three laymen, including my two great-grandfathers, Richard Webster and Charles Everson, and another layman, Mr. Taylor Parkin, took the services.

It was heated by a box stove. One Hallowe'en night some boys took Edwin Worsley's milking stool and set it beside the box stove. When the Sunday services came there was the milking stool. He never did take it home.

Sometimes they had revival meetings lasting for weeks, with services every night, all well attended, and prayer meetings every week. There was a service nearly every Sunday in the church.

In the summer they came to church by wagon and oxen, and in the winter they bumped over the rough roads in sleighs. On New Year's Eve, Watchnight services were held to watch the old

81

year out and the new year in. One Watchnight service long ago, Taylor Parkin, watch in hand, with his congregation, sat at five minutes to twelve. On the first stroke of twelve he heaved a mighty groan and at that the children snickered. A New Year was born!

The zeal and courage of the people who built this church have been passed on from generation to generation. Our prayer is that the sacred light of this torch may never go out."

Cambray:

By 1850 there was a congregation at Cambray meeting in a shed just south of Main St., or so old records say.

In 1871 James Roy sold one fifth acre to the Trustees for $50.00. The trustees were John Smith, Henry Chambers, Laurence Mason, Jacob Warder, John Holmes, and Thomas Douglas.

The church,

The Cambray Chapel, 1871-1937
The Methodists likely bricked the outside after Union in 1884.

however, had already been built on that parcel a year earlier as reported in The Observer, September 21, 1870, page 3 ...

"The corner stone of the new church at Cambray will be laid on Thursday, 29th inst, at 1 o'clock by J. Clarke, Esq. A sermon will be preached by Brother W. Hooper of Cobourg."

From the Bible Christian Property Book, housed at the United Church Archives in Toronto, Ontario, we find that the chapel was of frame construction and measured 24 feet by 34 feet, located in Lot 5, Conc. 1. A Sabbath School was begun here in 1873.

At one point in the old records, Minden is mentioned as being part of this circuit, but I don't believe there was ever a chapel constructed there, though meetings were likely held at the schoolhouse or in private homes. It was served by supply ministers whenever someone was available.

Ministers serving this circuit included:

1861 - by supply
1862-64 - Thomas R. Hull
1865-66 - George Dunkley
1867-68 - John Harris
1869 - William Hodnett
1870 - Robert Baker
1871 - George Smith
1872-73 - Robert Hurley, James Collins
1874 - Robert Hurley, William Henry Butt
1875 - Henry Newcombe, John Gilson
1876-77 - Henry Newcombe
1878-79 - John M. Tredrea
1880-83 - Moses Metherall

Note: Fenelon Falls had the only parsonage in the township and Zion at Cameron had the only Bible Christian cemetery in the township.

Mariposa Circuit

Along with Darlington Township in Durham County and Usborne Township in Huron County, Mariposa had one of the highest chapel counts in the Province, with eleven chapels.

Some of the chapels in Mariposa were very early chapels, their congregations coming together in the late 1830's and early 1840's and their chapels constructed shortly thereafter.

From the diary of Rev. John Kemeys, we have this report from Monday July 23, 1838 .....

"Rode 12 miles and preached in the afternoon at Nicholas

Mark's house in Reach Township, from thence two men accompanied me to Scugog Lake. We obtained the loan of a canoe, with which we proceeded 6 or 7 miles down the Lake, and a little before sunset we landed on a small clearance in the Township of Cartwright (now Mariposa). We had then 8 miles to travel in order to reach the persons I had promised to visit. As night came on we arrived on a small clearance, where we found a man preparing to take refuge on some logs of wood raised together for the purpose and a shower of rain falling just then. We proposed to take our abode with him for the night but as the shower soon passed off, the stars again appeared and our place of refuge was uncomfortable and we had but 4 miles further to go. We resolved to proceed although we were strangers to the road. We made torches of the cedar bark and having the tracks of travellers to guide us we travelled on trusting in the Lord. It being calm our torches gave good light. At 10 o'clock we arrived a another clearance and began to look around for the settlers. After a little observation we made towards a light which we saw in the distance which brought us to John Mark's (Little Britain) former a local preacher in the Luxillian [Luxulyan] Circuit [in Cornwall UK].. Our friend soon arose and furnished us with refreshment and after commending ourselves to God in prayer we retired to rest about one o'clock. Early in the morning friend Mark and his family spread the news of our arrival and at half past 10 o'clock as many as could get the information assembled at his house and at the conclusion of the meeting they pressingly invited us to repeat our visits. I intend to visit them again God willing on the 18th September."

From this entry we see that one of the earliest congregations was at Little Britain. In about 1839 they built a log church in what is now called 'the old cemetery', and called it Siloam. It served the village until 1851 when it was destroyed by fire. This old chapel was replaced by a frame chapel built on the same site in 1852. It was nearly twice the size, measuring 30 feet by 40 feet.

The first recorded baptisms in this new chapel were by

John Brown Tapp, for Greenway, Webster and Rodman.

In 1849 it was reported that there were two chapels in Mariposa, the second one perhaps at what John Brown Tapp referred to in 1847 as "the Irish settlement in Concession 2" - would this be Fingerboard, also known as Port Hoover?

In September of 1850, Thomas Green wrote ..."*We hope to open our chapel on the 9th line soon ...*" In another letter he mentioned Copeland's, Providence and Ham's Corners as meeting places.

Indeed, Ham's Corners, later known as Monticello, opened a chapel in 1851. The land for this chapel was "freely given" by Robert Edwards. Upon this quarter acre was erected a "neat little chapel", 36 feet by 24 feet.

The report of 1857 says there were now 5 chapels in Mariposa with 8 meeting places. These five would be Little Britain, Monticello, Providence, Salem and Oakwood., with the preaching places being Ramsay, Black's Schoolhouse, Bethel, Ebenezer, Fenelon Falls and Moynes meeting. Some of these places are not familiar, but the congregations of others will erect chapels in the years ahead. Some were separated off to other circuits in later years.

After this brief overview of the early years, here is what the circuit looked like ....

Little Britain:

Little Britain is on Lots 15 and 16, concessions 4 and 5, four miles straight south of Oakwood on the old grain route to Port Hoover. It was founded by Harrison Haight, who settled here in 1834 and built the first mill in the township in 1837.

The chapel was located in the village on 1/3 acre of land. The first chapel was of log construction. John Mark provided space for it on his land in the northeast corner of Lot 15, Concession 4. It was called Mark's Chapel. It burned down in 1851, and was replaced by a frame chapel in 1852, called Siloam. Men and women sat in separate sections of the church, as was the custom in church at that time. The frame chapel was replaced in 1870 with a brick chapel, 40 feet by 65 feet on a knoll just to the east of the old site.. A parsonage was built at Little Britain on another 1/2 acre at #9 King St. East, and a cemetery in Lot 21, Concession 5 on a 1 acre parcel.

Manilla:

We read earlier about a meeting place at Ham's Corners, and the building of Monticello Chapel there. Ham's corners was the first name given to the community that began with Jacob Ham who opened up the first log store here in 1837 and ran the first post office in the township. This place eventually came to be called Manilla and straddles the boundary between Victoria and Ontario Counties on the line between the 8th and 9th Concessions. Robert Edwards gave land in 1851 to trustees Charles Keeler, George Pearce, Adolphus Short, William James and Thomas Moon.

A frame chapel was built in 1851 at 14 East Church St. A parsonage was built at 13 West Church St., in 1862, measuring 22 feet by 28 feet, on a quarter acre town lot, but the preacher had been living at Manilla since 1856, no doubt in rented premises.

A new brick church was erected in 1869 and dedicated February 11, 1870. Measuring 36 feet by 56 feet it had eleven Gothic windows and seated 350 people. The steeple and tower was over 100 feet high, the first steeple in the Township. It was among the very few Bible Christian chapels to be given a steeple, as this was Church of England styling, not the plain style preferred by the Bible Christians.

Oakwood:

Located in Lot 18, Concession 7, in the village of Oakwood, was Ebenezer Chapel. It was a brick chapel, 36 feet by 56 feet, erected in 1871 and dedicated on January 19th, 1872. It was located on a quarter acre town lot at # 4 King Street E,. Trustees were John Janes Williams, John Astor Mason, Philip Steven Mark, William James, Charles Eck, John Flynn Cunnings and Dr. William Rear.

The organ stood in front of the orchestra which formed a half circle in the southwest corner. The choir was led by J.F. Cunnings. The congregation sat with their backs to the choir. There were three rows of seats and two aisles. Two stoves one on either side, with a long stovepipe leading to the chimney at the front, heated the building. A pail at the chinmey caught the drip of creosote from the pipes.

Samuel Casey Wood was in the chair for the public meeting at which the money that had been collected at the dedication services and teas was handed over to pay for the church. Mr. Wood said, *"With a long pull and a strong pull and a pull all together we raised the needed funds!"*

This was probably a difficult job for the local people, because the first settler at Oakwood, James Tift, had arrived only 17 years previously in 1833. The first store had been opened about 10 years later by Peter Perry of Whitby, and this housed the first post office in the village, with post master being A. McLaughlin. So, you see that the village was very young and people were still finding their way and building their farms. It was a mighty pull for some of them to come up with their share of the funds.

Zion Chapel:
The original log church was built in 1852, eight chains east of the southwest corner of Lot 11, Concession 3. This log building served the community for 21 years, when a new brick chapel, just east of the old one, was constructed on a quarter acre of land. This new chapel, measuring 32 feet by 48 feet was almost double the size of the old log chapel it replaced. This brick chapel served the congregation until 1965, probably the longest serving chapel in the township.

There was apparently a cemetery attached to this chapel, or the old log one, but further details have not been forthcoming.

Bethesda Chapel:
Constructed in 1861, on 1/5th acre of land, Bethesda Chapel was located in the middle of Lot 20 on the 2nd Concession,

87

on the east side of the quarter line. This was a frame chapel measuring 24 feet by 30 feet, a more or less standard size for a good country chapel.

The trustees were Thomas Green, Samuel W. Davidson, Philip Mark, Sr., John Dix and William Prouse.

There was a cemetery attached to this chapel, though it does not appear in the Bible Christian Property Book.

Some records refer to this church as North Valentia, but that name wasn't used until after the Union of Methodists in 1884, when a new church was erected and called North Valentia.

Shiloh Chapel:

Shiloh Chapel was erected in 1859 in Lot 19, Concession C. Concession C is similar to the Broken Front Concessions along Lake Ontario in the more southern Townships. It was located along the north shore of Lake Scugog, and was, until 1851, part of Cartwright Township in Durham County. Three concessions were deeded over to Mariposa Township, Victoria County, but by that time the concessions of Mariposa all had numbers, so these three were given letters, A, B, and C.

This little frame chapel, 26 feet by 36 feet, was built on a quarter acre lot. There was also a cemetery attached to this chapel, known as Lakeside Cemetery, and it was half an acre in size.

Trustees in 1859 were James Emmerson, Jesse Williams, Sidney Barclay, Robert Swain, William Swain, Thomas Emmerson, John Bruce, and John Silosky. Many of these surnames are also found across the lake in Cartwright Township, Durham County.

Some people referred to this chapel as South Valentia. When the new church was opened at Valentia in 1889, Shiloh Chapel was no longer used and was sold in 1890.

Ebenezer Chapel:

Taylor's Corners was the name of the location of Ebenezer Chapel, in Lot 19, Concession 8 of Mariposa Township. Prior to the erection of Ebenezer, the congregation met in the Plank

Schoolhouse in Lot 17 of the 10th Concession from about 1844. In about 1849, John Brown Tapp, the circuit preacher, purchased a parcel of land in Lot 19, Conc. 8 for £6 5s, from James Wallis, and in 1850 a small frame chapel was constructed.

Trustees at this time were George King, George Bateman, Henry Stevens, Henry McNeil, and William Bowes. Those on a list of contributors toward the church fund were: William Pedlar, William Bowes, John Williams, D. Grimston, Martha King, Henry Brockenshire, Dinah Wallis, William Ramsey and Mrs. Jarvis.

William Pedlar, a Cornishman, was the local or lay preacher who took 3 services per month at this chapel. The other service was taken by lay preacher John Cunnings.

By 1862 the chapel was repaired and re-decorated, but the congregation was small, many people having moved to Oakwood. When the new chapel was constructed at Oakwood in 1871, Ebenezer Chapel was closed and the congregation moved to the new chapel.

Providence:

Providence Chapel was built on the main road to Lindsay and to the Mariposa Grist Mill, in Lot 19, Concession 6. It was a frame chapel built in 1846 on one tenth acre. In the Bible Christian Property Book the chapel is listed as being 26 feet by 36 feet in size, but apparently it started out at 26 feet square. The extra ten feet were added about 1848.

After the new church was constructed at Little Britain in 1870 the congregation moved over there and this chapel was removed from the circuit. The building was sold at auction in 1880 and turned into a private home.

Bethel:

From very early days meetings were held in the home of Hugh McDonald on the 10th Concession of Mariposa long before a chapel was built in the vicinity. Bethel Chapel was built in an area known as the Linden Valley. Located in Lot 17, Concession 11, this log chapel was built in 1855, however, the land was acquired in 1853 and held by trustees until they could erect their chapel. The trustees were Richard Julian, William Brockenshire, John Pedlar, John Osborne, and Samuel Pedlar.

By 1882, the congregation were thinking of building a new church, but the looming Union of the Methodists prevented them from doing so. By now the old log chapel had served the community for 27 years, and it went on to serve the congregation after Union until 1897 when it was closed. It was torn down shortly thereafter. The congregation moved to Oakwood.

A small cemetery on half an acre was attached to this chapel, though very few people were ever interred there.

Salem:

In 1857 a log chapel was constructed in Lot 5, Concession 6, on a parcel of land purchased for one shilling in 1853. It measured 24 feet by 30 feet and could seat 100 people. As mentioned earlier, men sat on one side of the church while women occupied the other. At Salem, the women had the north side of the church while the men sat on the south side.

An early list of trustees survives, but whether this is for the 1853-57 period of lab acquisition and chapel building, or whether it is of a later date I do not know. The names include Edward Maunder, Thomas Gilson, Joseph Perrin, William Chidley and Isaac Elford. It should be noted here that Thomas Gilson is, I believe, the father of Rev. John Gilson, and that William Chidley is the same person as Rev. William Chidley.

There was a cemetery associated with this chapel, on the same parcel of land and is still in use today.

This is another log chapel that remained to serve its congregation after Union in 1884.

Fingerboard:

This location has had many names, among them Port Hoover, and much earlier, The Irish Settlement. The land for the chapel was purchased in 1847 and a chapel raised in 1849. Located in Lot 6 of Concession 2, it was a frame chapel. It is

90

reported that this chapel closed when the new Zion Chapel in the 3rd Concession was built in 1873, and that the building was moved 40 rods to the east and used as a private dwelling.

Old records tell us that trustees for the year 1867 were John Frise, Thomas Gilson, Isaac Elford, Curtis Thurtell, John Dix, George Rodman, Thomas Broad and George Davey.

In an early history of Little Britain Chapel it stated that there were ten other chapels in the circuit, making eleven altogether. I have presented those eleven, but there was one more in the north end of the township which was likely left off this list ....

Peniel Chapel:

This congregation started out in early years meeting in private homes, and the congregation went by many names, depending on where they were meeting at the time - Copeland's, Whylie's as examples, but by about 1857 they were meeting at Black's Schoolhouse and so the congregation was called Black's. They continued in the schoolhouse for 20 years until a parcel of land in Lot 5 Concession 11 was acquired from John Carmichael who donated it to the Bible Christian cause. The congregation wanted to call their chapel Providence, but as there was already a chapel by that name in the circuit, it was decided to call it Peniel. Locally it continued to be called Black's, after the old schoolhouse days, and some referred to it as Carmichael's, upon whose land it had been constructed.

Near where the old schoolhouse stood is a cemetery where many pioneer families are buried, and it assumed that this was attached to the congregation at Black's Schoolhouse. No chapel is known to have existed at that spot.

Trustees at the time of construction of Peniel were Thomas Smith, William Philip, J. McIndoo, R. Trethewey, F.J. Nancekivell, Thomas Squires and George Wilson. As you can see, there are many Cornish names among this number!

91

Ministers serving this circuit include:

Up to 1845 - John Hicks Eynon and John Kemeys
1845-46 - Robert Hurley
1847-49 - John Brown Tapp
1850-52 - Thomas Green and John Pinch
1853-54 - Abraham Morris
1855 - Robert Miller
1856-57 - John Hicks Eynon
1858-59 - Arthur Doble, John Hooper
1860 - David Cantlon, Archibald Clarke
1861 - David Cantlon, T.C. Pickard
1862 - Henry Kenner
1863 - Robert Hurley, William Wade
1864 - Robert Hurley, Henry James Colwell
1865 - Thomas Raynor Hull
1866-67 - Thomas R. Hull and Jacob Gale who was at Manilla
1868-69 - Jesse Whitlock and Thomas W. Glover
1870 - Jesse Whitlock and Walter Ayers (they also did Lindsay)
1871 - Richard T. Courtice and Joseph Archer
1872 - Jesse Whitlock and William Henry Butt
1873 - Archibald Clarke and John Kinsey
1874 - Archie Clarke, John Kinsey and Matthew Nichols
1875 - Archie Clarke and Fergus O'Connor Jones
1876 - Archie Clarke, Anselm Schuster and William Rollins
1877 - William Kenner and John Pooley at Little Britain
        Anselm Schuster at Manilla
1878 - William Kenner, and John Wesley Cannon at Little Britain
        James D. Kestle at Manilla
1879 - William Kenner, James Kestle and A.S. Stone
1880 - William Kenner and James Kestle
1881-82 - William George Beer and Alexander Richards
1883-84 - William George Beer, Richard Edgar Mallet, Frederick
        Woodger

Lindsay Circuit

The Lindsay Circuit was a circuit of one, as were the chapels in most of the large towns in Ontario. The chapel was built at Lindsay in 1872 at a cost of $8400.^{00}. It was a white brick church on the east side of Cambridge Street between Wellington and Peel Streets.

An old sketch of Lindsay about 1830, much like it was when John Kemeys and John Hicks Eynon visited there later in that decade.

However, there had been a congregation meeting in the town prior to that date.

From the 1871 census we have these families belonging to this congregation:

BELL , Robert 30	HARDY , Alfred 39 England
BROOKS , Elizabeth 8 Ontario	HARTWICK , Arthur 39 Ontario
BROWN , Elizabeth 19 England	HOLMES , Phebe 15 Ontario
BROWN , Robert 36 Ireland	HOW , Elizabeth 78 Ontario
CHASTRE , Arthur 41 England	HUGHES , Melinday 18 Ontario
DELURY , Kate 18 Ontario	LAWRY , Julio ? 21 United States
DELURY , Timothy30 Ontario	MCELWANE , Mathew 59 Ire.
ELLIS , James B 61 England	PATTERSON , John W 32 Eng.
FITZGERALD , Maurice 30 Ont.	REA , Osborne 17 Ontario
FORD , James 41 England	RICHARDS , Thomas 48 England
FOSTER , John 32 Ontario	SHILL , George 35 United States
GREGORY , Catherine 52 Ont.	THOMPSON , Aphrim 20 Ontario
GREGORY , George 29 Ontario	THOMPSON , Richard 18 Ont.
GREGORY , John 23 Ontario	WALKER , Samuel 34 Ireland

WALLER, William H 25 Ontario   WINGROVE, William 26 Eng.
WALLIS, Elizabeth 28 Ontario

This congregation may have met prior to the construction of their church somewhere along Market Street, perhaps above a shop.

The handsome white brick church measured 42 feet by 60 feet and was on a town lot of one quarter acre. The parsonage was built next door on the same lot, but whether it was on the north side of the church or south side, I do not know. The church still stands, though the parsonage may not. No further information about the parsonage has been found.

Lindsay Bible Christian Chapel on Cambridge St., now Baptist.

The steepled bell tower, which is unusual in Bible Christian chapels, rises dramatically from the centre of the building. It has a pointed entrance and narrow lancet windows with louvers which are typical of church architecture in Upper Canada at that time, especially in the towns and cities. The church has changed little in the ensuing years, except that the clock is no longer in the bell tower. After the Union of the Methodists in 1884, the church was sold to the Baptists. It still houses their congregation.

The Preachers who served this congregation were:
1870-71 - Walter Ayers
1872 - James Collins
1873-74 - Edward Roberts
1875 - Edward Roberts and   W. Trethewey
1876 - John Guard
1877 - Samuel Jolliffe
1878-80 - Richard T. Courtice
1881-83 - William Limbert

Ontario County

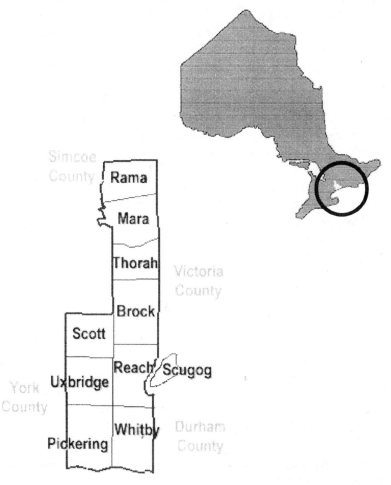

Circuits of Ontario County

Ontario County is located just about the centre of the province right along the north shore of Lake Ontario. It was settled at a very early date by United Empire Loyalist families who came in from both the west and east. By the mid 18teens, only lots in the back concessions were available in Pickering Township, but by the War of 1812-14 there were few settlers north of Moodie Farewell's tavern at the Ontario/Durham east county line. How different each edge of the county.

The Bible Christian Missionary, John Hicks Eynon and his wife, Elizabeth Dart, a renowned preacher in her own right, arrived in Upper Canada in 1833 and immediately set to work along the lakeshore. By 1835 there was an organized congregation at Oshawa meeting in the Union School.

As more and more ministers arrived from England or joined the itinerancy from the settler families already here, the circuits enlarged and the ministers found their way further and further back into the bush, until many of the townships of the old Ontario county had a circuit. These circuits included:

Oshawa Circuit:
Oshawa - In the village on Metcalfe Street, now the northern edge of Memorial Park.

Columbus Circuit:
Columbus - in the village, east of the 'four corners'.
Brooklin - in the village at Church Street and Cassel's Road
Elim - in the 6th Concession, north and east of Brooklin
Siloam - in the hamlet of Raglan

(Prior to 1867 this area was served on an infrequent basis from the Bowmanville Circuit)

Pickering Circuit:
Duffin's Creek - or Pickering Village as it came to be known, at

96

the corner of Kingston Road and George Jones St., just one block east of Church St.

Frenchman's Bay -

Cherrywood - in the hamlet - Lot 30, Conc. 2, Pickering Township
Providence - Lot 24, Concession 5, Pickering Township
Bethel - Lot 17, Concession 4 - near Brougham, aka - Hastings
Ebenezer - location unknown - no records found.

Uxbridge Circuit:
Uxbridge - in the village Lot 28, Conc. 6, Uxbridge Township
Bethesda - at Leaskdale Lot 24, Conc. 7, Scott Township
Zion - Lot 7, Concession 7, Scott Township

Prince Albert Circuit:

This circuit once served those chapels located in Cartwright and Manvers Townships in Durham County. In 1874 these two townships were withdrawn from the Prince Albert Circuit and given their own circuit status and came under the jurisdiction of the Victoria District. The following list deals only with those chapels left on the Prince Albert Circuit, the rest being on their own pages in Victoria County section.

Prince Albert - in the village, Lot 17, Conc. 5, Reach Township
Bethesda - Lot 6, Conc. 9, Scugog Township (Scugog Island)
Salem -
Bethany -

Oshawa Circuit

Originally part of the Bowmanville Circuit, Oshawa consisted of only one charge because of the size of the congregation and the size of the town of Oshawa which needed constant canvassing by the encumbent preacher.

In the early days, from about 1835, Bible Christian

meetings were held at the Union School house, a log building used not only for a school in the fledgling community, but shared by no less than five denominations for their meetings and Sabbath Worship.

From, *The History of the County of Ontario*, by Leo A. Johnson (page 167), comes this report .....

"When the Union Schoolhouse was built in Oshawa in 1835, it became the centre of worship for all denominations. The Wesleyan Methodists, Roman Catholics, Quakers, Baptists and Bible Christians all share the building until 1841 when the Methodists and Catholics built their own churches. The Bible Christians built theirs in 1842....."

So, by 1842, the Bible Christians were in a position to build their own chapel, and a piece of property, on Metcalfe Street, was acquired and a frame chapel erected. We know it was a frame building because of the record kept by the Bible Christians for the property they owned. In this book it is noted ....

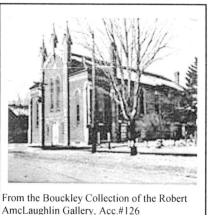

From the Bouckley Collection of the Robert AmcLaughlin Gallery, Acc.#126
Metcalfe Street Chapel, Oshawa, Ontario

"In 1864 a new brick chapel, 42' x 81', was erected to replace a frame church c1841"

The Bible Christians had a parsonage on Selina St (as the Property Book spells it) (should be Celina Street). This was a 20 by 26 foot frame house with a 16 by 20 foot kitchen wing. It was erected on 1/8 acre. Unfortunately, no date or exact address is given for this parsonage, the deed for which was kept ... "in Mr. Trewin's safe".

The chapel was enlarged from time to time to house the

growing congregation.. At the time of union in 1884, the congregation stayed on in the Metcalfe Street church, but eventually, with no more land either side for expansion, they decided to build a new church.

From McIntyre Hood's, *Oshawa*, we have this report ....

"In 1912, the cornerstone was laid for a new and much larger church, a few months later it was completed and formally dedicated."

Now, of course, this was in the time of the Methodists, but what an impact this must have had on the old Bible Christians who were still part of the Methodist congregation! Their former chapel was sold, not to be used as a residence, or a community centre of some description, but to *industry!* In 1912 R.S. McLaughlin acquired the building and turned it into his Buick Bumper Plant!!

There were a few old Bible Christians rolling in their graves over that, I'm sure!!!

The old Bible Christian Chapel served the community well, but was taken down in the 1960's or 1970's. For those of you who are familiar with Oshawa, it stood on Metcalfe Street, across the road from the bandshell in Memorial Park, Simcoe St. South.

Preachers who served this congregation include:

(See Bowmanville Circuit up to 1860)

1860-61 - John Pinch
1862 - unknown
1863 - John Harris
1864-65 - Henry Ebbott
1866 - J.T. Sencabaugh
1867 - by a supply minister as often as possible
1868-69 - W.S. Pascoe
1870 - J.J. Rice
1872-75 - John Kenner
1875-76 - William Kenner
1877-79 - Archibald Clarke
1880-82 - Walter Ayers
1883 - George Webber

Columbus Circuit

Columbus Circuit was located in Ontario County, in the township of East Whitby. It's most important chapel was at the village of Columbus about 7 miles north of Oshawa.

Because East Whitby Township was a well-settled area, there were only four chapels on this circuit, each having a large congregation.

Columbus:

Columbus was once called English Corners because of the great many English people gathered there. From W.H. Smith's Gazetteer of Upper Canada, 1850, we find this information .....

"Columbus contains about 300 inhabitants; it is a tolerable settlement, although it is too near Oshawa to do a large business. Indeed it appears to have remained nearly stationary for the last 3 or 4 years. It contains a grist mill with 2 run of stone, a saw mill, tannery, ashery, and soap and candle factory, a post office, 3 churches - United Presbyterian, Wesleyan Methodist and Bible Christian; and there is an Episcopal Methodist church one mile west of the village."

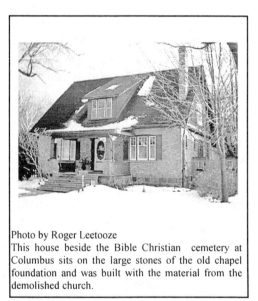

Photo by Roger Leetooze
This house beside the Bible Christian cemetery at Columbus sits on the large stones of the old chapel foundation and was built with the material from the demolished church.

The village is located in Lot 13, Concession 6, and it was on a one acre village lot that the Bible Christian chapel was built at an early date. The cemetery today has a sign which dates the cemetery at 1845 so the chapel may well date from a similar time. The Bible Christian Conference of 1855 was held at this chapel.

The Bible Christian Property Book tells us that the chapel was frame, 30 feet by 40 feet in size and with a Sunday School room 30 feet by 20 feet added on.

The circuit parsonage was built at Columbus in 1862. It was built on it's own town lot and was likely frame, but the records do not say which it was. It was 24 feet by 34 feet and the lot was 36 rods (probably square rods) in size. A cemetery shared the one acre parcel where the chapel was located. All that remains today is a small parcel with the stones gathered together in a memorial cairn. The foundation of the chapel still exists beside the cemetery, however, a brick residence was raised on it sometime early in the 20th century. It is said that the chapel, after union, was remodelled into a house. Rita Bone Kopp from Ohio has records that show her Bone ancestors lived in the remodelled chapel, though I believe the present house is of later construction

Siloam:

Located in the 9th Concession, this chapel was at Raglan. The first building was a log chapel, 15 feet by 20 feet, and by the size of it, it was probably put up as a settler's first house.

In 1861 a frame chapel was built, 25 feet by 40 feet, on a parcel of land 80 square rods. After Union it was moved over to Burketon in Darlington Township where it still serves the community as part of the United Church of Canada.

Elim:

The Bible Christian Cemetery sits astride two lots, Lots 13, and 14 in the 6th Concession of East Whitby Township. It marks the spot where Elim Chapel once stood.

Elim was built in 1860. It was a frame chapel, 20 feet by 30 feet, so we can guess the congregation was fairly small, probably only 30 or 40 families.

Brooklin:

Brooklin, once called Winchester, had a population of about 550 in 1850 when W.H. Smith compiled his Gazetteer of Upper Canada. Of Brooklin he had this to say ....

"Winchester contains 2 grist mills with 3 run of stone ea, one of which is built of brick, and another mill with 2 run of stones. There are also a tannery, a woollen factory, foundry, ashery and brewery; two saleratus (bicarbonate of soda) factories, and a soap and candle factory. The village also contains a circulating library."

Brooklin Chapel was by far the largest and most impressive chapel on this circuit, and why it was not the lead chapel on the circuit I wonder.

Brooklin Bible Christian Chapel became the community centre in the 20th century.

The only brick chapel on the circuit it was built in 1876. This was a late chapel because the Bible Christians had not started preaching at Brooklin until 1875. It was also a large chapel, the town growing by leaps and bounds. The chapel measured 35 feet by 50 feet and would likely hold about 300 people or more.

The contract for the masonry work went to Messrs. Gale and Dinner of Oshawa, and the wood work and painting to Messrs. Stephenson and Kirby of Oshawa.

At the time of dedication of the new chapel Rev. John Guard sent a description to The Observer.....

"The building is a handsome brick structure with a full stone basement, and a class-room partitioned off one end. The

102

audience room is neatly furnished, the walls being blocked and the ceiling having four ornamental centre pieces. In the front gable end, thre is a neat inscription stone, containing the name and date of the erection of the church. The building as a whole, is neat and tasty, and commands the admiration of all. In the rear of the church, the friends have erected a shed 80 feet long, and the whole is enclosed with a neat picket fence."

Prior to having a chapel, there was a small congregation who used Campbell's schoolhouse located about 4 miles northwest of the village. There was very little success at this location and so it was given up and preaching commenced in the village.

As early as 1856, a list of members from the Campbell's schoolhouse has been kept. These included:
Mrs. M. Newton, J. Medland, J. Clark, Miss M. Moffatt, Mr. H. Price and wife, T. Glyde and wife, Jos. Moffatt, W.Wage, Sr., Joseph Grose, J. Blight, R. Warder.

In 1869 the members included:
E. Tonkin (this is probably the minister), J. Medland and wife, J. Blight and wife, W. Wedge and wife, Thos. Moffat, J. Grose, Sr., J. Arscott, W. Newton, G. Ciphery, Jr., W. Brent, T. Taylor, W.H. Hull, G. Medland, M. Gaose, T. Wedge, W. Blight, G. Ciphery, A. Burns, Mrs. O. Clarke and daughter, Brent, Miss Susan Arscott, E. Wedge, E. Grose.

In that first year the chapel was constructed, members of the congregation included the families of Blight, Roberts, Medland, Holliday, Grills, White, Cowle, Baledon, Jeffery, Stork, Harper.

Ministers who served this circuit include:
1867 - Jesse Whitlock
1868 - ....
1869 - T.R. Hull
1870-71 - unknown
1872-75 - John Guard
1876-77 - William G. Beer and J.A. Dafoe

103

1878 - Archie Clarke
1879 - Alexander Richard, James Hoskin
1880 - Alexander Richard, Thomas Brown
1881 - William Ross Medland
1882-83 - Herman Moore
(Prior to 1867 this area was served on an infrequent basis from the Bowmanville Circuit)

Pickering Circuit

The Pickering Circuit, located in Pickering Township, Ontario County, had six chapels which included: Duffin Creek, Frenchman's Bay, Cherrywood, Providence, Bethel and Ebenezer.

Duffin Creek:

Duffin Creek is an early name for the village of Pickering, located in the 1st Concession of the township of the same name. This was an early village in the township and grew along the York to Kingston Road. Not only did it draw people because of the milling operations along Duffin's Creek, but it was also an important stagecoach stop before getting into Scarborough and York.

Although it was an early village, it was fairly late when the Bible Christians built their chapel here, in about 1871, though they likely met prior to that in the schoolhouse, or rented time from the Methodists. The chapel was built one block east of Church Street, at the corner of Kingston Road and George Jones St. in the village, on a one acre lot. It was a yellow brick chapel, 34 feet by 50 feet. A parsonage was also built in Pickering about 1875. The Bible Christian Property Book lists it as being on half an acre, but whether this was half the church lot, or another parcel of land I do not know. The parsonage was of frame construction, 26 feet by 28 feet.

At the time of Union the chapel was sold to the 'Fast' Quakers, otherwise known as the Hicksite Quakers.

In later years the old chapel was converted into a service

station.

Frenchman's Bay:

Siloam Chapel was built at Frenchman's Bay in 1878. The lot size upon which this frame chapel was built, was 80 feet by 52 feet.

The church was dedicated on July 7th, 1878, and an article about its erection appeared the following week in the Observer, in the July 17th edition.....

"Frenchman's Bay has, for more than 12 months past, been the scene of efforts, on the part of our people and a good measure of success has attended their labours. Here, as in very many other places, where we have sought to promote the cause of God, we had no church to work in. But God disposed the heart of Mr. J. Fisher to give us the use of his ballroom, rent free to hold religious services in. Brother George Smith and friends fitted it up to suit their purposes. In the fall of last year, Mr. Fisher sold the property to Mr. Ure, who very kindly allowed us to occupy the hall until the spring when he needed it.

One Friday, March 22 [1878] a meeting was called to consider the propriety of building. A committee was appointed and on the 27th of May the first work was don on it.

On Saturday July 6th at 7:00 p.m. we had the satisfaction of seeing the church in such a state as to be comfortable for the purpose of dedicating it to the worship of God."

A second parsonage was constructed here in 1879. This house, probably for the assistant, or *young man*, as he was referred to, was of frame construction and rough-cast, an old term used for concrete. This was often the technique used in houses, the front portion being rough-cast and the rest (away from the street) being frame. A cemetery was also located at Frenchman's Bay on a separate three-quarter acre parcel.

Cherrywood:

Not much is known about the Cherrywood Chapel. There may have been two chapels on this site. According to information at the Pickering Library, there was a log chapel on the site that served until 1850. I would imagine that a frame chapel was constructed to replace the log building at that time.

In the Bible Christian Property Book, there is reference only to a frame chapel constructed in 1870, which would be the chapel in the accompanying photograph, which measured 30 feet by 40 feet.

From the Digital Collection of the Pickering Library Archives
Cherrywood Bible Christian Chapel

Providence:

Providence Chapel, a frame chapel built in about 1853, at Lot 24, Concession 5, now resides at Greenwood, at the Pickering Museum Village. It was built on leased land, the lease of which expired in 1890. Whether or not the chapel was removed at that time, or whether it was removed when an airport was being planned for the area, I do not know. Probably the latter, as most of the historic buildings in the pioneer village were gathered from various places at that time.

Bethel:

The land for both Bethel and Providence (above) was donated by the Hastings family, and for that reason Bethel Chapel was sometimes known as Hastings Chapel. Located in the north part of Lot 17, in the 4th Concession, this

From the author's collection:
Providence Chapel, moved from Lot 24, Concession 5 to the Pickering Pioneer Village at Greenwood.

chapel stood on the southwest corner of the 16th sideroad and the 5th Concession Road. This would satisfy the mile and a quarter rule that the Bible Christians followed when building chapels in nearby vicinities, as with Providence and Bethel.

Situated near the village of Brougham, this was a frame chapel, 24 feet by 40 feet - quite small, really - built in about 1862.. According to the Bible Christian Property book, the chapel stood on 1 acre of land, but this also housed a cemetery. The Chapel has long since disappeared, but the

From the Digital Collection at Pickering Library Archives
Bethel Chapel near Brougham, also known as Hasting's Chapel.

small country cemetery still remains to mark the site.

Ebenezer:

No location has yet been found for Ebenezer Bible Christian Chapel, and no information was found in the Bible Christian Property book. The only suggestion I can make is that this chapel was at Scarborough Township, as it too had an Ebenezer Chapel I can not find.

The following is an article from the Bible Christian Magazine, dated September 1st, 1849 telling about the Pickering Circuit in it's early days .....

"We held our quarterly meeting near Brother Thomas Courtice's, one of our old and tried friends. It was the first meeting of the kind ever held in that place, I believe; as there was a quarterly meeting about two miles and a half from ours, I did not expect a large congregation; but more came than I anticipated. The Great Head of the Church was present, and a most gracious influence was felt from the beginning of the meeting to the end,

such, I trust, as will not be forgotten for a long time to come. We have only seven places open for preaching in this mission yet, and three of these had no preaching when I came on the station. It has been rather unfavourable for enlarging our borders since I came here. Just after I was relieved from Darlington station, hay-making and harvest came on, so that the people have not been able to attend as much as they would like. I hope by the help of the Lord to be able to break up more groung in a few weeks; however, great good is being done, and I believe we shall see better days. On the whole, the prospect which presents itself at present is of a cheering nature..... Brother John Edwards"

Preachers who served this circuit included:
1848-49 - John Edwards
1850 - Philip James
1851-52 - Richard Lyle Tucker
1853-54 - John Brown Tapp, and John Hodgson (who may have
        been the young man on this circuit)
1855 - Paul Robbins and R. Miller
1856-57 - Arthur Doble
1858-60 - Thomas Green
1861-63 - H. Stevens
1864- H. Stevens and Martyn Mennear
1865 - Henry James Nott
1866-67 - Henry James Colwell
1868-70 - John Williams
1871 - Joseph Hoidge
1872-74 - Anselm Schuster
1875-76 - George Smith
1877-79 - Andrew Gordon
1880-83 - William R. Roach

Many thanks are extended to Bob Martindale at Ajax for his assistance in locating the Bible Christian Chapel at Pickering Village.

Uxbridge Circuit

Although many miles into the 'back' of the townships, the area around Uxbridge was settled fairly early, with the settlement at Uxbridge itself being founded about 1820. Many of the people who came to live in the area were Quakers, and it is the Quaker population, both here and further south at Pickering Village, who are most often remembered as making early contributions to the growth of the area.

The earliest Bible Christian records in the area are for The Scott Mission in Scott Township in the year 1857, though I would suspect there was a congregation at the township at a much earlier date, meeting in private homes, in barns and in the local school house.

In 1871, the 'mission' status was changed to full circuit status.

Bethesda:

In 1857 John Tiffen gave one acre of land to the Bible Christians for the erection of a chapel and for a burial ground. This parcel was located in Lot 24 of the 7th Concession of Scott Township, Ontario County. That same year a chapel was erected. It was a frame chapel measuring 26 feet by 38 feet, according to the Bible Christian Property Book. However, Allan McGillivray, of Uxbridge, who wrote '*The Churches of Uxbridge-Scott*', tells us the size was 30 feet by 42 feet.

Photo Courtesy Scott-Uxbridge Museum
The Parsonage at Leaskdale, today a branch of the Scott-Uxbridge Museum

To help defray the cost of the chapel, anyone who gave five dollars into the fund ... "*got in return a 6 x 16 feet plot in the burial ground.*" So says Allan McGillivray.

In 1866 a parsonage was built at Leaskdale, just north of the village. It was a frame house 18 feet by 24 feet, and sat on one eighth acre. It must have been built well for it still serves as a private residence today.

Zion:

Zion chapel was also located in Scott Township, in Lot 7 of the 7th Concession. A society had been formed there a number of years, meeting in private homes at first. In 1861, the circuit trustees purchased the Primitive Methodist Chapel. This was a frame church built in 1852 and sat on one acre of land. It served the need of the Zion congregation until 1874 when the chapel was re-built.

Photo Courtesy Scott Uxbridge Museum
Zion Chapel and Cemetery, Lot 7, Conc. 7 Scott Twp.
The church shed is in the background.

This new frame church was 24 feet by 36 feet, and served the congregation who continued to meet here as Methodists after Union (1884) until 1886 when they built a new church.

There was also a cemetery on this site, but whether or not it was in use when the Primitive Methodists occupied the property is not known.

Uxbridge:

The congregation here started about 1857, being part of the original Scott Mission. In 1862 the congregation built a small frame chapel, but as Allan McGillivray tells us .....

"The chapel was close to where the railway station was built later. After the railway arrived they moved the chapel from

110

this 'smokey' location to the southwest corner of Church and Mechanics Streets and it was re-opened in 1874."

(It can be assumed that the railway went through within a year or two prior to 1874).

McGillivray also goes on to say that there was already a house on that village lot which was converted to a parsonage. The Bible Christian Property Book says this was a frame house, 24 feet by 30 feet, much the same size as the Leaskdale parsonage. This became the parsonage for the circuit and the Leaskdale parsonage was rented for $24 a month, so says Allan McGillivray in his book, 'Decades of Harvest, A History of Scott Township'.

After Union the chapel was rented to the Salvation Army for a couple of years, then sold and used as a private dwelling.

One other chapel was located in Scott Township, known as Bethel, but it was over on the western edge of the township right on the County line at Zephyr, and was part of the Georgina Circuit. See that section in York County Chapels for Bethel Chapel.

Ministers who served this Mission and Circuit included:
1856 - Arthur Doble and Robert Miller (served from Pickering)
1857-58 - Joseph Dix
1859-60 - Abraham Morris (served from Perrytown)
1861-62 - Abraham Morris and Henry Stevens (served from Pickering)
1863-64 - John Hooper
1865 - John Williams and Richard T. Courtice (with Prince Albert)
1866 - Robert Hicks
1867-68 - George Dunkley
1869-70 - William Woodman
1871 - Charles J. Pearce
1872-75 - Joseph Archer
1876 - Richard Mallett
1877-79 - John Holmes
1880-81 - Andrew Gordon
1882-83 - J.W. Cannon

111

Prince Albert Circuit

Prince Albert Circuit was based at the village of Prince Albert, near Port Perry, Reach Township, Ontario County. It included four, perhaps five chapels, four of which were in Reach Township and the fifth in Scugog Township, which was Scugog Island.

There were scattered settlements and farms in the bush of the vicinity in the early 1830's, and the Rev. John Kemeys made the rounds to each place, much of his travel done by canoe up and down the Scugog River. Then the Purdy's built a mill at the place now called Lindsay, then called Purdy's Mill, and the daming of the river caused much flooding further south, creating Lake Scugog, and further need to travel by canoe to most places. It was much easier to go by canoe than to try to fight one's way through the bush which separated these small settlements.

Prince Albert Circuit also came to encompass the chapels in Cartwright and the meeting places of Manvers. But in 1874 these two were withdrawn from the circuit, made into a circuit of their own, some further chapels built in Manvers,

From the Author's Collection:
An old plank road near Prince Albert c1870

and the whole new circuit given to Victoria District. Prince Albert worked under the direction of the Bowmanville District.

Prince Albert:

The Bible Christians built a chapel at Prince Albert in 1864. Settlers had been coming into the area in any number for the

112

past 30 years, so it was no longer an isolated place, though the roads were still nothing to boast about.

The frame chapel was fairly small, only 28 feet by 36 feet in size. It was on a town lot of 4400 sq. feet. The Pine Grove Cemetery, open to all denominations, was the local burial place.

In 1869 a parsonage was erected. It too was of frame and situated on its own half acre parcel. In those days lumber was plentiful and cheap, and so a congregation could put up a good house and a good chapel for very little money.

Bethesda:

This chapel was built in Scugog Township, which at one time comprised Scugog Island that was formed when Purdy's dam flooded the land south of Lindsay.

The chapel was located on Lot 6 of the 9th Concession. It was of frame construction and was erected on one eighth acre in 1868. On the 1877 Atlas, this chapel is shown on the corner of the farm owned by D. Jackson, and this was in fact the man who gave the lot for the chapel. The chapel was dedicated on June 31, 1869. In a book written by Rev. F.G. Weir in 1927, *Scugog and its Environs*, he tells us that the Bible Christian Chapel and the Christian Chapel nearby were raised on the same day. The people likely made a competition out of it to see who could put up their chapel more quickly - a chapel bee!!

Describing not only the chapel dedication but the area as well, Rev. David Cantlon wrote an article for the Observer ....

"To the numerous readers of the Observer unacquainted with the locality a brief description of the Island will not be out of place. It is the largest of these islands which stud the beautiful and romantic 'Lake Scugog', and was for many years called by way of pre-eminence the 'Big Island', but has been for some time formed into a township and designated 'The township of Scugog, in the County of Ontario'. It is connected with the mainland at the rising Village of Port Perry, the anticipated terminus of the 'Whitby and Port Perry Railway', by a floating bridge, three fourths of a mile long. The soil is for the most part good, and is occupied by an

industrious, intelligent and moral class of men, to whose praise I would record the fact, that there is no tavern on the Island. Here some five years ago, during the Pastorate of Bro. John Pinch, at the earnest request of the settlers the Gospel message, was proclaimed in a little log school house, and soon a few members were united in church fellowship. During the Pastorate of Bro. John Williams, our members were stirred up to arise and build a house for the Lord, a site was sought, and obtained from Mr. David Jackson, a subscription list passed around, and the sum of $400 subscribed towards the object. Immediately after my appointment to the charge of this mission, steps were taken to commence the work, the contract for a frame, on a stone foundation, 24 x 36, with an entrance porch 10 x 12, was let for the sum of $545, and the members supplying material for foundation and frame, so that the whole expense of the church is about $600. The Trustees and building committee, knowing the friends on the Island had subscribed to the full extent of and in some instances, even beyond their ability, and that $150 would be required to meet the contract engagement, were filled with anxious fears; many thought it unwise to provide a tea, in connection with the opening services, as the burden would necessarily fall on a few, however, being encouraged to proceed they went to work with a will, and made the necessary preparations. The state of the roads did not tend to allay their fears, there being no sleighing, but on Sunday morning hope began to dawn, for long before the hour announced for the first service had arrived, sleighs and cutters from the environs of the lake, and wagons and buggies from a distnace, streamed along in quick succession and many asked, where have they all come from ...... from Reach, Cartwright and Mariposa, the various vehicles well laden with friends came pouring along..."

(Note: The Rev. Weir gave the dedication date as June yet Rev. Cantlon says they came in sleighs across the lake - perhaps dedication was Janr. and transcribed incorrectly by Rev. Weir as June)

The Rev. Weir also tells us that the chapel was enlarged by about 20 feet (added to its length) during the pastorate of L.W.

Wickett. Rev. Wickett did not serve this circuit prior to Union, but he did continue with the Methodists, so this may have happened after 1884.

The members of the congregation in 1871 were:

Joseph Abbott and family
Henry Aldred and family
John C. Burk - great grandson of John Burk, Loyalist
George Hodgson and family
Robert Homer and family
James Jackson and family
Phillip Rodney and family
William Stanton and family
Joseph Stones and family
James Sweetman and family
Rosan Trowbridge and family
Samuel Wakebard and family,
Michael Walsh and family
William Willwood and family

Salem & Bethany Chapels:

Old records do not say which of these is which. According to Samuel Farmer, in his book, '*On the Shores of Scugog*', a Bible Christian Chapel was erected at Seagrave shortly after the Methodists put up a church in 1875. Was Salem or Bethany this chapel? The Bible Christian Property Book does not give a location for either of these chapels, but they do give dates of construction - Bethany in 1862 and Salem in 1864 - neither matching the date of Seagrave Bible Christian Chapel.

From the disbursement of Bible Christian families on the 1871 census, it appears as if there was a congregation just about mid-township in Concessions 5 through 7, but where this was located is unknown. Was it Utica? There is an un-named cemetery there, though the Bible Christian Property Book lists no cemetery with either Bethany or Salem.

Although little information can be found for this circuit, we do know who served on it. Those Bible Christian ministers are as follows:

1860-61 - George Bodle

1862-64 - John Pinch

1865 - John Williams and Richard T. Courtice (with Scott Twp.)

1866-67 - John Williams

1868-69 - David Cantlon and Robert Baker

1870-71 - David Cantlon and Gersham Nott

1872 - Archibald Clarke and John Holmes

1873 - William Kinley and W.H. Butt

1874 - William Kinley and George Fulcher

1875 - William Kinley and William Rollins

1876 - William H. Quance and John Gilson

1877 - William H. Quance and S.J. Cummings

1878 - Roger Allin and James Dafoe

1879-80 - Roger Allin

1881-82 - William Kenner

1883 - William Kenner and Andrew Cory Courtice

York County

The Circuits of York County

The circuits in this county were found at the extreme ends of the county - at Toronto in the south and at Georgina Township in the north. From an old history of York County there are a few places in between where the early inhabitants are credited with being Bible Christians, however, that author, like many others, likely confused the Christian Church with the Bible Christian Church, as no further indication has been found that there were either meeting places, congregations, or even attempts at setting these in place, at any place other than Toronto and Sutton area.

Toronto:
Agnes and Teraulay Streets - St. John's Ward
Lippincott and Buller Streets - St. Patrick'sWard

Georgina Township:
Sutton - in town
Egypt Chapel - possibly at the village of Vatchell
Ebenezer Chapel - near Virginia P.O.
Bethel Chapel - in Scott Township near the county boundary at
    Zephyr.

Toronto Circuit

At one time there were two Bible Christian Chapels in Toronto, one at Agnes and Teraulay Streets, and another at Lippincott and Buller Streets.

The chapel, sometimes known as Agnes Street Chapel, was located in St. John's Ward of the city, and the chapel at Buller was in St. Patrick'sWard. The parsonage was built at 248 Simcoe Street.

About 1867 the Bible Christians started seriously looking at Toronto for the site of a chapel and began to develop a congregation there. Immigration was reaching it's high-point at that time, and the city was filling up with people from Devon, and a few from Cornwall, though most of the Cornish gave the large cities a wide berth.

Ministers were appointed to Toronto on a supply basis for the first five years - in other words, when ever anyone had a chance they would go over to Toronto to preach to the congregation and offer words of encouragement toward the formation of their congregation.

Lippincott and Buller:

In 1872 a small frame chapel was erected at the corner of Lippincott and Buller Streets. It was on a small city lot 93 feet by 138 feet, and the chapel itself measured only 30 feet by 45 feet.

This seems to have been a short-lived

Church Choir 1907 Photograph by William James
Fonds 1244, Item 2373 Toronto Public Llbrary
The interior of the chapel may be much the same as it was when the Bible Christians had it.

chapel. By 1877 it is no longer listed in the city directories and by 1881 the Directory for the City of Toronto indicated there was nothing but vacant lots at that corner.

Teraulay and Agnes:

In 1873 a grand brick structure was erected at the corner of Teraulay and Agnes Streets. This chapel was 55 feet by 99 feet, capable of holding nearly 1000 people for Sabbath services. It took up the whole of the city lot on which it stood, the lot being only 69 feet by 100 feet.

After the Union of 1884, the chapel was purchased by the Black Methodist Episcopal (BME) Congregation. Of the accompanying photograph, the photographer''s son identified this church as ...." *on Terauley (now Bay) Street. It may have been the Agnes Street Methodist Church, which was on the southeast corner of Bay and Dundas (formerly called Agnes) streets."*

This whole area was levelled in order to build the now famous Eaton Centre.

The parsonage, which was built sometime later at 248 Simcoe St., was *rough cast*, the term at that time for concrete. This was

Bible Christian.

BIBLE CHRISTIAN.—Rev. George Webber, minister. Hours of service, 11 a.m. and 7 p.m.; Sabbath School at 2½ p.m. Cor. Agnes and Terauley.

BIBLE CHRISTIAN.—Rev. J. M. Tredrea, assistant minister. Hours of service, 11 a.m. and 6½ p.m. Sabbath School at 2½ p.m. Lippincott street, cor. Buller.

From the Toronto Directory , 1876
The listing for the two chapels. In 1874 & 75 the lsitings had shown J.J. Rice at Lippincott and Buller and George Copeland at Terauley St. By 1877 the Lippincott chapel is no longer listed.

scribed to look like hewn stone and was usually only at the front of the building the rest being of frame construction. The parsonage was 30 feet by 36 feet, while the lot upon which it stood was 30 feet by 120 feet.

Ministers who served this circuit included:
1872 - J.J. Rice
1873-74 - George Copeland
1875 - George Webber and J.H. Tredrea
1876-78 - George Webber
1879-80 - William Jolliffe
1881-83 - Edward Roberts.

Until 1877, this circuit fell under the jurisdiction of the Bowmanville District, as did the rest of the chapels in the County of York. But in 1878 they were placed under their own District.

Sutton Circuit

Sutton Circuit was located in the township of Georgina in the county of York. Georgina is at the northern edge of the County, is on the south shore of Lake Simcoe.

Just prior to the coming of the Bible Christians, Sutton was called Bouchier Mills. When the village got their first post office it was called Georgina Post Office, and the village was generally called Georgina. Then, when it took on town status in 1864 the name was changed to Sutton.

The Sutton Circuit was made up of at least four chapels -
Sutton - in town
Egypt Chapel - possibly at the village of Vatchell
Ebenezer Chapel - near Virginia P.O.
Bethel Chapel - in Scott Twp near the county line at Zephyr.

Sutton Chapel:

Although we have not yet found a physical address for this chapel, we do know that it was a frame chapel, 32 feet by 50 feet, which is large for a frame chapel. It was built on a town lot of one quarter acre in 1872. That same year a parsonage was built, also on one quarter acre, but whether it was built on the church lot, or whether it had it's own parcel of land I do not know. Because the Parsonage and chapel were constructed the same year, it suggests to me that the congregation had been meeting for some time, though the records for the various itinerant preachers shows no one visiting that area prior to the building of the chapel. In that same year there was a congregation at Beaverton which was attached to Sutton Circuit, but only for that one year. Beaverton seems not to have taken hold and was abandon for it was not mentioned again.

Egypt Chapel:

Egypt chapel was south and east of Sutton, and on the Belden's 1878 map of the township, a Bible Christian Chapel is shown one concession south of Vatchell, in Lot 6 Concession 4. This was a frame chapel, 25 feet by 30 feet, built in 1874.

Ebenezer Chapel:

This chapel was also referred to as Georgina Chapel, which would lead one to think it was located at Georgina P.O. aka Sutton. But, it was a little country chapel, measuring only 24 feet by 30 feet. It was of frame construction and is shown on the Belden's Atlas, map of Georgina Township at Lot 12, Concession 7 near Virginia P.O. Although no dates are available, it seems that there were two buildings here previously. A log schoolhouse, used for both school and church which was replaced by a ..... *"building of planks"*, which would be a frame building. Possible dates for these buildings have been suggested as 1836 and 1870. The church there now, Virginia United Church, was built in 1897, and the school was replaced in 1913.

Bethel Chapel:

Located at Zephyr, in Scott Township, this was a much earlier chapel, starting out life as an abandon settler's log cabin I would think, being just 18 feet by 22 feet. The Bible Christians either built this cabin in 1850 or started using it about that time. By about 1860 a brick chapel was erected to replace the log building. The chapel was on 1 acre and there was a cemetery attached to this chapel, possibly called Mount Pleasant.

In 1872 this circuit was part of the Victoria and Peterborough District, but in 1878 it was made part of the Toronto District. Preachers to serve this circuit were .....
1872 - George Dunkley and Arthur Kelly, a probationer that year
1873-74 - George Dunkley
1875-76 - Isaac Ashley
1877-78 - John Guard
1879-80 - Daniel Williams (accepted into full connexion in 1880)
1881-83 - John Pooley

Wentworth County

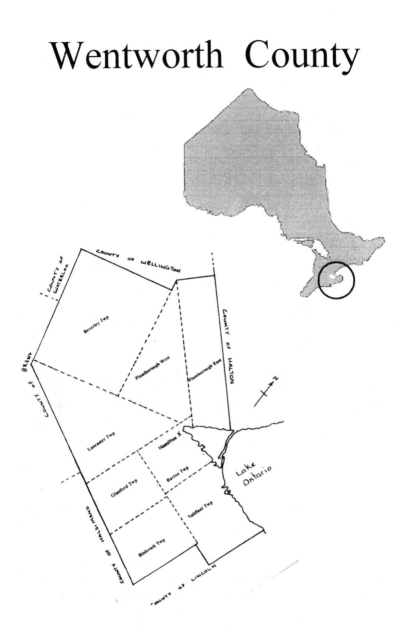

The Circuits of Wentworth County

Like most metropolitan areas, Hamilton was the only circuit in the County, and there was only one chapel on that circuit. In the years leading up to the building of a chapel at Hamilton, it would not surprise me to discover that there were meeting places out through Barton Township at least, as the Bible Christians worked to build their presence in this area, but reference to them so far has not surfaced.

Hamilton Circuit

Located on Emerald St, near Wilson, the building that housed the Bible Christian chapel was purchased from the congregation of St. Thomas' Church of England when they built a new church. Their new church was built in 1869 but it wasn't until three years later, in 1872, that the Bible Christians purchased the old church.

An account from the Hamilton newspaper, The Times, dated December 6, 1873, tell us the Bible Christians expended $1200.^{00} for renovations to the building which had been built in 1856 .... *"most of which sum has been raised by subscription among the church members and the citizens generally."*

The article goes on to say .... *"The Bible Christian church on Emerald Street has been undergoing extensive alterations and improvements during the past two months, and is now nearly finished, and presents a greatly improved appearance, both on the exterior and in the interior. In fact, now it is a little gem of a church."*

This 'little gem of a church' measured 32 feet by 72 feet, a good size for a town chapel. It was built of frame and brick construction (some sources say frame with stucco) - likely the front of the church was brick (or stucco) and the back frame. It seated 350 in the main body of the church and another 100 in the gallery.

The dedication service for the re-dedication of the building to the use of the Bible Christians, was held on December 21, 1873. The Rev. Cephas Barker gave the morning sermon, Rev. George Smith gave the afternoon sermon, and Rev. Cephas Barker gave the evening sermon. The Rev. Walter Ayers, who was the incumbent at that time, closed the dedication ceremonies by announcing a tea and further speakers on the following Tuesday. To capitalize on the enthusiasm of the audience at any dedication, the ceremonies usually lasted a week or so and the donations toward the building fund just kept pouring in - in many cases the debt on the church was completely paid off at the close of the dedication ceremonies.

The parsonage was next door at 45 Emerald Street. It stood on its own piece of property, 52 ¼ feet by 121 ½ feet, and had it's own deed, so it can be assumed that each was purchased from a different vendor. The parsonage was a frame house, 22 feet by 30 feet and was already built when the Bible Christians purchased the lot in 1872. Perhaps it was the old Church of England parsonage.

Courtesy: The Anglican Diocese of Niagara
The first St. Thomas church purchased by the Bible Christians in 1872

Hamilton was served in the early years by which ever preacher could spare a few days to go over to Hamilton and visit the congregation who were generally lead by lay preachers. This supply preaching was from about 1866 through to about 1872 when William Kenner was stationed there to build the congregation. Others to serve Hamilton included:

1873 - Walter Ayers

1874-75 - Stephen H. Rice

1878-78 - George Copeland

1879-81 - J.J. Rice

1882-83 - James H. Collins.

With Union in 1884, James H. Collins continued as the minister here when it became a Methodist congregation.

It should be noted too, that in Hamilton there was a strong *Temperance* movement. The Hamilton Spectator, April 22, 1878 edition reported on a temperance meeting at the Bible Christian chapel on April 21st, when Rev. J.J. Rice (who would take over that congregation the following year) was invited to speak on the subject .... *"The Rev. gentleman preached an eloquent sermon on 'Gospel Temperance'. ..."*

Many thanks are extended to Margaret Houghton at the Hamilton Public Library, and to Janet Forjan of the Hamilton Postcard Collection website, both digging out portions of the above material from old and obscure places!

Oxford County

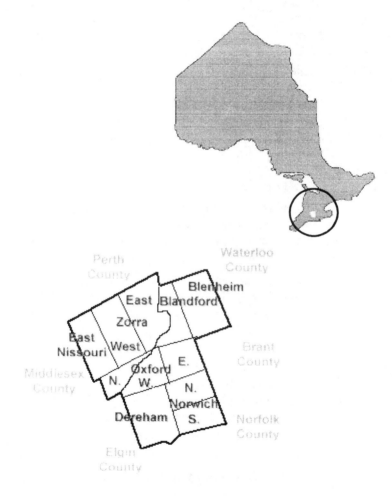

Perth County

Waterloo County

Blenheim

East Blandford

Zorra

East Nissouri

West

Brant County

Middlesex County

Oxford

N. W. E.

N.

Norwich

Dereham S.

Norfolk County

Elgin County

Oxford County Circuits

Like its neighbour Middlesex, Oxford County had two circuits, Dereham Circuit being all rural, and Ingersoll Circuit being partially rural. These rural congregations were, for the most part, started in the early 1850's when people like John Hicks Eynon, Philip James, and that ilk, were itinerant preachers going from place to place seeking out families in the bush and bringing the gospel to them.

As roads and trails were improved, these people were gathered together each Sabbath at a central place, perhaps the local schoolhouse, and active congregations were formed.

Dereham Circuit:
Bethel -aka the Old Delmer Chapel
Zion - built 1859 north of Ostrander - on the Williams farm
Salem - at Zenda on the Dereham-Norwich Township Line
Not listed in the Bible Christian Property Book -one others - near the Brownsville Road on the 9th Concession

Thanks go to the Mary Liley at the Oxford Historical Society, and to Mary Gladwin at the Oxford County Archives for all their help in sorting out the very vague Bible Christian Property Book information.

Ingersoll Circuit:
This circuit had only two chapels:
Ingersoll - on Oxford Street in the town
Putnamville - in Westminster Township, but no longer exists.

Dereham Circuit

Dereham Township is found in Oxford County in the west end of the province of Ontario. Within Dereham Township were at least three Bible Christian Chapels. The Bible Christian

128

Property Book did not list them all, I'm sure.

Dereham, and that part of the country was settled fairly late, compared to some of the settlement in that western end of the province, the majority of the pioneering families not arriving until the 1820's. By the early 1850's the Bible Christians had located most of the little settlements and small but faithful congregations were meeting in private homes and local schoolhouses.

Bethel:

Bethel Chapel was built in 1858. It was a small frame chapel only 27 feet by 36 feet in size. The small parcel of land upon which it sat was only 9 square rods in size. As far as can be ascertained today, Bethel was the chapel that used to sit beside the 'old' Delmer Cemetery. From *The Brownsville Pastoral Charge*, a booklet prepared on the occasion of the 70th anniversary of the United church of Canada in 1995, it tells us there were three Bible Christian Chapels in the township, this one being *north of Delmer between the 8th and 9th Concessions*. Sadly this chapel was not named, but the location would put it at the 'old' Delmer cemetery, and so there can be no question, as this was a Bible Christian cemetery.

Zion:

Located north of Ostrander in the 7th Concession, Zion Chapel was the second one to be built on the circuit. Erected in 1859, it too was of frame construction measuring 20 feet by 40 feet. The lot upon which it sat was 50 feet by 105 feet. The chapel was constructed on land given to the Bible Christians at a token cost of five shillings, by Richard Williams and his wife. The Williams farm was located on the Plank Road, in Concession 7, Lot 8. The Plank Road ran diagonally from just about where the Bible Christian Chapel was built northward to Salford.

The trustees at the time the land was transferred in 1861 were Josiah Miners, Richard Butler, James Whitlock, Thomas Allin, James Allin, William H. Roy and Samuel Philip Lobb.

Salem:

Salem Chapel was the third chapel to be constructed on the circuit. Built in 1872 it was a frame chapel, much the same size as Bethel, being 26 feet by 36 feet. The parcel of land upon which it sat was a little bigger, 13 square rods in size. Located at Zenda (called Salem before it had a post office) it was snuggled against the township line between Dereham and Norwich Township, but it was actually across the line in North Norwich Township.

From the booklet, *Brownsville Pastoral Charge*, we find another chapel listed besides these three - *the other was near the Brownsville Road on the 9th Concession* - on the 1876 Historical Atlas of Oxford County stars mark the position of all the township churches. There is a star in the 9th Concession beside the Brownsville Road, near a little place called Culloden - could this be a Bible Christian chapel not mentioned in the Property Book? The Property Book appears to have been written in 1874 and so any chapels constructed after that date would not appear.

Dereham:

The parsonage was the only Bible Christian property in this village. It was fairly small brick house, being only 20 feet by 28 feet in size. It was in a fairly central position being almost equal distance to Salem as it was to Ostrander or Delmer. In fact, the village was in the exact centre of the township, and was often called Dereham Centre, most likely intended to be the 'hub' of the township.

This house was not built until 1878, and was a hurried entry on the last page of the Property Book. Until that time the ministers may have lived in rented premises.

In 1874 when the first attempt at unifying the various Methodist bodies occurred, both Bethel and Salem congregations joined the union at that time. This was a strange occurrence for a Bible Christian congregation, as most went screaming and kicking into the Union of 1884. Their financial situation must have really looked dreary for them to have made that decision at that early date. Bethel Chapel sat empty for many years, but it is possible it was used for funeral services from time to time. It was eventually taken down. What became of Salem Chapel I do not know.

In the very early days this circuit was under the jurisdiction of the Huron District, but in 1860 it was given to the Exeter District for administration. In 1868 the division of the province once again took place and Dereham came under the jurisdiction of London District.

Preachers to serve this circuit included:

1858 - supply
1859 - Andrew Gordon
1860 - Robert Miller
1861-63 - John Edwards
1864-65 - John Kinsey
1866 - Thomas Greene and Martin Mennear
1867 - Thomas Greene and W. Heysett (served with Ingersoll)
1868 - William Wade and William C. Beer (with Ingersoll)
1869 - William Wade (with Ingersoll)
1870 - William Wade and William H. Quance (with Ingersoll)
1871-72 - unknown
1873 - W. Trethewey
1874-77 - John Veale
1878-80 - T.R. Hull
1881-82 - Henry A. Newcombe
1883 - Joseph Archer.

Ingersoll Circuit

The Ingersoll Circuit consisted of 2 chapels, one at Ingersoll in the town and another in the village of Putnamville, located in Westminster Township, Middlesex County. Being in different counties makes these two places sound very far apart, but they were not. The distance between Ingersoll and Putnamville is probably no more than 10 miles.

Ingersoll was named after Thomas Ingersoll, an early settler in the western end of the province. It was Ingersoll's daughter, Laura Ingersoll Secord, who went to warn the British during the War of 1812-14, after overhearing the American plans of attack, though most historians figure that Laura Secord never visited the town named for her family.

Ingersoll was incorporated as a village in 1852 and as a town in 1865, and it was in Ingersoll town where the world famous cheese was made and toured all over the world on dispaly. It certainly raised awareness that Canada was no longer a wilderness and that we were indeed open for business.

Ingersoll:

The Bible Christian Chapel at Ingersoll opened for business in 1868. It was built on a vacant town lot on Oxford Street. It was a fairly large frame church, measuring 32 feet by 46 feet, dimensions usually reserved for brick chapels. The same year a parsonage was built on the church lot. It was also of frame construction, 24 feet by 30 feet.

After Union in 1884, the chapel was purchased by Peter Kennedy and moved to the corner east of Trinity United Church on King Street, but what it was used for at that time I do not know. In later years it was used as the P.T. Walker Funeral Home and residence.

Putnamville:

Putnamville, because it no longer exists, seems not to have

been written about. Located in Westminster Township, it was named after the first settlers there, Seth and Joshua Putnam. When they arrived, or whether or not they were Bible Christians I do not know. The chapel at Putnamville was built in 1865, suggesting that there was a congregation there for a while prior to that date. This too was a fairly large chapel for a frame building, measuring 30 feet by 40 feet. It was built on a quarter acre village lot.

In the early days of the congregations on this circuit, the two charges may have been served as "by supply", that is, whenever anyone had a free moment to go over there to see them.

Records of the ministers who served this circuit begin in 1868 with the building of the chapel at Ingersoll ....

1868 - Thomas Greene and William C. Beer

1869 - William Wade and William C. Beer

1870 - William Wade and William H. Quance

1871 - William Roach and William H. Quance

1872 - William Roach and Alexander Richard

1873-74 - Robert Baker

1875 - John Watson Butcher

1876 - Thomas Broad

1877 - John Chapple

1878 - John Chapple and Thomas Broad

1879-82 - Joseph Archer

1883- R. B. Rowe

Middlesex County

Middlesex County Circuits

Two circuits were organized in Middlesex County - London Circuit and Lambeth Circuit. London Circuit was all within the city of London, while Lambeth was mainly country chapels.

It is very surprising to me to find that the chapels in London were built before the chapels in the countryside, for the Bible Christians had started out with the idea that they would have only country chapels for the everyday working family, in other words, the agricultural folk that they were used to in Devon and Cornwall.

London:

London Centre - chapel located on Horton Street - built 1855
London East - on Dundas Street - no dates given
London South - Wortley and Bruce Streets

Lambeth Circuit:

There were three chapels on the Lambeth Circuit:
LambethVillage - in the village on a 'town lot'- Westminster
    Township
Sharon - probably Lot 13, Concession 3 - Delaware Township
Westminster aka White Oak - probably Lot 17, Conc. 5,
    Westminster Township.

London Circuit

The city of London, Ontario was located in Middlesex County, in London Township. Today, this is a large 'regionally governed' area with little resemblance to former days.

The London Bible Christian Circuit was made up of three chapels, all within the boundaries of the city and in the early days, of 'missions' in Delaware and Westminster Townships that eventually formed the Lambeth Circuit. The three city chapels included: London Centre, London South and London East. This is how they were identified in the Bible Christian Property Book.

London Centre:
This chapel was also called Horton Street Chapel. It stood on the north side of Horton Street, east of Wellington. This chapel is listed in the city's first City Directory of 1856-57. The preacher at that time was Richard Lyle Tucker. The Stewards in that year were John Isaac from Westminster who likely became an integral part of White Oak in later years, and Thomas Heard from 'the Junction' - probably Lambeth at the Junction of the North Talbot Road and Commissioner's Road. He, too probably took an active role in developing Lambeth Chapel in later years.

This chapel was built in 1855. It was a brick building measuring 34 feet by 66 feet and was on a lot 66feet by 50 feet. A parsonage was built near this chapel in 1867, however, no address is available for it. It was a substantial brick house, 28 feet across and 48 feet deep on a rather large city lot 90 feet across and 130 feet deep.

The Bible Christian Property Book doesn't say so, but research by Mr. W. Glen Curnoe, retired Librarian from London, tells us that the chapel was rebuilt in 1872.....

"From the London Free Press, August 25, 1919:

After having been a landmark for nearly 50 years, the old frame church which stands at the corner of Wellington and Horton Streets, where, since 1872 the Bible Christians worshipped is being torn down to make way for another building. It has not served as a church for a number of years for after worship in it had been discontinued due to dwindling of the congregation, it was sold and has been used as a carpenter shop by Tambling and Jones. To the older residents of the city, many pleasant memories of church life in the earlier days of the city's history center about the old building.

Mrs. John Isaacs, an old lady of 85 years, remembers the founding of the congregation quite clearly. She stated that the first pastor was Rev. Robert Hurley and he was succeeded by Rev. Mr.

Haycroft.

Another Londoner who has many happy memories of the old edifice, is Mr. Hubert Ashplant, the well-known retail shoe merchant. He identified himself with the congregation very soon after coming to Canada from Devonshire in 1878, and for a number of years he was organist at the church. The pastor at that time, was Rev. Mr. Jolliffe whose home was in Cobourg, Ontario and he and his wife were very earnest Christians, and the congregation prospered under their leadership. Mr. Jolliffe was greatly interested in young people's work and founded an improvement class.

Mr. Ashplant recalls with a good deal of relish the tea meetings which were a popular institution of that day. Everybody used to attend them, and an unusual feature of the excellent menu was Devonshire cream in quantities only dreamed of nowadays. The congregation at that time numbered over 500, and the work developed to such an extent that a branch church was opened at the corner of Dundas and Elizabeth streets and another one shortly afterward in South London.."

Here we have an excellent collection of events that took place at this chapel. Mr. Ashplant also went on to say that after Union there were four congregations of Methodists which proved unwieldy, and so Wellington Street Methodist Church was built to serve all four congregations. It was at this time that *"the little frame church was sold and put to secular service"*.

Odd, how Mr. Ashplant thought the church was frame and the Bible Christians thought they owned a brick chapel! There was also an error in Mr. Ashplant's information - Rev. Jolliffe's home was at Bowmanville rather than Cobourg, where he and his son, also William, were Methodist preachers after Union.

Mr. Ashplant's memoirs leads us to the next chapel ...

London East:

This chapel was located at the corner of Dundas Street and Elizabeth Street. It was a frame chapel, but no year was listed in the Bible Christian Property Book for it. This book mentions a parsonage too, but no further details were entered, so this may have been a rented premises.

London South:

Located at Wortley and Bruce Streets, this frame chapel was leased from the Presbyterians in 1874, though in the Bible Christian Property Book it is listed as being on Northey Road. Perhaps it is an easy mistake to misspell Wortley and Northey. Another discrepancy is the fact that in the sketched picture below it looks as if this is a brick chapel, yet the Property Book clearly says 'frame'. This was a short-lived chapel, likely opened in the 'old' south end of the city to investigate the possibilities of a congregation there. But in 1877 this was found impractical and the chapel was once again put to use by the Presbyterians as a Sunday School until it was sold to the

Sketch of chapel, London South, Wortley Road

Baptists. When the Baptists erected a new church in 1897 the old chapel was demolished. It should be made clear that the Bible Christians never owned this building, it was always rented from the Presbyterians.

In the very early days of this circuit, London was part of the Huron District, and as such was served by Huron preachers, sometimes on a substitute basis as time allowed. However, by 1852, London had it's own preachers and these were:

1852 - George Rippin
1853-55 - Richard Lyle Tucker
1856-57 - Paul Robins
1858 (& St. Thomas) Paul Robins with probationer Andrew Gordon
1859 - Robert Hurley

At this time, Huron District was now divided into Huron and Exeter Districts, and London continued on with Exeter District.

1860-62 - Joseph Hoidge

1863-65 - William Hooper

1866-67 - Edward Roberts

The circuits in the US and London was separated from Exeter District and the new London and Cleveland District was formed.

The preachers who served on the London Circuit were....

1868 - Edward Roberts and William Hodnett, a probationer

1869 - William Jolliffe and William Kinley who was accepted into full connexion in 1870

1870-71 - William Jolliffe and James Collins

1872 - William Jolliffe

At this time, Cleveland was put with the rest of the American Districts and the preachers who continued with the new London District, London Circuit were ....

1873-74 - William Kenner

1875 - J.J. Rice

1876-77 - J.J. Rice, F.M. Whitlock

From this time each of the London Chapels had their own resident ministers ....

London Centre:

1878-80 - William H. Quance

1881 - Cephus Barker

1882-83 - William Henry Butt

London East:

1879-81 - George H. Copeland

1882-83 - Lewis W. Wicket

London South:

1879-80 - W. Rollins

1881-82 - Andrew Cory Courtice

1883 - T.W. Blatchford

The London Mission, which was likely White Oak on the Lambeth Circuit, was looked after in 1878 by J.J. Rice.

Lambeth Circuit

This circuit, located in Middlesex County, and stretching across both Westminster and Delaware Townships, had three chapels: Lambeth, Sharon and White Oak.

This circuit extended from the London Circuit at an early date, first reaching Lambeth in 1854. Then in 1868 the congregation of the area built Sharon Chapel. Lastly, White Oak chapel was constructed in 1875. Not all chapels are built when a congregation is formed. Some congregations wait many years for a "proper" chapel, meeting in the interim in private homes, in the local schoolhouse, and sometimes in a converted barn or store room. So, knowing this it is difficult to say which is the oldest congregation, however, Lambeth is likely the oldest. According to the 1871 census, there were a number of Bible Christians at North Dorchester Township, at Putnamville, however, this congregation was on the Ingersoll Circuit in Oxford County, and information on that congregation will be found with Ingersoll.

Lambeth:

Lambeth Village is located in Westminster Township. It was a "T" shaped community at the junction of North Talbot Road and Commissioner's Road. It hugged the roadside for about a quarter of a mile in all three directions from the junction

The chapel, a 21 foot by 30 foot frame building was built on a 'town lot' of one quarter acre in 1854, but it was not until 1874 when a brick parsonage was built in the village, 30 feet by 37½ feet also on a quarter of an acre, just two years after the Lambeth Circuit had been separated from the London Circuit.

In a local history book, it says .... *"In 1870 the Lambeth Chapel was undergoing renovations and repairs"*, but in the Bble Christian Property Book, it states the Chapel was rebuilt in 1876. Though it was still a frame chapel, it was nearly twice the size, now being 36 feet by 40 feet - a good indication that the population of the area was growing.

Westminster or White Oak Chapel:

From the history book mentioned above, 'Westminster United Church', it states that (in 1870) ...... *"The Cause at White Oak was most hopeful"*. In other words, the congregation was in earnest and there were a few members already.

At this time, this congregation was served by a lay-preacher, and every now and then Rev. William Jolliffe would come over from the London Circuit. There are a few records surviving with Rev. Jolliffe's signature from that time. By 1872, the Westminster congregation were part of the new Lambeth Circuit and the first preacher on this new circuit was Rev. John Harris who now had responsibility for three chapels.

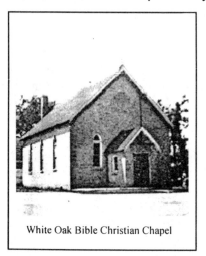

White Oak Bible Christian Chapel

It seems that he was influential in this circuit, for in 1875, trustee Emanuel Manning was able to purchase from Captain John Shore, one acre of land for $100. This seems rather steep, but Shore was a Unitarian and the Bible Christians meant nothing to him other than a chance to do some business. Placing this chapel exactly has been difficult because it does not appear in the 1878 Atlas of the County. But, John Shore owned two parcels of land, one in Concession 4, Lot 17 and one in Concession 6 Lot 19. I would assume that the acre bought by Manning was in Lot 17, Concession 4 as Manning lived right across the road in Lot 17, Concession 5.

A chapel was constructed here that same year. It was a frame chapel and measured 26 feet by 36 feet. The Gerry construction company was hired to erect the building. It was furnished with straight-backed wooden seats, which were later converted into long benches, which were used in the Christian Education Building many years later. The Chapel was heated with two square wood burning box stoves, and was lighted with chandeliers consisting of five kerosene lamps covered with one very large china lamp shade.

On a platform, raised four or five inches at the front of the chapel was a pulpit, organ with large lamp brackets at each side, and cane bottom chairs for the choir. Some of these chairs continued in use in various parts of the church for many years until recent times, and there may still be some there today.

Members of the congregation included William Vanstone and John Courtice. Other families from Devon and Cornwall in the immediate area were Vail, T. Burgess, James Davey.

Sharon Chapel:

Sharon chapel was located in Delaware Township. For it, too, there are two possible locations - Lot 10, Concession 2 or Lot 13, Concession 3.

From '*The History of Sharon Chapel*' we find out that the Bodkins, the Bignells, the Weylers and the Howletts were all Bible Christians in the neighbourhood of Sharon Chapel. The 1878 Atlas of the County tells us that the Bignells lived across the road from Lot 10, Concession 2, where the map also shows a chapel in the south-west corner of the Gilbert Harris farm. Next to the Bignells were the Bodkins and next to them the Weylers. The Howletts lived directly behind the Bignells out on the Concession Road. But here we have our dilema. The Howlett's were deeply involved in their church and possibly more than any other settler family in the area (according to their descendants). They held another property, about 50 acres in Lot 13, Concession 3 - not far from the first chapel. Upon this 50 acres was another chapel, according to the Atlas. Which one was Sharon? A search of the 1871 census tells us that Gilbert Harris was an Episcopal Methodist, and so the chapel in the corner of his farm in Lot 10, Concession 2 was likely an Episcopal Methodist, leaving the chapel out on the Concession Road to be the Bible Christian Chapel.

143

Constructed in 1868, this chapel was on a quarter acre and measured 32 feet by 45 feet - remarkably large for a country chapel. At that time, Lambeth and Sharon were part of the London Circuit and had only recently been upgraded from Mission status to Chapel status. This was likely due to the hard work of Rev. Edward Roberts who had served the outlaying areas of the London Circuit since 1866. In 1868 he was joined by William Hodnett, who was still a probationer, or 'young man' as the assistant was called.

Ministers to preach on this circuit after it was separated from London were:
1872 - John Harris (also served St. Thomas)
1873 - Thomas Greene
1874-75 - Thomas Broad
1876-78 - Jesse Whitlock
1879-80 - Thomas Mason
1881-83 - J.G. Yelland

Elgin County

The Circuits of Elgin County

There were only two circuits in Elgin - St. Thomas and Talbotville. St. Thomas was a circuit of one chapel and it was an urban circuit, while Talbotville was a mix of town and rural congregations - one at Talbotville and one at Middlemarch.

St. Thomas Circuit

St. Thomas was already a settlement at the time of the War of 1812-14. It was burned twice by marauding American soldiers.

But it was rebuilt each time and by 1844 it had a population of 1000 people. The growth was not very rapid considering its position on the Talbot Road, one of the provinces settlement roads that took people back into the bush.

But the west country people began arriving in the early 1830's and many of that 1000 population were from Devon and Cornwall, and many of those were Bible Christian.

The Bible Christian congregation there began in about 1848 or 50 and the first full time preacher to serve the small community was George Haycraft. In 1852 St. Thomas was large enough to be incorporated as a village.

But even so, the village of St. Thomas was experiencing hard times. In 1856 a railway was built across the southern portion of the province between London and Niagara Falls, and this undermined the importance of the trade at St. Thomas and the village began to go into decline. The congregation could not afford to build a chapel until 1873.

But build they did. One fifth of an acre, a double town lot, was acquired and a 36 foot by 45 foot brick chapel was erected on John St. A frame parsonage was built on the other half of the lot which measured 101 feet across the road frontage and 110 feet deep.

By Union in 1884, there were a few gas lights on the main street. Some electric lights, powered by a coke burning power plant, were also found in the town, whose population was now about 10,000. The streets were still unpaved.

There were a number of Bible Christians in the township of Yarmouth, some may even have lived close enough to drive into town each Sabbath, however, many lived near or at Sparta, a small hamlet in the southern portion of the township. Though there was never a chapel at Sparta it can be safely assumed there was a meeting place there either in the schoolhouse or in rented space perhaps in a Methodist or Presbyterian church.

The records of the preachers to serve the town are not complete, but from those records that do exist they included:
1851-52 - George Haycraft
1853-57 - unknown
1858 - Andrew Gordon and Paul Robins
1859 - Robert Hurley
1860-71 - unknown
1872-74 - John Harris
1875-76 - Henry James Nott
1877 - Alexander Richard
1878 - Richard Mallett and Daniel Williams (with Talbotville)
1879-80 - William Hooper
1881-83 - John Holmes.

Talbotville Circuit

At Talbotville, in Southwold Township, the congregation was started in 1876. To understand the politics found even in Christian congregations, one must have all the facts. In 1874, the Methodists held their first attempt at unifying the various Methodist branches, without much success. However, here and there a few New Connexions congregations and a few Bible Christian congregations took the offer. These were struggling congregations who could see no way out from under their debt (those with a mortgaged chapel) or who could see no way of ever affording the luxury of even a tiny chapel.

The Bible Christian congregation at Talbotville were

147

among those who joined this first union, along with the local New Connexions congregation. But differences soon arose ......

In the book, *The Families of Five Stakes: The History of Talbotville Royal, 1811-1851, by Morley Thomas, we find this* reference.....

"*Then, in 1876, many members withdrew from the church ..... and built a Bible Christian Church near the site of the present Talbotville Cemetery. In 1878, a new brick church was built by the Methodists on Lot 41 East and a few years later, in 1884, the congregations were reunited. This [1878] church still serves as the Talbotville United Church of Canada. The Bible Christian church on the Back Street was taken down and the materials were used to build a Congregationalist church at Frome*"

Many thanks to Morley Thomas for sending this information to the project.

The Bible Christian Property Book tells us that this chapel was 30 feet by 44 feet and was of brick construction.

In the book, *Historical Sketch of the Talbotville United Church,* by Rev. J.W. Hedley, 1938, comes this further information...... " *[The Bible Christian congregation] used as a parsonage the house enlarged and now occupied by Mr. Lewis Jones.*" (I guess one of us will have to find an old city directory in order to know the address).

This part of the circuit history was found by Pat Temple of the Elgin Branch of the Ontario Genealogical Society. Many thanks, Pat.

According to the Property Book, the parsonage measured 28 feet by 24 feet with a kitchen wing 16 feet by 22 feet. It was a frame house built in 1879. The chapel and the parsonage do not seem to be on the same parcel of land

James McCallum, also a member of the Elgin OGS, says this ....

"*A deed was found for a lot in the north part of Lot 40 south side of the North Branch Talbot Road, dated April 12, 1876, from Richard B. Nicoll to the trustees of the Bible Christian church.*"

148

The lot by the cemetery where the church was located was Lot 43, south side of the North Branch Talbot Road. Based on 200 acres per lot, that would be 3/4 to 1 mile further along the road from Lot 40. I would suggest that this deed may be for the land where the parsonage was built.

The Bible Christian Property Book lists a second chapel on this circuit, on Front Street. Again, Jim McCallum of the Elgin Branch, Ontario Genealogical Society came to the rescue ....

*"A Bible Christian church was located in the community of Middlemarch, also in Southwold township. Bible Christian preachers and lay-preachers came out to this community and held meetings in the schoolhouse and in homes. It was decided to build a church, and land was donated by Peter Smoke & his son Caleb. This was on lot 33, North Side Talbot Road East. (*The Talbot Road was also known in various places as The Front Road, and in Middlemarch they called it Front Street.*)The congregation was formed on June 3, 1879, and became part of the Methodist church in 1884, when it was linked with the Fingal circuit. It was later part of the Southwold & Iona charge, along with Fingal. In 1907 a cyclone blew out both end walls of the church, but it was rebuilt. The church was closed in 1954 and sold in 1956 to Mr. H. Duff to be converted into a chicken hatchery."*

This chapel was a small brick structure, 26 feet by 40 feet, built in 1879.

Many thanks are extended to Jim McCallum for his research, which comes to this project from that branch's work in compiling their county *Places of Worship* book, as well as from Sim's *History of Elgin County*.

Peter Smoke, who gave the land for the chapel at Middlemarch, was, by 1881, living at Tuscarora in Brant County, South. He was a native of Canada, and listed on the census as "pagan". Four of his children had Christian names but four did not. The census taker didn't even try to enter them in the record but simply made a note for them "No English Christian names." Caleb was not among those with English names at home on the census report, nor could he be found anywhere in Ontario.

Further information from Sim's, *History of Elgin County,* tells us the preachers from Talbotville boarded with Thomas Futcher when they came over to Middlemarch. Oddly, Thomas Futcher and his family were all Anglicans!

Also from this book, we find that John Curtis and John Stubbs teamed the lumber for the chapel from Lambeth and London, and that the church was erected with a "bee".

Preachers to serve this circuit include:
1877 - Francis Metherall Whitlock (son of Jesse Whitlock)
1878 - Richard Mallett and Daniel Williams (with St Thomas)
1879 - Richard Mallett (with St. Thomas)
1880-82 - J.H. Rice
1883 - Samuel J. Allin

Essex County

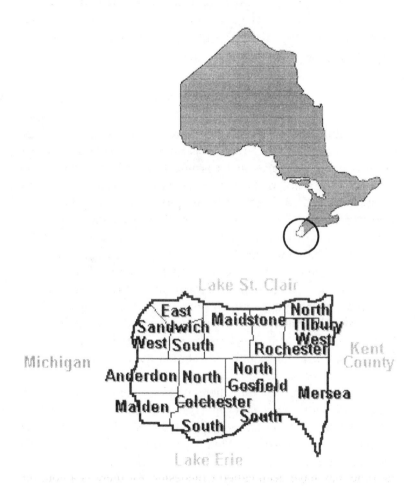

The Circuits of Essex County

Essex County is right against the far western edge of southern Ontario, tucked up beside the Detroit River, looking across to the State of Michigan, U.S.A. There were two circuits in Essex - Colchester and Windsor.

Colchester Circuit

Although the Bible Christian Property Book says there was only one chapel on this circuit, it is my belief that there were at least two meeting places and possibly three, likely not all with chapels. The one in the property book was likely in North Colchester, and from the concentration of Bible Christian adherents on the 1881 census, I would suggest there was one somewhere in Gosfield Township.

The chapel was likely located at Gesto, though no written proof of this has yet been found. At the time of Union, Rev. Samuel Muxworthy, still a probationer, was stationed at Colchester, then he appears with the Methodists at Gesto. This makes me think that Gesto was the location of the Bible Christian chapel (a number of Bible Christians were found at Gesto on the 1881 census) and he retained his station there when the formal handing over was done.

It is my belief that there was another Bible Christian Chapel at Harrow almost straight south of Gesto. There was a standard look to little brick Bible Christian Chapels, and the chapel at Harrow, now an African Methodist Episcopal church (AME) looks as if it was at one time a Bible Christian chapel.. Harrow at one time may have been called Colchester, for there is a note on the page in the Bible Christian Property Book ... *"south of Windsor on the Lake Erie shore".*

The Preachers who served this circuit were:

1872 - J. Kinsey

1873 - J. Ball
1874 - Moses Metherall
1875 - W. Davis
1876 - Herman Moore
1877 - Daniel Williams
1878 - Joshua Elliott
1879 - S.J. Cummings
1880 - by supply probably from Windsor
1881-82 - W.H. Spargo
1883 - S.W. Muxworthy

Windsor Circuit

The chapel at Windsor was located on Mercer St. It was a brick chapel measuring 35 feet by 52 feet - more or less standard measurements for a village church. Built in 1877 it stood on a village lot with 75 feet frontage. The parsonage also had a frontage of 75 feet, but no address has been located for it. The parsonage was of frame construction, measuring 22 feet by 30 feet. It apparently had two wings (one would have

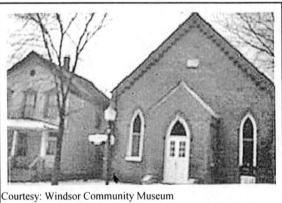

Courtesy: Windsor Community Museum
Mercer St. Bible Christian Chapel. It was sold to the Baptist congregation at the time of union. This photo dates to c1950.

been a kitchen wing) measuring 26 feet by 18 feet, and 20 feet by 10 feet. The lot on which it stood measured 160 feet deep - lots of

153

room for the preacher to have a garden, which most of them did in order to eat well (a preacher's pay was miserably small!)

Heather Butt, from the Windsor Community Museum, tells us that the 1885 Fire Insurance map for the town shows the chapel at the corner of Mercer St., and Assumption St., on the south east corner. The map says it was a brick building with a wooden structure attached to the back. This was probably a Sabbath School room.

The report from Heather goes on to say that by 1891-3 this was a Baptist church, and by 1894 it was owned by the African Methodist Episcopal congregation.

Unfortunately the whole block was demolished in the early 1960's.

Many thanks to Heather Butt for her input into this project. Her information has rounded out the history of this chapel.

Preachers who served this congregation included:

1874-78 - Walter Ayers
1879 - Francis Metheral Whitlock
1880 - William Limbert
1881-83 - Thomas Mason
(I have not been able to find out where the congregation met prior to the building of the chapel.)

Huron County

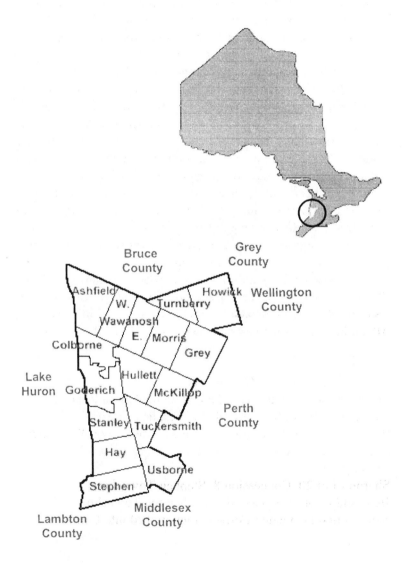

Bruce
County

Grey
County

Ashfield

W.

Turnberry

Howick

Wellington
County

Wawanosh

E.

Morris

Colborne

Grey

Lake
Huron

Goderich

Hullett

McKillop

Perth
County

Stanley

Tuckersmith

Hay

Usborne

Stephen

Lambton
County

Middlesex
County

Huron County Circuits

The history of this county is the history of the whole of the Huron tract, and the colonization of the western end of the Province of Ontario. Far too involved to go into it here, suffice it to say that once the London Colonization Road was opened into the interior, and once the Canada Company took over the selling of land to settlers, the settlement of this area took off at a rapid pace.

From about 1830 settlers started to pour into the townships, some of which were not yet fully surveyed. But people made their way to all corners of the county, and within a very short space of time they began to meet in one another's homes for worship. Most were farmers, but some were merchants and some became lumbermen, settling along the shores of Lake Huron and shipping timber down the lakes. Many of these settlers were Bible Christians prior to coming to Ontario, and many others were converted after their arrival. But the missionaries and itinerant preachers found them, congregation by congregation and added them member by member to the chapel rolls.

Usborne Township had the densest population of Bible Christians, with three very large circuits: Exeter, Crediton and Usborne. Numerous small circuits were also found in this county. Altogether, Huron County had seven circuits of varying sizes.

Exeter:
Exeter - at James and Main Streets
Ebenezer - at the Adams Settlement on the Huron Road
Providence - Lot 20, Concession 2, Stephen Township
Bethel - at Devonshire Corners, Lot 11, Concession 1, Stephen
Eden - Lot 5, Concession 3, Usborne
Crediton - in the village
Sharon - Lot 20, Concession 8, Stephen Township
Bethesda - Lot 25, Concession 2, Usborne Township
Salem - first at Whalen Corners, then moved into Centralia

Crediton:
(Separated from Exeter in 1878)
Crediton - in the village
Centralia - at the south end of the village
Bethel - Devonshire Corners, Stephen Township
Eden - 1 ½ miles east of Devonshire Corners, Usborne Township
Sharon - Lot 20, Concession 8, Stephen Township
Dashwood - On the Township line between Stephen and Hay

Usborne:
Bethany - Lot 18, 6th Concession - Usborne Township
Siloam - Lot 16, Concession 8, Usborne Township
Rehoboth - 10th Concession, Usborne Township
Eldad - 8th Concession, Usborne Township
Prospect - Lot 12, Concession 13, Hibbert Township, Perth Cty
Freewill - on the townline between Biddulph and Blanshard
Zion - Lot 'A' of the 8th Concession, Usborne Township
Bethel - 11th Concession, Usborne Township
Staffa - Lot 16, Concession 9, Hibbert, Perth County
Elim - Lot 10, Concession 6, Usborne Township

Hensall and Bethesda:
Hensall - in the village (north of Exeter)
Bethesda - Lot 25, Concession 2, Usborne Township

Clinton:
Clinton - in the town on Huron Street
Holmesville - on Highway 8 between Clinton and Goderich
Alma - Lot 6, Huron Road Concession, Hullett Township
Ebenezer - Lot 33, Concession 10, Hullett Township
Summerhill - Concession 6, Hullett Township
Mount Pleasant - Fullarton Township, Perth County

Colborne:
Ebenezer - Lot 33, Concession 10, Hullett - this chapel was likely
    on the Colborne Circuit rather than Clinton though it

would have been easier for the Clinton ministers to serve it.
Bethel -Lot 5, Conc. 1, Colborne Township - Eastern District
Zion - Lot 1, Concession 6, Colborne Township
Fisher's Corners - early name for Benmiller in Colborne Township
Oasis - unknown, but was likely Eden on the Usborne Circuit and
not part of this circuit.

Grey:
Providence - in the town of Cranbrook, Grey Township
Salem - Lot 25, Concession 9, Grey Township

Exeter Circuit

The Exeter Circuit comprised nine chapels, all about a mile
and a quarter from one another. Exeter did not see it's first settler
until 1832. According to the Huron County Atlas of 1984 ......

*"Sometime in the winter of 1832 James Wills made his way
northward along the London Road Survey stopping at a point
between London and Goderich in the Huron Tract in the heart of
Upper Canada. Wills chose Lot 20, Usborne Township for the site
of his homestead. Thus the Exeter we know today had its humble
beginnings with a log cabin set in a small clearing carved out of
what was then a vast and virtually unknown wilderness."*

This was a late start, and so we do not see many people
there until a decade and a half later. In about 1846 John Hicks
Eynon went to Huron County to see what was there, and started
many congregations in the little clearings dotting the forest. These
small groups met in the cabins of their neighbours and sometimes
in the local schoolhouse if there was one, but by the 1850's chapels
were being erected.

Exeter:
As early as 1854 there was a congregation of Bible
Christians at Exeter, meeting in the home of lay preacher James
Pickard at the corner of James and Main Streets. At that time,
members of this small group were James Pickard and his wife,

Richard and Ann Welsh, James and Fanny Bissett, Richard and Dorothy Handford (Hanaford?), Robert and Margaret Frayne, Henry and Elizabeth Westcott, John and Ann Jones. On February 24, 1856, the first Bible Christian chapel was dedicated. Added to the membership at this time were Charles and Mary Ann Snell, Thomas and Grace Oke, Paul and Jane Wilcox, John and Ann Crocker, and James and Mary Down.

James Pickard was the driving force behind this church and personally guaranteed payment of all costs associated with it's construction not covered by subscription and collections. He and his wife also provided free lodgings for the junior ministers of the circuit while at Exeter. Located on Main Street, this chapel was moved early in the 1900's and used as a storage facility. It is now gone but the original site has been turned into a lovely parkette.

The first chapel was likely of frame construction and was replaced in 1862 by a brick church, probably of white brick made nearby from local clay. It measured 38 feet across and 72 feet deep - a good large town chapel! This second church was located at the corner of James and Andrew Streets. It had a stone foundation and a full basement. It had ten Gothic windows and was heated with a hot air furnace. Mr. Vosper was the builder and it cost $4500. This cost too was guaranteed by Mr. Pickard, though whether or not he was called on to support any of the cost is unknown.

The ladies of the congregation served a tea (a full meal) at the dedication on June 25, 1862. They served 1400 people between 2 p.m. and 7 p.m. - without the aid of refridgeration, microwaves, coffee makers or electric kettles!!

The first parsonage in Exeter was built in 1852 on one third acre, located on Huron Street, but I think it was replaced in later years by a brick parsonage, still on Huron St. at the corner of Elizabeth St. It still stands today, however, the first one was taken down many years ago.

The first circuit preacher at Exeter was Robert Hurley in 1851 or 52. He was followed in 1853 by John Edwards. It has been recorded of John Edwards ..... "[that he was] *a very godly man whose knees were callous from much praying.*"

159

Ebenezer:

In 1852 a Bible Christian chapel was built one and a quarter miles east of Exeter on Huron Street, or The Huron Road as it is called today. It was called Ebenezer. At this cross-roads was the Adams Settlement, named for the first family to settle there. A cemetery was included on this small corner parcel, the stones of which have been gathered into a memorial cairn with a plaque commemorating the chapel that once stood there, and the pioneers who worshipped there.

Photo by Roger Leetooze
The commemorative cairn
at Ebenezer

Providence:

Providence Chapel was south of Exeter, on the London Road. If you were to find this chapel today you would travel out of Exeter and turn west along the Fourth Sideroad to where the 2nd Concession Road crosses it. This would put you about one and a half miles west of Exeter, the same distance as Ebenezer was east of the town. It was the practice of the Bible Christians, whenever possible, to erect their chapels one and a half miles apart.

Providence Chapel was not in Usborne Township, as was Ebenezer, the London Road being the township boundary road. It was in Stephen Township. The first chapel built of logs was erected in 1855 in lot 20, Concession 2. The church trustees at that time were Richard Sweet, James Shapton, Thomas Dearing, William H. Penhale and William Heaman. It was sometimes known as Shapton's Chapel. A second chapel was built in 1872 kitty-corner to the first chapel on Lot 21 of the first Concession. This was a brick chapel on one fifth acre of land. The original log building remained standing and was eventually sold to W. Sims, the timbers of which were used in his barn.

This second chapel was fairly small, measuring only 24 feet by 36 feet. The Bible Christian Property Book does not

160

mention a cemetery, but local historians credit this site with one, reports saying that until 25 or 30 years ago some stones could still be seen in the old cemetery. They may still be there.

Although this chapel served the community for many years, it was taken down a number of years ago.

Bethel:

Bethel Chapel was located at Devonshire Corners. This place was first known as Balkwill Corners because of the Balkwill brothers who owned land on each of the four corners of this cross-roads. Later, some of this land was purchased by William Rollins and so was known for a time as Rollins Corners. Still later, it was Twilight Corners for the two families that resided there, the Days and the Knights. But because of the large population of immigrants from Devonshire, England, the name Devon Corners, or Devonshire Corners became its name.

Bethel Chapel was constructed in about 1851 or 52, on 1/5th acre of land in Lot 11, Concession 1 in Stephen Township, on the west side of the London Road. This parcel was left to the Bible Christians by Richard Bissett in his will.

It was a neat brick chapel, measuring 24 feet by 40 feet and served the local congregation well after Union in 1884. But, by 1900 it had stood empty for a few years and was taken down.

Eden:

East of Bethel about one and a quarter miles is Eden Chapel, in the township of Usborne, in Lot 5 of the 3rd Concession. The deed for the transfer of the land is dated April 3, 1863 between John and Nancy Luxton, and the trustees for the chapel, Thomas Allaway, Richard and William Easterbrook, John Murley, William Essery, George Rook and Thomas Hull.

We can draw a pretty good picture of this chapel using various sources. From the Bible Christian Property book we find that the dimensions were 24 feet by 34 feet and the building was of frame construction. From the book, Between the Fences, by the Usborne Township Historians, we are told .....

161

"The lumber chapel has six circular windows and has a neat appearance. The inside is neatly finished and it is admired by all, to be one of the most comfortable and neatest country chapels. Total Cost $600.

Upon the three quarter acre parcel was also a cemetery, and when the church was sold and taken down in 1910, a contract was drawn up that the cemetery should have perpetual care with the proceeds from the sale of the chapel furniture,etc.

In 1963 the broken stones were put into a memorial cairn and a dedication

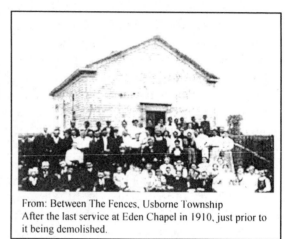

From: Between The Fences, Usborne Township
After the last service at Eden Chapel in 1910, just prior to it being demolished.

service was held to honour the pioneers who lived in the vicinity and were buried at Eden.

The Luxtons, who gave the land for the chapel and cemetery, were from Hatherleigh, Devon, and by 1879 their son Frederick had taken over the farm.

Crediton Village:

In 1996, the Huron County Historical Society published, in their *Huron Historical Notes*, a short history of each community in the county and the various names by which they were known down through the years. Here is what they say about Crediton ...

"Crediton extends along County Road #4 in Stephen township from the Aux Sables River west to Concession Road 6-7 and is the township's dominant village. The crossroads was first

settled by William Sweet from Devonshire, England, and became known as Sweet's Corners. By the 1860's the community with its several mills was flourishing and growing. In 1861 a post office called Crediton was opened here, named after Crediton in Devonshire because it also was six miles from Exeter......"

Although there are no records in existence to say when meetings first began at Crediton, we know that some were held at David Stahl's log house. Sunday School was organized there in 1860 and was conducted in David Stevens' log barn. While the Rev. Edward Roberts ministered on this circuit meetings were held in the schoolhouse, and members of this congregation included such families as: Banes, Broderick, Gardner, Hall, Harris, Hill, Krause, Lewis, Lloyd, Mitchell, Parsons, Stanley, Stevens, Sweet, Trevithick, White, Zwicker.

Rev. William Hooper followed and it was his energetic work that prompted the people to lay plans for a chapel. On January 16th, 1867, William Sweet, Sr., the original settler on Lot 10, Concession 7, donated land for the church site, which is lot 27 in the village survey. This consisted of a half acre located on the south end of the village. The chapel was constructed two years later.

From: A Century of Service, Crediton United Church History
Crediton Bible Christian Chapel, built 1869

Measuring 30 feet by 40 feet, this chapel was built of local white brick from the Crediton brickyards. It had a full foundation in which some of the ladies served tea on the day the chapel was

163

dedicated. The rest of the ladies were apparently across the road at Wagner's blacksmith shop baking for the tea. Trustees for this new chapel were Michael Stevens, John Parsons, George Lewis, John Trevethick and William Banes.

Sharon:

The congregation at Sharon started when a number of Bible Christians in the area met in one another's homes for worship. Later, they met in the schoolhouse. In 1869 they erected their own chapel which was located west of Exeter and 2 ½ miles north of Crediton, in the 8th Concession of Stephen Township. This was a frame chapel, measuring 26 feet by 40 feet and was erected just across the road from the Sharon schoolhouse.

This chapel cost $750 to build. The entrance was at the side instead of at the end and about half the seats were elevated, rising from the centre to the end of the building opposite the pulpit. One of the congregation gave a communion carpet, another the pulpit trimmings.

Families connected with Sharon Chapel include kestle, Amy, Rowe, Pedlar, Brokenshire and Lewis. Some of the lay preachers in this congregation were Michael Stevens, George Lewis, John Parsons and William Lewis. All were well versed in the Bible and the work of the church, and most could pray and expound as well as any ordained minister!

Bethesda:

To find this chapel, we now must travel to the north-east past Exeter to Usborne Township, where we find the chapel in Lot 25 of the 2nd Concession.

The chapel here was a small country chapel, measuring only 22 feet by 30 feet, put up on 8 rods of land. This did not likely include the land where upon sat the cemetery, but it may have.

The chapel was rebuilt in 1872, this time a brick chapel 34 feet by 48 feet, and the land was increased to half an acre.

Salem:

Salem Chapel was located at Centralia, an early settlement on the London Colonization Road, or The London Road as it is called today. The spot where the town would grow was settled in about 1833. Thomas Trivitt arrived in 1848, and by the early 1860's he had taken a portion of his land and set it aside, divided up into town lots. And so Centralia began, and Bible Christian families moved in and started meeting in private homes, and probably in the school house.

But Salem chapel was not always at Centralia. It began life as a small country chapel at Whalen Corners in the southeast corner of Huron Township. It was probably built in the 1860's, though no date has been found for it's erection. It was a frame chapel, measuring 22 feet by 30 feet, on the Crediton Circuit, but the congregation there soon dispersed or attended other meetings and the chapel was no longer required. In 1876, the congregation that had formed at Centralia needed a chapel, and so the old frame chapel at Whalen Corners was moved over to Centralia, where it served that congregation until Union in 1884.

Ministers to serve this circuit include:
1856 - John Williams
1857-59 - David Cantlon, John Edwards
1860-61 - John Hooper, H.J. Colwell
1862 - John Hooper and Henry Ebbott
1863 - Edward Roberts, Henry Ebbott and John Kinsey
1864 - Edward Roberts and Lewis W. Wickett
1865 - Edward Roberts and Martin Mennear
1866 - William Hooper and Richard T. Courtice
1867 - William Hooper and W.G. Beer
1868 - William Hooper and James Collins
1869 - William Hooper
1870 - Henry Kenner and Stephen H. Rice
1871 - Henry Kenner and Mark Hardy
1872 - Henry Kenner and William H. Quance
1873 - Jesse Whitlock and John Holmes
1874 - Jesse Whitlock and William Trethewey

1875 - Jesse Whitlock, John Ball, Herman Moore
1876 - John Watson Butcher and John Holmes
1877 - John W. Butcher, J.P. Price and William Davies
1878 - John Watson Butcher
1879-82 - George Webber
1883 - W.S. Pascoe

Usborne Circuit

This was the third circuit in the area of Usborne and Perth Townships, and had nine chapels along it's length, all built between 1855 and 1868. Usborne, along with its neighbours Exeter and Crediton, comprised the densest population of Bible Christians in Ontario, and probably in Canada and the United States as well. Darlington Township and Bowmanville in Durham County have always been sited as being the hub of the Bible Christians in Ontario, but in all honesty, I think it was Huron County and these three townships. Granted, there was the Bible Christian Observer being published at Bowmanville, and in the 1850's Ebenezer Thorne published the first Bible Christian newspaper, The Day Dawn, at Orono, and John Thorne and his family lived at Providence just outside Bowmanville, but if having dignitaries in the area is the reason it got its reputation, well, in my book its just not enough.

Bethany:
The early history of Bethany Chapel comes from missionary reports and tell us that, in 1856 land was given in Concession 6 of Usborne for the purpose of building a Bible Christian chapel. Subsequent reports go on to say ...

"1858 - A hewed log chapel 30' x 24' has been recently opened, 20 persons just brought to God united in church fellowship."

"1866 - At Bethany, they intend to build a new sanctuary and $700 has been provided toward it"

"December 1868 - Bethany Chapel, Usborne Circuit was opened Wednesday, October 14. Mr. A. Clark preached the first sermon. About 900 persons took tea the first day and the proceeds were $250."

The agreement to buy land was registered on April 16, 1860 at the registry office in Goderich. The trustees, William Passmore, Donald McInnes, James Fanson, Robert Campbell and Andrew Campbell, bought 20 rods (.26 acres) of land from Walter Madge and his wife Mary Webber for $1.00. This parcel of land was in Lot 18, on the 6th Concession, the land upon which Walter Madge settled in 1850. This agreement bears the signatures of the witnesses, John Mowbray, likely a member of the congregation, and Garrance Tink Colwell, a Bible Christian Itinerant Preacher. The chapel was 30 feet by 40 feet and was of brick construction and served the congregation until 1923, when a terrific wind storm all but destroyed the chapel.

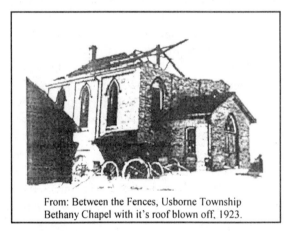

From: Between the Fences, Usborne Township
Bethany Chapel with it's roof blown off, 1923.

Siloam:

Joseph Dinnin and his wife Margaret, deeded to the trustees of Siloam Chapel, 12 ½ rods of land in Lot 16, Concession 8 of Usborne township. The trustees who signed the transaction were William Trewin, Thomas Clark, Jonathon Cooper, and Henry Taylor. The agreement was also signed by John Edwards, superintendant of the District and by David Cantlon, resident minister at Exeter. The witnesses were Titus Tremere, yeoman and Joseph Dinnin, both of Usborne. The transaction is dated December 18, 1859, but was not signed until April 16, 1860.

According to the Bible Christian Property Book this was a log chapel built in 1859, 20 feet by 30 feet in size. There is not indication that a frame or brick chapel followed in later years as was usually the case.

Members of this congregation at various times included in 1865: Mrs. Isaac G. Westcott, Samuel Isaac and wife, John Shadick, William Trewin and wife, Titus Tremere and wife, Philip Reed and wife.

1866: Mr. William Trewin, Samuel Isaac and wife, C.I. Pearce, John Shadick, Robert Wilson, Mrs. Jane Tremere, Mr. D. Knight, John Knight, A Hodgert and wife, David Mills.

Rehoboth:

Located in the 10th Concession of Usborne, this chapel was built in 1862. Robert and Mary Creery sold to the trustees, 24 rods of land for $1.00. The deed was dated March 25, 1862. The Bible Christian Property book says that this was a log chapel, 20 feet by 30 feet, but other old records say the chapel was built in 1864 and constructed of brick, perhaps the brick chapel replaced the log one.

The trustees to whom the property was sold were Thomas Clarke, Chancey Fuller, Matthew Routley, and Samuel Skinner. Brother George Dunkley, Bible Christian minister was also included in the list of trustees. The witnesses to the agreement were John Hooper, minister, and Joseph and Robert Creery.

One of the funny tales to be handed down from Rehoboth Chapel is told in the book, Between The Fences, by the Usborne Township Historians ......

"*It had been a warm day and the sheep decided to rest on the church steps. Somehow the door seemed to open and the sheep went inside out of the sun and when Mrs. John Fletcher, Norma Hooper's grandmother, and Sarah Francis arrived at the church to get it ready for prayer meeting they had an unexpected chore to do. The sheep were hurriedly chased out, and the ladies had to clean and scrub the church before anyone arrived.*"

The church was closed at the time of Union in 1884.

Eldad:

Located in the 8th Concession of Usborne Township, Eldad Chapel was built in 1855. It was a small log chapel measuring 26 feet by 36 feet, built on 40 Rods of land purchased from Andrew and Margaret Stewart for $1.00. The trustees to whom the land was sold were Francis Ashton, William Kernick, James Vance, John Fulton and John McInnes. The transaction was witnessed by Charles James Pearce, and Bible Christian Minister, John Edwards. This transaction was sworn before township clerk Thomas Trivitt of Centralia who had given land for the chapel there.

Some of the members of this congregation were James Vance who lived at Lot 17 on the North East Boundary; John Pybus who lived on Lot 25 in the 8th Concession; William Bray who lived on Lot 12 of the North East Boundary, and John Fulton who lived on Lot 16 in the 14th Concession of Hibbert Township, Perth County.

This chapel did not survive until Union. On June 12, 1881 the trustees for the chapel, Francis Ashton, John Fulton and John McInnes agreed to sell the land back to Andrew Stewart for the sum of $30, a figured agreed upon at the Bible Christian Conference earlier that month. It was torn down the following year.

Prospect:

Prospect Chapel had three faces. In 1862 the congregation erected a log chapel. This was replaced by a frame chapel, measuring 24 feet by 34 feet, in 1865. And in 1876 a third and final chapel was erected. Whether all these chapels were located at the same place I do not know, as old records are not clear on this point. Neither is the Bible Christian Property Book. The land upon which the third chapel was constructed was in Lot 12, Concession 13 in Hibbert Township. It was also known as Butler's Chapel, as it was from William Butler that the ½ acre of land upon which it sat was purchased in 1876 for $12.

Freewill:

This chapel was one of the last chapels to be built in the area, being constructed either in 1875 or 1880. It was built of white brick, probably from the Crediton brickyard. It measured only 22 feet by 32 feet and seated less than 100 people. It was built on the farm of John Hodgins on the township line between Biddulph and Blanshard. The church shed was across the road on Philip Brooks' farm.

Some of the members of this congregation included George Cook, William Duffield, William Hodgson, Philip and James Brooks, William and Albert Gunning, Benjamin and John Morley, James Sutherby, Jim Kernick, John Millson, Jabez Millson, Joseph Morley, John Walker, Samuel Gunning, Frank Morley.

The chapel closed in 1905.

Zion:

Very little is known about Zion Chapel. It was located in Lot 'A' of the 8th Concession of Usborne on a parcel of land 16 Rods in size. The small brick chapel was built in 1865, and beside the chapel was a cemetery on a further ½ acre.

Bethel:

Bethel Chapel was built in 1865 on the 11th Concession of Usborne Township. It was a small brick chapel, 26 feet by 36 feet, on 14 rods of land, and located at Munro. There is no further information about this chapel or its congregation.

Elim:

By far, the most well known today of all the chapels on the Usborne Circuit is Elim Chapel, located in a small rural community that took its name from the chapel, called Elimville. It was so well known that the circuit was often called Elim Circuit. Elim was just off the Huron Road on the Elimville Line where it crosses the Kirkton Road, in Lot 10 of the 6th Concession. The first recorded meeting of the local people for the purpose of worship was in the home of Silas Whitlock, so say the authors of the 1984 Huron County Historical Atlas. Old records indicate that this may have been Isaac Whitlock. They erected their first chapel in 1865 on ½ acre parcel, likely donated by Mr. Whitlock. This first chapel was built of logs and measured 24 feet by 34 feet, a standard size for a log chapel. In 1874 the congregation had set aside enough money to begin a new chapel, this time a brick chapel which would measure 34 feet by 50 feet - just double the size of

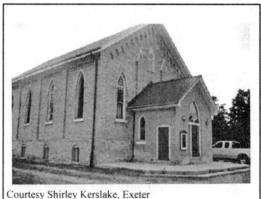

Courtesy Shirley Kerslake, Exeter
Elimville Chapel just prior to its demolition in recent years.

their old log house of worship.
Elimville also had a parsonage from which the circuit preacher made his rounds. It was a brick house built in 1867, but it was a pretty small house, measuring only 20 feet by 27 feet. It occupied half an acre. In 1878 the house was replaced, or re-built. Again, it was a brick house but this time it was 32 feet by 24 feet

Elim Chapel had a cemetery attached, and even though the chapel no longer stands, the cemetery is well maintained.

Ministers that served this very large circuit included:
1852-54 - Robert Hurley (Henry Ebbott joined him during 1853)
1855 - Joseph Dix and John Williams
Records missing for 1856-1864.
1865 - John Edwards and Charles J. Pearce
1866 - John Edwards and Garrance Tink Colwell
1867 - Mark Browning and Garrance Tink Colwell
1868 - Mark Browning
1869 - George Bodle and James Collins

1870 - George Bodle and Roger Allin
1871 - George Bodle
1872 - David Cantlon and John Veale
1873 - William C. Beer and Moses Metherall
1874 - William C. Beer and Herman Moore
1875 - William C. Beer and William Limbert
1876 - T.R. Hull and Daniel Williams
1877 - T. R. Hull and J. E. Elliott
1878 - Henry A. Newcombe and John Gilson
1879 - Henry A. Newcombe and William Henry Spargo
1880 - Henry A. Newcombe and William Coombe
1881-82 - William Quance and William Coombe
1883 - William Quance and G.F. Cannom.

Hensall and Bethesda Circuit

Hensall Bible Christian Chapel has a unique history. It was a late chapel in this area, not constructed until 1877 at the village of the same name, north of Exeter at the junction of the road to Mitchell and the road to St. Joseph's. It was a frame chapel measuring 22 feet by 45 feet, a long narrow chapel which was not the design used in this part of the country by other circuits and congregations. It seems that this chapel was rebuilt at some time, probably on the same

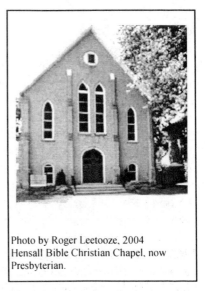

Photo by Roger Leetooze, 2004
Hensall Bible Christian Chapel, now Presbyterian.

foundation, the second being in white brick from local brickyards, perhaps Crediton.

172

The congregation grew and eventually found that their church was just too small. The Presbyterians on the other hand were finding a smaller congregation year after year, and eventually their church was just too big for them. So the two congregations switched churches.

Bethesda:
We've already seen this chapel on the Exeter Circuit, located in Lot 25 of the 2nd Concession of Usborne Township. It had always been an out of the way chapel on the Exeter Circuit, and because it was in closer proximity to Hensall than any other place, it was withdrawn from Exeter Circuit in 1878 and joined with Hensall to form one circuit.

Ministers who served this late circuit were:
1878-79 - S.J. Allin
1880-82 - Francis Metherall Whitlock
1883 - William Henry Spargo

Colborne Circuit

Colborne is the township in the north west corner of Huron County, north of Goderich along the shore of Lake Huron. An official circuit was not devised until 1866, the meeting places of the pioneers likely being visited when ever possible by the ministers at Goderich. There were chapels in the circuit long before the circuit became official, but they were most often looked after by local lay preachers.

Ebenezer:
The Bible Christian Property Book lists Ebenezer in Lot 33 of the 16th Concession of Hullett, but seeing as there are only 14 Concessions in this township, it can be safely assumed that this was the chapel by that name at Lot 33 in the 10th Concession.

Hugh Radford from England purchased this lot from the Canada Company in 1855. On 13 May 1857 he and his wife Sarah sold a half acre to the trustees of the Bible Christian congregation for 1£ 5s 0d. The trustees were Hugh Radford Sr., Robert Douslin, John Armstrong, yeomen of Hullett and Goderich Townships. Witnessing the transaction were Bible Christian ministers John Edwards, then stationed at Clinton and David Cantlon who was serving at Bridgewater. The first chapel to be erected was a log chapel built in 1857, the year the land was transferred to the trustees. It was a small chapel measuring only 20 feet by 30 feet, the same size that settlers usually built their first cabins.

By 1878 the congregation were able to erect a better chapel, this time a frame chapel 24 feet by 30 feet.

Along with the chapel a cemetery was started at this site and many of the area pioneers are buried there. Today, no trace of the chapel remains, but the cemetery, which stands atop a knoll and surveys the surrounding countryside, is a testament to the work and toil of our ancestors.

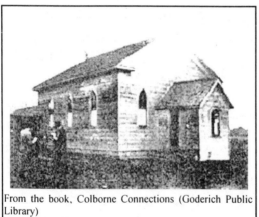

From the book, Colborne Connections (Goderich Public Library)
Bethel Chapel c 1925

Bethel:

Today, if you take Road 15 (upon which we've just found Ebenezer Chapel) in a westerly direction from Ebenezer, you will come to Bethel Chapel in Colborne Township. A small country chapel it was built in 1868 on 1/8 acre located in the Eastern District of the Township on Lot 5 in the 1st Concession.

In the history book, Colborne Connections, they say the chapel was constructed in 1874, so perhaps the first chapel was replaced by another frame chapel in that year. Or, 1874 was likely the year the deed of transfer was finally signed by all parties.

174

There was often a gap between the time the land was given and used and the time when it was all made official.

Bethel was a frame chapel measuring 25 feet by 32 feet, and served its community until the Union which created today's United Church of Canada. It was taken down about 1925 when the congregation moved over to Benmiller.

Zion:

Zion chapel was the hub of activity on the Colborne Circuit. The chapel was located on Lot 1 of the 6th Concession on the southwest corner just one mile south of Carlow.

This congregation first built a frame chapel in 1857 on a quarter acre plot. This quarter acre also housed the parsonage built here in 1864, a frame house 28 feet by 30 feet in size.

In 1875 the congregation purchased, or were given another plot of land where on they built a new white brick chapel.

From The Colborne Connection (Goderich Public Library)
Zion Church as it looked about 1925

Where this site was in comparison to the original site I do not know, but Zion School was built later on the original site.

From the book, Colborne Connections we learn this about Zion chapel .....

"A second church, an imposing white brick structure, was built in 1875 at a cost of $2,287.00. At the entrance end of the church, there were six rising seats which gave a very attractive appearance. The walls inside were plastered to represent block stone and the ceiling was adorned with three pretty centre flowers.

175

A moulding of Plaster of Paris was run in the angles of the ceiling, and a vase of fruit of the same material was suspended from the centre. The church was lighted with four three-branch chandeliers, suspended over the aisles and two brackets fastened to the posts at the pulpit."

Zion continued to serve the Methodists until the next Union in 1925, at which time this chapel was closed and like many others across the province, was torn down.

At one time, the roofs of the vestibules (one on either side of the church) had wrought iron work gracing the tops, and the pillars either side of that central front window were topped with mini-spires. These changes were likely made between 1884 and 1925.

Fisher's Corners:

According to Lorine McInnis Sholz this is the story behind the naming of this community ....

"The first settler to come to Colborne Township came because the Canada Company tried to interest several Toronto men (1828 or 1829) who were known to be professional settlers and provided a schooner to take them to Goderich to see the Huron Tract for themselves. In this group were John Wilson, Jacob Cromer and Michael Fischer (later spelled Fisher) and his son Valentine. Michael Fisher was one of the Pennsylvannia Dutch settlers who had followed the trail of the Black Walnut. He promptly set out exploring the vicinity and legend says that he went up the Maitland River on a small row boat and followed the tributary up to the present site of Benmiller. This apparently pleased him because he returned to Goderich and purchased 5,465 acres outright at a cost of ££2,049 7s. 6d. On his holding he built first a log shanty, then a log cabin, and in 1836 a big stone house which still stands.

Only a year later a second settler came to this section of Colborne, Benjamin Miller, from whom the present day Hamlet takes its name (Benmiller). He erected and operated a Tavern on this site which in those days was known as "The Hollow"."

The frame chapel at Fisher's Corners was not built until 1875, but it likely replaced a log chapel built by early settlers to this area about 1850 or so. This little country chapel was only 24 feet by 30 feet. No record has been found saying who gave or sold the land to the Bible Christian congregation, nor any information about how long this chapel stood at Benmiller.

Oasis:

This is the final chapel on this circuit, though it was not the last to be built. Very little information can be found for this chapel. It was of frame construction, it was erected on 1/4 acre of land, and it measured 20 feet by 36 feet. It was built in 1862, but the Bible Christians did not put the location of it in their property book. After much searching, it is felt that this chapel may not belong to this Circuit afterall, but refers to Eden in Usborne Circuit further south, however, seeing as it is listed in this circuit in the Bible Christian Property Book, I will leave it listed in this section.

At an early date the Bible Christians were visiting this area, and even though there was no chapel for many years they met in the schoolhouse as was often the case in most circuits in the early days. Unfortunately, no exact location is given for this schoolhouse. However, a short narrative from Brother Philip James has been found in an 1848 edition of the Bible Christian Magazine from Britain which gives us a very good image of the circuit at that time ...

"February 19th ... A few friends met together at the school house in the eighth concession of Colborne to settle our quarterly accounts; and as this was our last meeting before the District meeting, we had more business than usual and but few of the official friends present; the state of the roads being such that brethren from the other societies in the mission could not come. But by the help of the Lord, we got through our business comfortably and were much pleased to realize an over-plus in our quarterly accounts. This was affected by a few friends who collected from house to house toward defraying the expenses of the

mission. We felt thankful that the Lord had crowned our feeble efforts with such a degree of prosperity. Some improvements have been made during the year and unity and peace still reign in all our borders. Praise the Lord.

The next say, Sunday, were the public religious services of our quarterly meeting. In the schoolhouse above mentioned by half passed ten the preaching commenced A goodly company were present and there was a good feeling during the lovefeast and sacrement. The Lord was truly present.

Saturday, 26th ... On my way to my Sabbath appointment I called on Sister Olver, and found her struggling under heavy affliction and bereavement. She has sustained an irreparable loss, in the death of her husband and son, who both died at Stratford of Typhus fever...."

Many thanks are due Reg Thompson of the Goderich Public Library for his assistance in identifying some of the Colborne Township places.

Ministers who served the Colborne Circuit were:

1848 - unknown date - Philip James

1866-67 - William Wade

1868 - John Kinsey

1869-1871 - George Dunkley

1872-74 - unknown

1875-78 - Thomas Mason

1879-81 - James J. Broad

1882-83 - T.J. Sabine

Grey Circuit

Located in the far eastern corner of Huron County, we find that the early settlers to this township were mostly Scottish and English with some Irish and a few Germans. The first settler however, was a French Canadian by the name of Beauchamp who was a squatter who had taken up a holding in the township long before it was put up for sale as Crown Land and so can't be determined exactly where he settled. The second settler, John Mitchell, took up land in 1852 where the village of Molesworth stands. Other early settlers in the area of Brussels were - John and Duncan Ferguson, Robert and Ronald McNaughton Peter McDonald, a family called Hyslop, Thomas Blackie, James J. Ford, five McFadzean brothers, three families of Lamonts. The population grew quickly and within ten years was almost 2,500.

And so into this mixture came the Bible Christians in about 1856, the first preacher in this area being Joseph Dix. Two congregations were started in Grey Township, one at Cranbrook in the village, called Providence, and one at Lot 25, Concession 9, called Salem.

Providence:

Located in the little town of Cranbrook, Providence Chapel was built on a town lot of half an acre. Constructed in 1864, this frame chapel was fairly large, measuring 30 feet by 40 feet, measurements usually reserved for brick chapels. Cranbrook was/is in the far eastern end of the township.

Salem:

Salem Chapel was built on Lot 25 in the 9th Concession of Grey Township in 1869, on a parcel of land measuring 1320 square feet. This small frame chapel was only half the size of Providence

Chapel, 20 feet by 30 feet.

The Parsonage was built at Brussels on town lot #24 and was called Beach Cottage. The lot was 1/4 acre in size, allowing plenty of room for the preacher and his family to have a large garden. Beach Cottage was built in 1862. It was of frame construction and was fairly small measuring only 22 feet by 24 feet. The parsonage was placed almost halfway between the two chapels, Salem being directly north of Brussels at the northern edge of the township.

Brussels village is on the western side of Grey Township, and along with Cranbrook, is located on the main east-west arterial road that crosses both Grey Township and Morris Township next door to the west.

Ministers who served this circuit were:

1856 - Joseph Dix

1857 - no one

1858-59 - Robert Miller

1860-61 - Andrew Gordon

1862 - John Shortridge

1863 - Thomas Greene and George Dunkley

1864 - Thomas Greene and Mark Browning

1865 - Thomas Greene

1866-67 - John Kinsey

1868-69 - W. Heysett

1870-71 - none recorded

1872-75 - George Bodle

1876 - John Ball

Records seem to end in 1876. Was this circuit added to another? Were the chapels closed at this time? A small mystery indeed.

Perth County

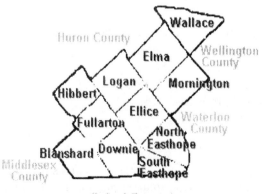

Perth County Circuits

Perth County, like Huron County, was settled when the Huron Tract was open for colonization, though being farther from the waters of Lake Huron it was settled at a later date.

There was only one circuit in this County, the Mitchell Circuit which spanned 3 townships, however, this circuit soon became too large and was divided, giving Perth two circuits, the second one called Fullarton Circuit.

Mitchell:

Mitchell - in the town on Toronto Street
Fullarton - Lot 22 of the Woodley Plan(1860's) in the village
Bethel - at Monro, Fullarton Township
Staffa - Lot 16, Concession 9, Hibbert Township, Huron
Providence - Lot 16, Concession 6, Logan Township
Carlingford - Lot 8, Concession 6, Fullarton
Zion - Lot 5, Concession 7, Hibbert Township

Fullarton:

In 1874 this circuit was split, with Fullarton, Bethel and Zion being drawn off to form Fullarton Circuit. Added to this was:
Russeldale - just a meeting place in the village
Mount Pleasant - (south of Russeldale) transferred over from
    Clinton when Fullarton was formed.

Many thanks are extended to the Stratford-Perth Archives for their assistance in collecting data on these chapels, and most especially to archivist Lutzen Riedstra.

Mitchell Circuit

The Mitchell Circuit comprised the chapels in Fullarton, Hibbert and Logan Townships of Perth County, with the chapel at Mitchell more or less the main chapel with the parsonage for the Circuit Preacher. Another parsonage was located at Fullerton for the assistant, or probationer.

This part of the country started settling in about 1842. Almost from the very beginning of settlement, the Bible Christians had an itinerant preacher in the townships. In 1848 it was a lay-preacher by the name of Jones and in 1849 he was joined by Rev. Arthur Doble. Within the first ten or twelve years of settlement three of the seven chapels on this circuit were erected. They were log chapels built in the early 1850's, as was the case at Bethel, and was likely so at each location, though the Bible Christian Property Book does not mention any of the log chapels.

At times on this circuit, as on many of the circuits both in Canada and UK, there was difficulty in raising enough money to pay the ministers' salaries. Petitions and letters were often sent to the district meetings and the annual conferences asking to be allowed to retain part of their Missionary receipts to help with their cash flow. On the Mitchell and Fullarton Circuits, as on all the circuits in Ontario, frequent circuit teas were held which also raised money. Often, an I.O.U. had to be given to the preacher on payday! In the Mitchell Circuit minute book on May 16, 1870, in large letters is this message: *SETTLED UP IN FULL THIS DAY WITH THE PREACHERS.*

Mitchell:

Mitchell was the hub of the circuit, having one of the earliest chapels. It was also the location of the parsonage for the circuit preacher, with the parsonage for the assistant, or probationer being at Fullarton.

The Mitchell chapel was built on Toronto Street in 1856 on 1/4 acre lot. It was a large brick chapel, 31 feet by 62 feet, and could likely seat 300 people. A Sabbath School wing was built onto this chapel, 31 feet by 21 feet. The cost of the building of this church was $1600.^{00}, a hefty sum in those days!

The parsonage was also a fairly large house. Built in 1867, it was a substantial brick dwelling, 30 feet by 32 feet with a kitchen wing on the back (probably frame) 16 feet by 21 feet.

Whether or not the parsonage was adjacent to the chapel is not known, but it stood on its own half acre lot. The Bible Christians owned considerable property at Mitchell, for the cemetery there was one acre in size.

A report from the October 1865 quarterly meeting for the circuit tells us there were 9 charges on this circuit: Mitchell, Bethel, Fullarton, Zion, Providence, Ebenezer, Union, Robbs and Shipley's with a total membership of 273. Union, Robb's and Shipley's were meeting places and by 1869 the numbers had diminished and so were discontinued. However, Ebenezer chapel is a mystery. The only other mention of it is in connection with the building of the parsonage at Fullarton, when Ebenezer chapel was sold in 1874 to help pay the debt. This would explain why it does not appear in the Bible Christian Property Book, written in about 1874, but it does not help us locate this old chapel.

Fullarton:

Fullarton was the other 'anchor' in this circuit. Though the community was not nearly as large and bustling as Mitchell, Fullarton served the circuit as the place of residence of the assistant ministers and probationers who worked on the circuit.

The congregation here had apparently been meeting in private homes in this area since about 1844. In the book, *History of the County of Perth*, by William Johnston (1903) the author says this ....

"Rev. Philip James established a mission in 1844 at Fullarton Corners. Services were held in the shanties erected by the settlers and in a log building which was built for a school. In 1848 a Sabbath School was organized by James Moore who came a long distance through the woods to discharge his duties in this self-imposed task."

The chapel at Fullarton was built in 1858. It was a small frame chapel only 26 feet by 36 feet, and stood on a small village lot 31 feet by 93 feet.

The parsonage, built in 1865, was also a small frame building, only 18 feet by 24 feet, and sat on a quarter acre lot. At that time it was Lot 22 of the Woodley Plan for Summervale, which was another old name for Fullarton. The lot was purchased from John Woodley in July of 1862 for $30.^{00}

From the book, *Water Under the Bridge*, we find that prior to the building of the parsonage ..... *"The first two ministers for the Fullarton Circuit lived in a log shanty but in 1875 [sic] that shanty was rebuilt, enlarged and made considerably more comfortable. The Rev. J.P. Rice was the new parsonage's first occupant."*

Many dates abound for the building of this parsonage. 1865 comes from the Bible Christian Property Book. Another record says 1868. In the 1868 account of things it points out the Bible Christian ministers weren't above making a profit in God's cause, for in that year Rev. Paul Robins loaned the circuit $530 at 8% interest for the purpose of building the parsonage. A further $75 was found by selling off the old Ebenezer Chapel (location as yet unknown) in 1874 and applying it to the debt, which was finally paid in 1876.

The cemetery at Fullarton was located in Lot 22, on the 8th Concession and was 1 ½ acres in size. Even though the Bible Christians were using the plot of land at an early date, the deed of transfer was not drawn up until 1869 when William and Mary Ann Francis officially transferred it for the sum of $120.^{00}. Trustees of the congregation at that time were James Baker Sr., William Vanstone, William Munro, William Rogers, all yeomen of the area. The preacher, who was included in the list of trustees, was Thomas Greene.

Bethel:
From a letter written to and published in The Bible Christian Magazine in England, from Rev. Philip James, we see how conditions were in this area in 1847. The letter is dated Sept.

5, 1847 .....

"*The work started in the form of a Sabbath School. The school was commenced early this summer under many discouraging circumstances. There is no school house or any convenient place for teaching. The roads are bad and many have a great distance to come. However it was decided to hold meetings alternately in the three most central shanties even though they were small and dark and there was scarcely room nor light for writing. By the above date, after four summer months, a platform was erected and children gave a program, which was proof of the instruction given.*"

Rev. Arthur Doble wrote another letter a year later in which he confirms the date of this Sabbath School. He also tells us something about the population of the area ....

"*We are much encouraged since three years ago there could scarcely be found the trace of anyone. Now they are coming from the east, west, north and south ....*"

Bethel Chapel at Monro in Fullarton Township was the third early chapel to be constructed on this circuit. It too was built in 1858, and replaced a log chapel that may have been erected as early as 1854 when Rev. Philip James started the original congregation. For a country chapel it was quite substantial. Measuring 30 feet by 40 feet it was of brick construction and was erected on a lot 80 square rods in size. The cost of construction was $1200.[00]

The land had been in use for at least six years prior to its official transfer in 1860, when Samuel Harris sold to the Bible Christians the said property for the sum of £5. The trustees at the time were Jasper Pridham, James Moore, Henry Heal, William Yeo, Philip Greenwood, Charles Curtis, Jonas O. Coles.

A description of that first church tells us that there were individual doors at the ends of each pew, each of which were numbered and a rental of $1.25 per family was charged for the use of each pew. Mr. Lewis F. Goodwin held the office of Pew Steward for twenty-five years. Several reports survive telling of teas that were served in the shed which was decorated for the occasion with cedar boughs, etc.

There is a cemetery with Bethel chapel and it was opened at an early date with many of the pioneer families of the district buried there.

Bethel Chapel no longer exists. It was replaced in the early 1900's by the present church and is still used today by the descendants of the early pioneer families.

Staffa:

Located on Lot 16 of the 9th Concession of Hibbert Township, in Perth County, this chapel is just north off the Staffa Road, on County Road 180, also known as The Perth

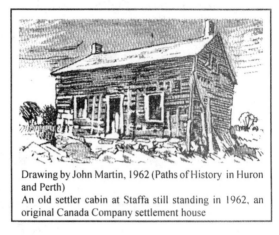

Drawing by John Martin, 1962 (Paths of History in Huron and Perth)
An old settler cabin at Staffa still standing in 1962, an original Canada Company settlement house

Road. No sign remains of where the chapel once sat, but a small cemetery at the crest of the hill as you enter Staffa from the south, marks the spot.

Staffa used to be called Springhill, the congregation there starting about 1856, meeting in George Weese's barn in Lot 17, Concession 8. In 1860 they were finally in a position to erect a chapel, and did so that year in Lot 16, Concession 9, apparently also part of George Weese's farm.

The day of dedication had been set for the Sunday, and on Saturday Joseph Moffat went to Mitchell to bring over the Minister who would dedicate the church. According to records, that would have been Paul Robins.

While he was gone, Peter Drown started cleaning up the shavings that were still laying all over the ground, getting the place all spruced up for the big day. He had taken some of the shavings

187

to the edge of the road where he had set fire to them, and had returned to gather some more to put on the blaze, when a strong wind came up and carried some sparks to some of the shavings still all over the ground. It wasn't long before the flames engulfed the new chapel, and with no one around to assist, the flames could not be put out. When Mr. Moffat returned with Brother Robins they found the chapel nothing but a pile of ashes.

History does not tell us if a second attempt was made to erect a chapel, but I would think there was one, for the congregation continued, and the little cemetery is there to remind us that the Bible Christians were still active down through the years.

Providence:

In the book, *Legacy of Logan*, it says .... *"The annual report of the Missionary Society of the Bible Christian Church of Canada for the year 1856-57, showed the Bible Christian Church in Logan Township as part of the Mitchell Mission. The following contributors were listed: G. Ward, J. French, Elizabeth Hornibrook, Simon Elliott, Ann Barchall, J. Mills, W. Boyd, J. Hornibrook, J. and F. Boyd , E Hornibrook, J. and A. Wade and Charles French...."*

Providence chapel was apparently the only Bible Christian chapel in Logan Township. It was located in Lot 16 of the 6th Concession. Built in 1862, it was a frame chapel, 30 feet by 40 feet, erected on 21 square rods of land granted to the Bible Christians by John Wade Sr. and his wife Mary. The fee charged was $1.⁰⁰ and was transferred May 1st, 1863. The trustees to whom the land was granted were Thomas Coppin, Thomas Leake, Sam Hornibrook, William Anderson, Henry Squire, Thomas Elliott and Thomas Roe.

Beside the chapel was constructed a shed for the horses, buggies and wagons of the congregation, measuring 20 feet by 25 feet.

At Union in 1884 this chapel was chosen as the meeting place for the three congregations who came together at that time, the Bible Christians, the Primitive Methodists and the Wesleyan Methodists, so Providence served the community at large until 1901 when a new church was constructed beside it, and the old one taken down. It was sold to James Graham who moved the material away with horse and sleigh and later used for house building purposes.

Carlingford:

Although the Bible Christians met here from an early date, they never had a chapel of their own. They shared the Carlingford Church with both the Wesleyan congregation and the Episcopal Methodist congregation. It was the Episcopal congregation who originally purchased the land, in Lot 8, of the 6th Concession, from Charles Brogden in 1856 and erected the chapel which would serve everyone. The cemetery also served all three congregations.

Zion:

Located west of Mitchell in Lot 5 of the 7th Concession of Hibbert Township, Zion was a frame chapel constructed in 1864 on 1/4 acre of land purchased from Samuel Gerry. In 1874 the land was finally transferred to the congregation for the sum of $1.^{00}.

This chapel continued to serve the people of the neighbourhood after the Union of 1884, but records seem to indicate that by 1889 it was in disuse and was likely taken down at that time.

In about 1874 Bethel, Fullerton and Zion were withdrawn from the Mitchell Circuit to form the Fullerton Circuit. On the Fullerton Circuit Plan for 1884 is Russeldale, which was likely just a meeting place, as no chapel has been found there. At that time James Kestle held services there every Thursday evening at 7:30 p.m.. The first meeting in this area was held in the shanty of Nicholas Roach who lived at Lot 19, Concession 14. Roach is said to have been a member of Mount Pleasant chapel and he received his mail at Russeldale Post Office.

Also listed part of the time with Mitchell was a chapel called Mount Pleasant, but it seems to appear in more than one circuit. Mount Pleasant is found on Highway 23, just north of Kirkton, and could very well have been included on the Usborne Circuit. A check of the preachers who were suppose to have served this chapel show that from 1850 through 1870 this chapel was on the Clinton Circuit, though I wonder why because it is no where near the other places on that circuit. After 1870 Mount pleasant is with the Mitchell circuit where it should have been all along.

Ministers who served both Mitchell and Fullerton Circuits were:

1848-49 - Arthur Doble
1850 - John Brown Tapp
1851 - John Hodgson (he also looked after Clinton)
1852 - J.W. Chitley and John Brown Tapp
1853-54 - John Williams
1855 - Robert Hurley and Paul Robins
1856-57 - Andrew Gordon
1858 - Robert Hurley
1859 - Paul Robins
1860 - Paul Robins and T.C. Pickard
1861 - Paul Robins and Adam Curry
1862 - Paul Robins and George Dunkley
1863 - Joseph Hoidge and Henry James Colwell
1864 - Joseph Hoidge and Henry Ham
1865 - Edward Roberts and Richard Hicks
1866 - William R. Roach and William G. Beer
1867 - William R. Roach and Robert Baker
1868-69 - Archie Clarke and Thomas Greene
1870-71 - Archie Clarke and Paul Robins
1872-73 - John Watson Butcher and Paul Robins
1874 - John W. Butcher and Edwin Tonkin
1875 - William Hooper and George Dunkley
1876-78 - William Hooper
1879-82 - W.S. Pascoe
1883 - Walter Ayers

Wellington County

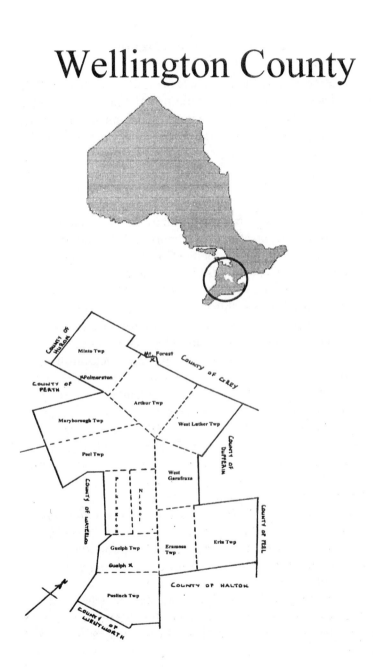

Wellington County Circuits

Palmerston was the only place in the county where a Bible Christian chapel was erected. Apparently at Palmerston, or in the vicinity of Palmerston, there were three preaching appointments, but old records do not give the location of them - most likely in the countryside outside the town.

Palmerston Circuit

Like Cobourg and Belleville in the east, Palmerston was a circuit of one chapel. The town of Palmerston is located in the 6th Concession of Minto Township in the County of Wellington, and this was the only chapel ever built in this county.

Located on a town lot of a quarter acre, on the corner of Lowe and Victoria Streets, this was a log chapel in about 1870, which is very surprising because few log buildings were erected at this time. Some accounts say that this chapel was put up in 1874, and if this is the case it replaced the original log structure. In about 1878 this building was 'remodelled', and in a letter to the editor of The Observer, printed in the edition of September 4, 1878, Rev. John Veale tells about the work on the chapel ....

"There is wainscoting put around the building. The posts that stood in the aisles, that the stove pipes rested upon, are taken away, the stove pipes put nearly up to the ceiling, the lamps put on the sides of the church and nice reflectors put behind them. A very nice chandelier hangs in the centre of the church.

The pulpit remodelled and made a lot smaller, and a beautiful arch put behind and two nice lamps put in the arch.

We have a little more painting and white washing to do. Notwithstanding the hard times up this way, all the improvements have been done without increasing our debt."

A parsonage was located at Palmerston, but whether it was located close to the church I do not know. It was a frame house, 18 feet by 30 feet in size, and was likely constructed between 1876 and 1878.

This chapel had three preaching appointments attached to it, but where these other meetings were held is not known at this time. Five local preachers assisted the itinerant preachers who served this chapel and the surrounding area. At Union in 1884, there were 69 members, and two Sunday Schools with a combined attendance of 108 students.

At the time the chapel was built at Palmerston, it was a boomtown, it's prosperity due to the railroad. Half the town worked for the railway - general labourers, linemen, section bosses, etc. The other half of the town were either merchants or skilled workmen such as plasterers, carpenters, masons. There was no lack of variety in the kinds of shops along the main street, including three butchers! The town was busy enough to give employment to three lawyers.

The spiritual life of the inhabitants was also well served with six churches - Anglican, Presbyterian, Episcopal Methodist, Canada Methodist, Catholic and Bible Christian.

The ministers who served this circuit were:

1874 - T. Mason
1875-77 - William H. Butt
1878-79 - John Veale
1880-81 - T.J. Sabine
1882-83 - George Smith

Bruce And Grey Counties

St. Edmunds

Lindsay

Eastnor

Georgian Bay

Cape Croker

Albemarle

Lake Huron

Amabel

Saugeen Indian Reserve #29

Saugeen

Arran

Bruce

Grey County

Eldersie

Kincardine

Greenock

Huron

Brant

Kinloss

Carrick

Culross

Huron County

Wellington County

Circuits of Bruce and Grey Counties

The United Counties of Bruce and Grey are, today, a vacationer's paradise offering wilderness camping, hiking, boating of all kinds on Lake Huron and Georgian Bay. I doubt it was such a paradise in the early years of settlement, though the rugged beauty of the place has likely never changed.

There was only one circuit in this large northern area, with it's base at Wiarton, Bruce County, hence the name, Wiarton Circuit.

Even though the Bible Christian Property Book gives no listing for a chapel at this town, there was indeed a chapel here, on the same lot as the parsonage. Unfortunately, because the Bible Christians knew where their chapels were they never, or seldom, entered an address in the property book.

Three other chapels were on this circuit, being next door in Grey County included:
Oxenden - in the village
Colpoys Bay - possibly Lot 26, Concession 24 of Keppel Township
Keppel - probably at Kemble, south and east of Oxenden

Wiarton Circuit

The Wiarton Circuit was made up of two appointments - one at Wiarton in Bruce County, and the other at Oxenden in Grey County.

Wiarton:

Although no sign of a Bible Christian church can be found at Wiarton in any of the local 'histories' that have been written, the Bible Christian Property Book says there was a parsonage constructed there, for the Wiarton Mission, on a town lot measuring 72 square rods, in 1871. It was of frame and concrete construction. In 1875 a chapel was built on the parsonage lot, measuring 30 feet by 40 feet. It was a frame chapel, but whether or not it was taken over by the Methodists, or taken down at Union in 1884 I do not know.

Oxenden:

There was another church built by the Bible Christians at Oxenden in Grey County, on the shore of Colpoys Bay. It should be noted that even though Wiarton is in Bruce County and Oxenden is in Grey County, the two places are only about two miles apart.

No sign of a parsonage has been found in the records so it is possible that the parsonage at Wiarton continued to serve the circuit.

The chapel at Oxenden was on town lot number 8, on Havelock St., beside the Mallard Hotel, and across the road from the cemetery. Behind the cemetery the Gleason River meandered toward Colpoys Bay. The chapel was built in 1877 and was of frame construction.

From the book: Beautiful Stoney Keppel, by the Keppel Township Historical Society
Oxenden Chapel, while it stood at Purple Valley

The trustees of that chapel were: C. Barfoot, George Atkey Sr., John Scott, and Henry Atkey. Henry Atkey was in fact a Methodist and some time lay preacher, but he showed much community spirit by sitting as a trustee for the Bible Christians.

The chapel served the village and township until Union with the Methodists. In 1886 the chapel was lifted off its foundation and taken across the ice to Purple Valley where it served that community until it was destroyed by fire in 1981.

197

Colpoys Bay and Keppel:

The Bible Christian Property Book lists two other chapels in the area - at Colpoys Bay, built 1876, of frame construction, and at Keppel, no further information.

These chapels have not yet been located, but there is the possibility that one of these, perhaps the one listed as Keppel, was located at Kemble where William Westaway, probably from Bradworthy Parish in Devon, settled in 1856. The Westaway family, as well as most of Bradworthy Parish, were Bible Christians from an early date. Kemble is south and east of Oxenden.

The Colpoys Bay Chapel might be the one indicated on the map in Belden's Atlas at Lot 26, Concession 24.

The Reverend William Woodman, who began his Canadian career at Prince Edward Island, retired to Wiarton where he had preached for many years, and where some of his children had been born . He died here July 16th, 1900, age 79 years. I think even then Georgian Bay drew people to its shores because of its exquisite beauty.

Preachers to serve this circuit were:

1870 - George Smith and James Collins
1871-73 - William Woodman (and James collins for 1871 only)
1874 - supply
1875-77 Roger Allin
transferred in 1878 from Exeter District to Toronto District
1878-79 - George Dunkley
1880-82 - Thomas Dry
1883 - Henry Newcombe

Many thanks are extended to Betty Siegrist of Wiarton for finding most of the references to this circuit, and to the members of the Keppel Township Historical Society for allowing me to quote their work, much of which came from the memoirs of the older citizens of the area which had been written down and now published. Without their recollections of these places in their childhood, we would, today, be without our history.

Kings County

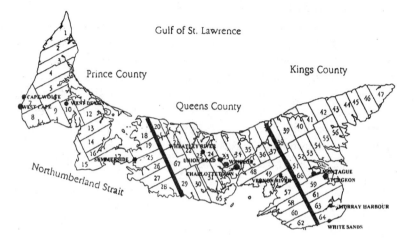

Kings County

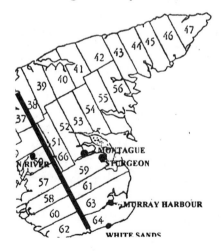

The Circuits of Kings County

Kings County includes Georgetown Royalty, as well as Lots 38 to 47, 51 to 56, 59, 61, 63, 64, and 66.

Although it was one of the earliest settled areas of the whole of Prince Edward Island, there were only two circuits to develop in that county. Had the economic climate of the island been a little better in the 1830's and 1840's, and had the settlers been able to own their own land at an earlier date instead of leasing it from absentee landlords, then another circuit may have been in existence, probably by the 1840's, with the division of chapels amongst the circuits quite different than it ended up.

As it is, the two circuits were Sturgeon and Murray Harbour.

Sturgeon:

The chapels on Sturgeon were taken from other circuits in 1874.....
Sturgeon - in the village
Montague - just beyond the bridge.

Murray Harbour:

Sturgeon - in the settlement with a cemetery
Murray Harbour - in the village with a cemetery and a parsonage
Three Rivers - no further information
White sands - with a parsonage

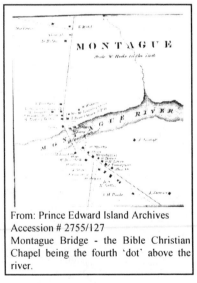

From: Prince Edward Island Archives Accession # 2755/127
Montague Bridge - the Bible Christian Chapel being the fourth 'dot' above the river.

Meeting places on this circuit, 1851-53 included:
Georgetown,
Bay Fortune,
St. Peters

Sturgeon Circuit

Sturgeon Circuit was withdrawn from Vernon River Circuit in 1874. There were two chapels on this circuit, Sturgeon and Montague.

Sturgeon:
The chapel at Sturgeon P.O. was built shortly after the arrival of the Rev. William Harris in 1844, on the coastal road at the edge of the farm of Matthew Young in Lot 59. It was a small frame chapel, 20 feet by 32 feet (just about the same size as a settler's first log house) and it was located on half an acre. A small cemetery was also on this parcel, located in Lot 61. At that time Sturgeon P.O. was a small settlement on the Murray River Circuit, just 4 miles from Georgetown but shortly the community started to grow, and eventually the Bible Christian congregation as well. By 1874 the congregation was large enough to demand more attention than the itinerant preacher could give it and so, along with Montague a new circuit came into existence.

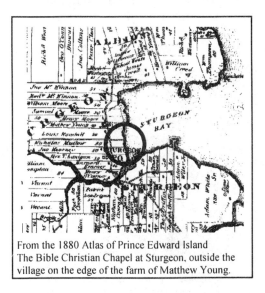

From the 1880 Atlas of Prince Edward Island
The Bible Christian Chapel at Sturgeon, outside the village on the edge of the farm of Matthew Young.

At Sturgeon the postmaster was Thomas J. Sabine, likely the son of Harry, or Henry Sabine, who would later be known as Rev. Thomas J. Sabine, Bible Christian minister. The Rev. Sabine's mother was the well known Bible Christian evangelist,

Martha Jago from Cornwall.

At the time of Union in 1884 the chapel was sold to the Baptist congregation and today the cemetery is called the United Baptist Cemetery.

Montague:

The Bible Christians were the first to establish a following in the town and the home of Philip Beers was used for services before a chapel was built. This was in the days when Rev. Francis Metherall was the itinerant preacher in the area, and he split his time between Montague, Georgetown, Vernon River and Three Rivers. In 1834 Philip James arrived on the island and took over the eastern end while Rev. Metherall went over to West Cape to develop that end of the island.

Montague was early on part of the Vernon River Circuit, but because the growth of the congregation it was withdrawn from that circuit in 1874 and coupled with Sturgeon made into its own circuit.

The chapel at Montague was built in 1853. It was a neat frame chapel, 25 feet by 32 feet. No cemetery was mentioned in the Bible Christian Property Book. Although old records do not tell us much about the

From the Prince Edward Island Public Archives and Records Office Acc. #2476/1-1
Montague Bridge in the 1870's. The Bible Christian chapel is on the left side, third building past the bridge.

building of this chapel, it is possible that Philip Beers, in whose house the congregation met prior to having a chapel, donated the lumber, or at least sold it at cost, to the congregation. Beers owned a saw mill on that branch of the Montague River known as Brown's Creek., not very far outside the village.

Ministers who served the circuit from 1874 were:
1874 - Fergus O'Connor Jones
1875-76 - John Pooley
1877-80 - William Bryenton
1881-83 - J. Wesley Down

Murray Harbour and Three Rivers Circuit

At some time, a short history of the Bible Christian Church at Murray Harbour was written. Below are some excerpts from that history that highlight the forming of the circuit.

"In 1834, the Bible Christian congregation in Vernon River erected a parsonage for the use of the resident missionary. The house continued as the residence of the minister until 1880, when a new one was built.

A barn seems to have been built later for the comfort of the horses of those attending the Church services. The construction of this barn marks the first recorded contact between the Bible Christian Church and the Murray Harbour area. The Sencabaugh brothers of Murray Harbour prepared the frame timbers at home, they left with them in the evening, and drove to Vernon River through the night a distance of twenty-four miles, put the frame together during the day, and returned the next night. '

The Sencabaugh brothers noted would likely have been those of William Sencabaugh Sr., the first Sencabaugh to settle in Lot 64. These were William Jr., Benjamin, James Sr., and Henry. They were the Sencabaugh sons that remained in the Murray Harbour and Guernsey Cove area and would have been of age to take on such a task.

In 1843, Rev. Metherall was asked to take over the old Methodist congregation which he did reluctantly, but with the prayers and sanctions of the Methodists. And so Murray Harbour became a part of the infant Bible Christian organization of the island.

William Calloway and William Harris arrived in the fall of 1844 to assist with the work on the island and to take on the work of the Murray Harbour area. This would result in four chapels eventually being erected to form a circuit:
Sturgeon - later transferred to its own circuit
Murray Harbour
Three Rivers
White Sands

Murray Harbour:

Murray Harbour was never a very large place. Even by 1871 the population had reached only 200 people. But a congregation here also drew on Murray Harbour North, just 2 miles away and Murray Harbour South, just 3 miles in the other direction.

The chapel at Murray Harbour was built in 1846. It was a frame chapel measuring only 27 feet by 37 feet. It was on a one acre parcel which it shared with a small cemetery. Like Sturgeon, the village straddled the line between two lots - Lots 63 and 64, but on which side of the line the chapel and cemetery were located I do not know.

Three Rivers:

By 1851, Jesse Whitlock was preaching at Three Rivers, dividing his time between three charges. At just about this time the congregation erected a chapel, though the Bible Christian Property Book does not mention it.

White Sands:

This was a late chapel for this circuit, built in 1860. It too was a small chapel, of frame construction, 24 feet by 30 feet. Although the Bible Christian Property Book does not mention a parsonage, the tourist board for the area says there was a 'manse' for the Bible Christians directly across the street from the chapel. This is quite likely, for the Bible Christians did not keep as good records of their property as they did their baptisms and marriages!

The same year that the chapel at White Sands was built, a parsonage was erected at Murray Harbour on a corner of a three acre parcel that was being used as a cemetery. The parsonage was frame, as were most buildings on the island at that time, though brick buildings were found at Charlottetown and in various other 'prosperous' areas. Often, the main minister, or elder one, would occupy one house on a circuit, while the assistant or probationer would occupy another. This is likely why there were two parsonages built on the circuit.

When Jesse Whitlock was minister on this circuit, he branched out to a few other places, holding meetings and trying to establish other charges on this circuit. Unfortunately, because of the great many other religious bodies on the island vying for every person, there was little success and these places were abandon after only about two years. They included:
Georgetown - served with Three Rivers 1851
Bay Fortune and St. Peters were added in 1852 and served through 1853 with Georgetown visits.

Visits by the ministers to these three places was likely on a 'supply' basis, when he had the time to go and see them, or perhaps regularly on a once in six weeks schedule - it was not often enough to build the congregation he envisioned. The island at that time was desperately short of manpower to build the Bible Christian holdings.

Ministers to serve the Murray Harbour Circuit included:
1832-1836 - Francis Metherall
1837-43 - Francis Metherall and Philip James
1844-46 - William Harris and William Calloway
1846-50 - William Calloway (with Vernon River)
1850-51 - John Watson Butcher
1851 - Jesse Whitlock
1852 - Jesse Whitlock and Richard Cotton (including Georgetown)
1853 - Jesse Whitlock and Jacob Gale
1854 - John Watson Butcher and Jacob Gale

1855 - J.W. Butcher
1856 - J.W. Butcher and William Woodman
1857 - William Woodman
1858 - J.W. Butcher and William Woodman (with Vernon River)
1859-61 - JesseWhitlock and William Woodman
1862-63 - Isaac Ashley
1864-65 - John Watson Butcher
1866-67 - J.W. Butcher and Alexander Richard
1868-69 - W.P. Hunt
1870-71 - R.B. Rowe
1872-75 - William Ross Medland
1876-78 - James H. Collins
1879-80 - William Ross Medland
1881-82 - Edwin A. Tonkin
1883 - dissolved

It should be noted here that there was a son of Murray Harbour to join the Bible Christian Itinerancy, in the person of John T. Sencabaugh, son of James Sencabaugh Sr., one of the brothers who had helped build the horse shed at Vernon River in the 1830's. He was likely the only person from Murray Harbour Circuit to enter the Bible Christian Ministry.

From the Collection of Kathie Sencabaugh

John T. Sencabaugh, grandson of a United Empire Loyalist who settled on St. John Island/PEI after the American Revolution.

Queens County

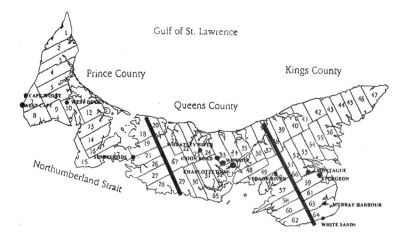

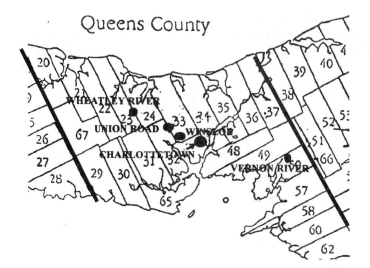

The Circuits of Queens County

Queen's County was the destination of the first Canadian Missionary, Francis Metherall in 1832. Henry Abbott of Union Road had written to England requesting preachers for his neighbourhood.

It was also at Queens County, at Charlottetown, where Cephas Barker set up a central administration for the Island in 1856.

And it is in Queens County that we find the most circuits, these being :

Charlottetown:

A circuit of one, as in most cities, the chapel located on Prince St. However, for a short time there was also a congregation at Grand River - not the Grand River near Bideford, but the Grand River that was also known as Bridgetown in Lot 35. I don't believe a chapel was ever erected at Bridgetown.

Union Circuit:

The circuit was formed from the old Kings Mission in 1850. Located in Lot 33 (for the most part) north of Charlottetown with four stations...

Winsloe North - the first chapel on the circuit built in 1850
Winsloe South - built in 1872 - 3 miles north of the parsonage
Rustico Road - possibly at Milton - frame, built in 1861
Union Road - located in Lot 35 - the largest of all the chapels on this circuit.
Parsonage at Winsloe, a large house on a large lot 40 rods square.

Vernon River Circuit:
Vernon River:
Cherry Valley:

Wheatley River Circuit:

There were four stations on the Wheatley River Circuit:
Wheatley River - the chapel being built in 1860
Princetown Road - possibly at Greenvale - built in 1840
Rustico Road - the chapel built in 1861 and enlarged in 1873
Hunter River - joined the circuit in 1879 - chapel possibly built that year.

New London:

Although this was one of the areas early visited by Francis Metherall in his 'drive' across the Island, it was not a long-lived circuit, though it did last about 20 years. It was an area where many Devon families had settled and Philip James went to work building the circuit in 1834 when he arrived on the Island.

It is unlikely that chapels were erected at any of the places where congregations were started, and these included:
Little York
Covehead Road
Mill River
South-west Bedeque
New London

Charlottetown Circuit

Charlottetown was one of the last areas of the island to see the thrust of the Bible Christian mission work. It had always been the aim of the missionaries to make this a religion for the common man - the labourer, the farmer - and leave the big cities alone.

However, when Cephas Barker arrived on the island in 1856 he saw a network of little circuits with no central place from which to administer them. They were all working in the dark and not being as effective as they might be. He decided, seeing as the island wasn't very large to begin with, that the city of Charlottetown, with its admirable central location, would make a grand central location for the work of the Bible Christians. And so, in 1857 the Charlottetown Circuit was begun.

Of course, at that time there just weren't enough preachers on the island to go around and so Barker himself took on the closest circuit to Charlottetown and served both the city and the Union Circuit.

In about 1862 Grand River was added to the Charlottetown Circuit, a community seven miles North east of the city. It has also been called Bridgetown. This appointment was also occasionally worked with Vernon River.

Charlottetown:

Queen Street, Charlottetown, 1860

The chapel at Charlottetown was built in 1858 on Prince Street, on a town lot 80 feet by 96 feet in size. Even in the city the chapel was a f r a m e building, but at t h a t t i m e lumber was still plentiful and cheap and it was likely the most cost effective way to get a central administrative position for the island circuits.

The chapel itself was fairly large, considering the size and importance that Charlottetown had gained in those days. It measured only 48 feet by 56 feet, and could house a congregation of at least 400.

The following year a parsonage was erected, but unfortunately the records do not give an address for this residence.

It was apparently not an ostentatious building, being only 22 feet by 36 feet.

Cephas Barker was sent to the Island to take a look at the finances, and the work to see how it could be improved. His stay was for ... *"perhaps twleve months"* ... He was on the island for nine years! During his stay he was instrumental in having Prince Edward Island join with Ontario, which was then known as the Canadian Conference, in 1865. He realized it would so much easier to administer it from the same side of the ocean. Once this union had been finalized, his work was considered done. From Warren Goss we have this statement ...

"Under the leadership of Rev. Cephas Barker, the condition of the Bible Christian Church had improved greatly in spiritual awakening as well as in growth in the number of church buildings and memberships. When he left the societies were peaceful, finances healthy, and the prospects were encouraging. The church in Charlottetown had grown to fifty members and the district membership had risen to six hundred and seven."

Market Square, Charlottetown, 1865. The round market building would have been known by the Bible Christians in their day.

Fifty members in a church large enough to hold four hundred seems almost laughable today, however, four hundred may well have attended. Not many in a whole congregation ever paid their subscriptions, that is, taken out membership in the society. So having fifty people actually pay for the privilege of attending the church was pretty good.

211

In 1883 a large fire destroyed the Bank of Commerce corner in downtown Charlottetown. The rebuilding gave rise to thoughts about what the community needed. It was decided that they needed a theatre. After the Union of Methodists in 1884, the Bible Christian Church was no longer needed, and it wasn't long before it was turned into *The Lyceum*, not a grand theatre, but large enough that some great performances could be presented to the people of Charlottetown.

Grand River:

This community was also called Bridgetown and was located in Lot 55 in King's County. Why this preaching place was not looked after by the Sturgeon Circuit is a question which may never be answered. Local politics no doubt.

It is doubtful that a chapel was ever erected at Grand

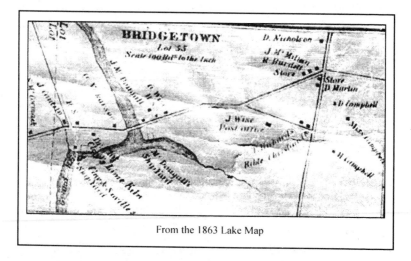

From the 1863 Lake Map

River, and no mention of it appears in the Property Book. It was a long, spread-out community, as you can see on the map above, and grew primarily around the ship building yards of Clay and Saville. This preaching place lasted only seven years and was dissolved three years after Cephas Barker transferred to Ontario.

Preachers who served Charlottetown and Grand River included:

For Grand River:

1862 - Cephas Barker with Charlottetown.
  Francis Metherall with Vernon River
  (It appears that this was served on a supply basis by whomever could give some time to it.)

1863-64 - T.J. Sencabaugh

1865 - W.P.Hunt

1866 - William Kinley

1867-69 - Alexander Richard

For Charlottetown:

1857 - Cephas Barker, Jacob Gale (with Union)

1858-61 - Cephas Barker

1862 - Cephas Barker, Francis Metherall, William Partridge
  (With Vernon River and Grand River)

1863-64 - Cephas Barker, William Partridge

1865-67 - Henry A. Newcombe and William Kinley

1868-69 - Alexander Richard and William Heysett

1870-74 - George Webber

1875-78 - W.S. Pascoe

1879-82 - John Harris

1883 - S.H. Rice.

Union Circuit

In the March 27th edition of The Observer, in 1878, there appeared an article by Rev. E.A. Tonkin who was serving on the Union Circuit. It was a description of the circuit for those who did not know the area already, which of course, was most of Canada. In part, this is what he wrote .....

"The Union Circuit, consisting of four appointments, lies chiefly in Lot 33, about 6 miles north of Charlottetown.

Four roads: Rustico, Winsloe, Brackley Point and Union Road, traverse this lot from North to South and each road forms a distinct neighbourhood.

On the Winsloe Road about 7 miles north of Charlottetown we have a small church built about 27 years ago during the pastorate of Brother Butcher, and around this little chapel, now old and hastening to decay, many hallowed memories cling to gracious outpourings during the ministries of Brothers Metherall, Gale, Barker and others.

From the collection of Heather Chevalier, Moncton North Winsloe Church, likely remodelled or altered about 1900.

The parsonage is very commodious, 2 ½ storeys with a French roof.

Three miles to the north on this road we have a very comfortable church dedicated in 1872 in a thickly populated neighbourhood.

One and a half miles west of the parsonage and on the Rustico Road, we have a small but neat church recently renovated.

At Union Road, 3 ½ miles east of the parsonage we have a large frame church dedicated in 1871. The neighbourhood is thinly populated and this thin population is devided between the Canada Methodists and ourselves."

Winsloe North:

This small community had the first chapel in the area, built about 1850 or 51, it was a frame chapel. The size of this first chapel was only 21 feet by 28 feet. The entry in the Bible Christian Property Book says this was at Winsloe South, but they

214

have reversed the two chapels. They do mention the renovated or rebuilt chapel in 1880, which was also frame, measuring 30 feet by 24 feet. There was also a cemetery with this chapel.

Winsloe South:
The chapel he mentions 3 miles north of the parsonage is the chapel at Winsloe South. Built in 1872 and dedicated in 1873 it too was of frame construction, but quite a bit larger than the chapel at Winsloe North, measuring 40

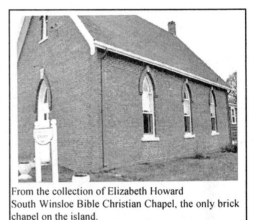

From the collection of Elizabeth Howard
South Winsloe Bible Christian Chapel, the only brick chapel on the island.

feet by 28 feet. Being that much closer to Charlottetown it may have had a larger congregation. Rev. Tonkin calls this "a very comfortable church", and being so much larger than its sister chapel, it likely was brighter and airier, and all around more comfortable. The parcel of land on which this chapel was built measured 80 feet by 80 feet, and appears to be a 'village size lot', and may have been donated by Jasper Pickard, a member of the congregation, and upon whose farm this chapel is built. This chapel was re-built after Tonkin's time. The second chapel was of brick, and is now a heritage site, not only because of the Bible Christian connection, but because it was the only brick chapel ever constructed on the island!

Rustico Road:
One and a half miles west of the parsonage on the Rustico Road one comes to the settlement called Milton, and this is likely where the third chapel in Rev. Tonkin's article was located. According to the Property Book it was constructed in 1861, and

rebuilt in 1873, the renovation that Rev. Tonkin said had taken place 'recently'. This new chapel was a frame chapel 28 feet by 40 feet, and according to the Property Steward's records, the lot it sat on was only 40 feet by 40 feet.

Union Road
The chapel at Union Road was located in Lot 35. Rev. Tonkin says it was a large frame chapel, it's recorded size being 32 feet by 44 feet, the largest of the chapels on this circuit. It was on one acre of land, possibly not right in the settlement, and no cemetery is mentioned with it.

The parsonage was located at Winsloe, just north of Charlottetown. It was a frame house, and not only was it 2 ½ storeys tall, as Rev. Tonkin describes it, it was 30 feet by 30 feet in size, a terrifically large house indeed. But if it had to house the assistant preacher, or the probationer who helped on the circuit, besides the preacher's family, and possibly be the venue for quarterly meetings, then it had to be large to serve all those purposes. It sat on a parcel of land 40 sqaure rods in size. In Rev. Tonkin's diary he speaks of growing turnips - he could grow an awful lot of turnips on that large lot!

From the records of Lot 33 found in the 1880 Meacham Atlas of Prince Edward Island, there are three Bible Christian properties identified. One is on Jasper Pickard's farm as I mentioned above. Another was 17 acres in size and a third one 6 ½ acres. I do not know which is which, and unfortunately Rev. Tonkin didn't go into their sizes in his description of the circuit. Needless to say, the Bible Christians owned a sizable chunk of Lot 33.

The preachers who served this circuit included:
1850-52 - Jacob Gale
1853-56 - Francis Metherall
1857 - John Ball and Jesse Whitlock
1858 - Jacob Gale
From this year served with Charlottetown

1859-61 Cephas Barker
1862 - Cephas Barker and Francis Metherall
1863 - Cephas Barker, William Partridge and William Woodman
1864 - Cephas Barker and William Partridge
1865 - John Chapple
1866-67 - John Chapple and Henry Newcombe
1868 - John Chapple
1869 - John Chapple and Alexander Richard
1870 - William E. Reynolds and William Heysett
1871 - William Reynolds and George Webber
1872-73 - George Webber
Separated to its own circuit again
1874 - John Pooley and R.B. Rowe
1875 - John Holmes and R.B. Rowe
1876 - R. B. Rowe
1877-80 - Edwin A. Tonkin
1881-83 - J.M. Tredrea

Vernon River Circuit

The Vernon River congregation of the Bible Christians, as in most of the area east of Charlottetown, began in 1832 with the arrival of Francis Metherall, the first missionary to the island. Richard Cotton took over in 1839 and Absalom Pickings arrived to assist in 1841. At one time the circuit covered most of Queen's County. It remained in 'mission status' until about 1850, everything in Queens and Kings Counties being called Kings Mission.

By 1850 it appears as if Vernon River had been withdrawn from the Kings Mission and began a life of its own as a full circuit, as did the other areas of Queens County.

Included in this new circuit was Cherry Valley. Montague was added in 1865, then withdrawn in 1874 and put with Sturgeon.

Vernon River:

Rev. Francis Metherall continued to reside at Vernon River for a while after going to the west end of the island to develop a circuit there which he called Ebenezer, later to be called West Cape Circuit. He remained at Vernon River until 1846. This was his first home on the island. Not only had he built his house here in 1834, but he had built the first chapel here too. He had sad memories of the place, too. It was here that his wife had died in 1840, and it must have been difficult to leave this place.

Some sources say that the first chapel here was built in 1840, other records say services were held at the substantial parsonage until 1842. The chapel was likely erected in 1842. It was a small frame church, only 22 feet by 30 feet.

The parsonage and the chapel were built on a 12 acre parcel which had been given to the denomination by James Laird ... *"for use by the missionary"* in 1834. The parsonage that was erected served all future ministers to the circuit until 1880, when, it is assumed, a new parsonage was

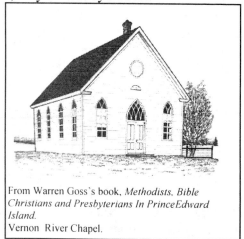

From Warren Goss's book, *Methodists, Bible Christians and Presbyterians In PrinceEdward Island.*
Vernon River Chapel.

built. This 12 acre parcel also housed a cemetery.

Members of this first congregation included Jeremiah Enman, John Van Iderstine and J. Fletcher. It should be noted that the first cabin occupied by Francis Metherall and his family was one that belonged to Jeremiah Enman.

The chapel was replaced by a new structure in 1872. Although still of frame construction, the new chapel was twice the size of the original, measuring 32 feet by 44 feet.

After Union the chapel continued to serve as a Methodist church. In 1970 the old church was dismantled, the church property and the cemetery were fenced in and the cemetery was named "The Vernon River Memorial Cemetery". It is here in this spot that Rev. Francis Metherall's first wife, Mary Langlois is buried.

Cherry Valley:
Although it did not hold the same importance as the Vernon River Chapel, this small chapel served the people of the Cherry Valley area for about 20 years. It was from Cherry Valley that Mary Nelson, Rev. Metherall's second wife, hailed.

The chapel was erected in about 1864. It was of frame construction and measured only 26 feet by 36 feet. It was located on half an acre on what has been described as *Irving land,* so it may be that the Irving's donated it to the local congregation. Unfortunately, no deed has ever been found transferring the land. This parcel was on 'The Loyalist Line Road' , also called locally, The Back Road.

The chapel here served the surrounding community until Union in 1884, when an offer of free land at the junction of three roads leading into China Point was received and a new church was erected. The old Bible Christian Chapel with its tower that looked more like a lighthouse than a church steeple, was moved into the town and used as a Community Hall, where, among other activities, plays were given.

Ministers who served this circuit included:
1832-34 - Francis Metherall
1834-40 - Philip James
1840 - Philip James and Richard Cotton
1841-42 - Richard Cotton and Absalom Pickings
1843 - Richard Cotton and Francis Metherall
1844 - William Calloway and Francis Metherall
1845 - Richard Cotton and Francis Metherall
1846 - John Watson Butcher and William Harris
1847 - William Calloway and Francis Metherall on occasion

1848-49 - William Calloway and Jesse Whitlock
1850 - William Calloway
1851 - Richard Cotton
1852-53 - John Watson Butcher
1854-56 - Jesse Whitlock
1857-58 - J.W. Butcher
1859-60 - Jacob Gale
1861-63 - Supply
1864 - J.J. Rice
1865 - With Montague - W.E. Reynolds
1866-68 - Isaac Ashley
1869-70 - J.G. Yelland
1871-72 - R.B. Rowe
1873-75 - James D. Kestle
1876 - William Ross Medland
1877-78 - George Smith
1879-83 - John Ball

Wheatley River Circuit

The Wheatley River Circuit came into being in those first few years that Francis Metherall was on the Island. In 1834, after two years of working by himself on an 80 mile-long circuit, Metherall was joined by Philip James who took over the preaching places in the Wheatley area, while Metherall went to the west end of the province.

In those early years the circuit included Charlottetown, Union Road, Vernon River, the Winsloes, Princetown Road, Rustico Road, as well as the Wheatley River area. It was a large area to cover and the burden was eased to some degree in 1839 when Richard Cotton arrived from England, and Absalom Pickings in 1841.

Together this team of dedicated ministers spread out across the province and tackled the job of building congregations and chapels.

In the early 1870's Charlottetown was withdrawn and made a circuit unto itself, while the western portion of the area was made into the Wheatley River Circuit, and the eastern end into the Vernon River Circuit, and the central portion into the Union Circuit.

The Wheatley River Circuit eventually looked like this....
Wheatley River
Princetown Road (Greenvale)
Rustico Road
Hunter River joined in 1879

Princetown Road:
The Princetown Road Chapel was the first to be built on the circuit. It was constructed in 1840 on a half acre parcel of land at or near Greenvale. It was a small frame chapel, 22 feet by 30 feet. A cemetery was also started on the same half acre. Brother Richard Cotton was the driving force behind its construction.

Wheatley River:
The chapel at Wheatley River was the next to be built, it being constructed in 1860. It too was located on half an acre with a cemetery beside it. Not much bigger than Princetown Road chapel, this frame chapel was 26 feet by 36 feet. Both Wheatley River and Princetown Road chapels could seat about 100-150 each Sabbath, but whether or not they saw congregations of this size, I do not know. It is possible that by the time this chapel was built, during the incumbency of Cephas Barker, the congregations indeed grew that large. He was a builder and achiever, and was sent to Prince Edward Island in the first place to get the financial viability of the place back on track. To do that he had to enlarge the member base, which is just what he did.

Rustico Road:
The first chapel here was likely built in 1861, measuring 28 feet by 40 feet. In the Bible Christian Property Book, it says the

old chapel was 18 feet by 26 feet - perhaps there were three chapels on this site! When the frame chapel was rebuilt in 1873 it was enlarged to 40 feet by 40 feet, indicating a growth in the congregation and therefore in the community around it.

Hunter River:

This chapel was added to the circuit in 1879, but unfortunately, it is not entered into the Property Book, this being made up in 1874. When this chapel was constructed, I do not know, but it was likely in 1879 when it first appeared on the circuit. It was located in Lot 23.

Preachers to serve this circuit were:
1832-34 - Francis Metherall
1834-39 - Philip James
1840 - Philip James and Richard Cotton
1841-42 - Richard Cotton and Absalom Pickings
1843 - Absalom Pickings
1844-47 - John Watson Butcher
1847-50 - Richard Cotton
1850-53 - Jacob Gale
1853-56 - Francis Metherall
1856-65 - Cephas Barker
1865-70 - John Chapple
1871 - George Webber and William Ross Medland
1872 - George Webber and James D. Kestle
1873 - George Webber and R.B. Rowe
1874-75 - George Webber and John Holmes
1876 - J. G. Yelland and John Holmes
1877-78 - J.G. Yelland
1879 - J.G. Yelland and George Smith
1880 - George Smith and James A. Dafoe
1881 - James A. Dafoe
1882 - J.A. Dafoe and W. E. Reynolds
1883 - W.E. Reynolds and William Bryenton
(William Bryenton continued on with the Methodists.)

New London Circuit

The New London Circuit is not often mentioned in the old records, as it did not last for very many years. Located near the north shore in Queen's County, it was originally part of the PEI Mission which in the early days was the whole of the island, but mainly in the eastern regions.

From the book, *Methodists, Bible Christians and Presbyterians in Prince Edward Island*, by Warren W. Goss, we find this .....

"Rev. Metherall turned his attention to Malpeque Road, commonly known then as Princetown Road, along which had settled many English families. He visited and set up preaching schedules in LittleYork, Covehead Road, Mill River which was near New London, and South West Bedeque. His missionary labours now extended 40 miles."

This took place in 1833 and 1834. Philip James arrived in the fall of 1834 and was appointed to all those places west of Charlottetown, from Union road to New London, while Rev. Metherall worked everything east of the Hillsborough River. Between them there was now 36 preaching places.

Up until 1842 the area of New London was part of the PEI Mission, but in 1843 it seems likely that the Bible Christians tried to make a separate circuit of the area, as there were specially appointed preachers assigned to it. It is doubtful that chapels were ever erected at any of the preaching places, for there are no records of any in the Bible Christian Property Book, and this makes it difficult to know how the area was actually progressing and developing.

Preachers were appointed to this circuit until 1854, when records cease, and none of the above mentioned five places appear in the records of surrounding circuits. It can be assumed that the New London circuit was dissolved at that time.

Preachers who served this early circuit included:
1843 - John Watson Butcher and Absalom Pickings
1844 - John Watson Butcher and Richard Cotton

1845-46 - William Calloway
1847 - J.W. Butcher
1848-50 - Richard Cotton
1851-52 - William Calloway
1853-54 - Richard Cotton

Prince County

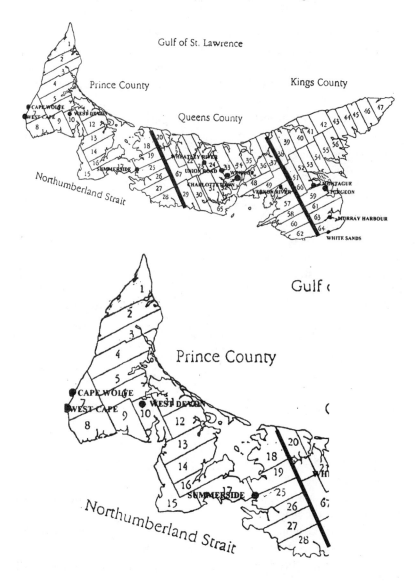

Gulf of St. Lawrence

Prince County

Kings County

Queens County

Northumberland Strait

Gulf c

Prince County

Northumberland Strait

The Circuits of Prince County

Prince County was the last area where the early Bible Christian missionaries worked to build a presence on the island. Francis Metherall was here about 1839, on and off, and he eventually moved here in 1847 to give his full time to the area.

Two circuits were eventually developed here - Summerside Circuit and West Cape Circuit. The area around Malpeque Bay, namely Bideford, Tyne Valley, and that area around Cascumpec (known today as Alberton) further to the west were worked for many years, however, few stations in these areas were included in later years in either circuit.

Summerside Circuit

Summerside was one of the more important centres in Prince County, not as large as Charlottetown, but growing in importance, mainly because of the large amount of ship-building in the area. It was also well known from a fairly early date, for the oysters that were caught in

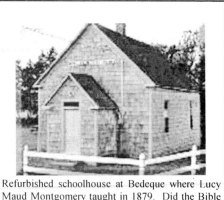

Refurbished schoolhouse at Bedeque where Lucy Maud Montgomery taught in 1879. Did the Bible Christians ever hold meetings in this building in the early days while trying to build a circuit?

Bedeque Bay and shipped all up and down the eastern coast of both Canada and the US.

Still known today for its oysters, Summerside is also the supply centre for the farms of Prince County.

Within the area of Summerside were four chapels, all

eventually allied with Summerside Circuit ...
Summerside
Northam
Bideford
Traveller's Rest
This was a long circuit with Northam and Bideford many miles away to the north-west.

Summerside:
Because Summerside was the 'home base' for the circuit preacher more has been written about it than any of the other stations on this circuit, and from the book, *Summerside Saints and Sinners, A History of Trinity United Church*, by George A Leard (1958), we have this description ....
" *A number* [of Bible Christians] *worshipped with the Methodists but felt in 1870 that they would like to have a church of their own.. Accordingly we find that at the 1871 district meeting of the Bible Christians it was recommended that Summerside be made an appointment.*"
This suggests to me that the congregation had been renting space from the Methodists, as was the custom in many places. Some of these people were John Cudmore, John W. Clark, David Cook, Mrs. Joseph Mallett, D.D. Crue, and Edgar Craswell, all members of that first congregation.
This little book tells us that Henry Newcombe, the preacher appointed to Bideford, was asked to work with this nucleus of a congregation. The following year James. H. Collins was sent over to Summerside, and he and George Webber, who at this time was the superintendent of the Island, together procured land and supervised the construction of a school room that would hold services until a chapel could be built.
The old Bible Christian records mention a chapel here, 15 feet by 40 feet, which was likely that first school room.
This school room became the vestry of the new chapel constructed in 1873-74, with the new chapel being 32 feet by 52 feet overall, constructed of frame and clapboard (so says the Bible

227

Christian Property Book).

The new parsonage built here in 1873, 26 feet by 36 feet, was apparently modelled on the one at Winsloe.

The chapel was located on Spring Street, and at Union in 1884, the Methodist church was sold and the Bible Christian Chapel became the circuit church. The parsonage also became the parsonage for the Methodists.

Northam:

Located in Lot 13, Northam was a very small settlement, but the chapel located there drew it's members from the surrounding area. Northam was in the middle of agricultural land and most of the members of the Northam chapel were farmers.

The frame chapel here was built the year prior to Summerside's chapel, 1871, and its size, 18 feet by 26 feet, reflected the size of the congregation.

Bideford:

From the records compiled by Douglas Walkington, housed at the United Church Archives in Toronto, Ontario, it appears as if Bideford was not a very early station on the Bible Christian circuits. According to that record 1865 was the first year that an itinerant preacher was appointed to Bideford, in the person of William Hunt. However, the Bible Christian Property Book lists an early chapel there, built in 1845 on one acre of land which also housed a cemetery. Rev. Philip James is said to have served the first gathering of Bible Christians here as early as 1835, and it was just about this time when the Grigg family from Devon, settled at Bideford, and whose children were christened as Bible Christians here at an early date.. No doubt Bideford was served from an earlier circuit, possibly West Cape when Francis Metherall went over that way in about 1845 or 46. It may have been served for about 20 years by the itinerant for that area, though it is not mentioned in Walkington's Directory as being associated with West Cape until 1875, and then only for one year.

Bideford was an area of much industry. It was one of the

most productive ship-building areas of the whole island. The Ellis family of Bideford were some of the most prolific builders in the vicinity and according to the 1881 census these families were Bible Christians, though these would be the children of George Ellis by that time, grandchildren of William Ellis. William and George arrived in about 1816 from Devon.

Unfortunately the appointments at Northam and Bideford did not last long enough to see Union. The ship building of the Bideford and Northam area had declined to such a state by the 1870's that people were beginning to move away, leaving the chapels virtually empty every Sabbath. I mentioned that Bideford had been administered by West Cape during 1875. Back it came to Summerside in 1876 and then both Bideford and Northam were discontinued for want of congregations.

Travellers' Rest:

In 1870 there was an appointment at Travellers' Rest with a small congregation and 56 people on probation for membership. Perhaps these probationers didn't work out, or perhaps the bulk of the circuit was given up before a chapel could be built at this place, but it has not been mentioned in the Property Book, nor in the Walkington Directory.

Traveller's Rest, also known as Townsend's Corners, is where Rev. Richard Cotton preached from time to time, and where he retired and farmed in later years.

Preachers who served this circuit included:
At Bideford:
1835-1864 - unknown - but likely Philip James in the early years
1865-67 - William P. Hunt
1868-71 - Henry A. Newcombe
1872-73 - James H. Collins
1874-75 - Thomas J. Sabine
1876 - E.A. Tonkin - partial year

At Summerside:
1871-73 - (with Bideford) Henry Newcombe and James H. Collins
1874-75 - James H. Collins
1876 - E.A. Tonkin
1877-78 - William Ross Medland
1879-81 - James Collins
1882-83 - James A. Dafoe

West Cape Circuit

While much of the island work was still in development, Francis Metherall moved to the western end of the Island in 1844 on a temporary basis, and by Christmas had established the Ebenezer Mission which consisted of West Cape, Bideford and Cascumpec congregations. He moved over permanently in 1847. Now that there was a permanent, full time preacher in the area, the Ebenezer Mission became Ebenezer Circuit.

The first church had been constructed in 1845 at Cape Wolfe, also known as The Lot 7 Chapel. The next chapel wasn't constructed until 1860 at West Devon in Lot 8. The other 4 chapels on the circuit were built after 1870.

You can see that it was a long drawn-out process to build the circuits on the Island, and in the early days the work was unbelievably difficult. The lack of good roads was the greatest problem, making it difficult, both winter and summer, to go from place to place on any sort of schedule.

In England, most of the preachers came from the West Country which broadly included not only Devon and Cornwall but Hampshire, Dorset and Somerset as well. These places rarely see snow, but when they do, it's what Canadians call "a sprinkling". So when the missionaries came out from England it was likely the first time they had encountered deep snow in the winter months and it must have been almost unbearable for them to learn how to travel in it. And being an island, the extra dampness meant lots of snow, and heavy, wet snow at that. Rev. Metherall recorded trying to go around his circuit, on foot, with snow three and four feet deep.

So the early days of West Cape Circuit, known then as the Ebenezer Circuit , were not easy. Is it any wonder it took over 10 years to get a second chapel built?

There were six stations eventually organized on the West Cape circuit and these included:
Cape Wolfe
Milburn
Bethel
West Devon
Knutsford
Miminegash

Cape Wolfe:

Also known as The Lot 7 Chapel, Cape Wolfe was the first congregation on the circuit to erect a chapel, in fact, they were the first congregation on the circuit. They called their chapel Ebenezer, after the first Bible Christian Chapel in England, built at Shebbear Parish, Devon. The circuit took that name for a number of years.

That first frame chapel, erected in 1845, was a modest affair. By July of that year, Rev. William Harris, who had come to the island in 1844, reported that the frame was up, the shingles were on, but the windows and floor were not yet put in. Most of the labour was probably donated by members of the congregation.

The congregation out-grew their little chapel in a few years, and in 1868 a second chapel was constructed on the same site. Warren Goss in his book, *The Methodists, Bible Christians and Presbyterians in Prince Edward Island*, says ....

" *The second Cape Wolfe, Lot 7, Bible Christian Church was built in 1868 on part of the sixty six acre farm of Samuel Kinley, located on the west side of the Shore Road, across from the Nauvoo Road. In its earliest history, the church was called the Ebenezer Mission Church.* "

Samuel Kinley was the son of James Kinley who had

231

owned the farm 23 years previously when the first chapel was erected.

A cemetery had been established across the road on a 1 acre parcel on the west side of Horatio MacWilliam's farm and in 1859 Rev. John Watson Butcher was instrumental in having a parsonage built on the east end of the same farm, occupying 3 acres. A parsonage had not been needed while Francis Metherall had the circuit, as he had purchased himself an 86 acre farm where he lived with his second wife and his family.

By 1883, the congregation hearing the first discussions about Union, decided they had better find a deed for their small holdings. In that year the people who owned the parcels of land in question were Frederick Peters and Arthur Peters, and so a deed between these two men and the trustees of the chapel and its associated ground, was signed. Trustees that year were James Farrar Stewart (Francis Metherall's son-in-law), William Fish, Samuel Lidstone, John Durdan, Sr., and Edward Lidstone. The transaction cost the congregation $1.[00]

When Union occurred in 1884 the West Cape Chapel became a Methodist Church.

Milburn:

From the Goss book mentioned above, we find that the people of Milburn had started a society about 1850, holding their meetings in the home of Nathaniel Boulter and being led mostly by lay preachers, with the occasional visit from the preacher at Cape Wolfe.

A chapel was never erected here. By the 1870's, the majority of people attending the services at the Boulter home were Methodist, and the names of the preachers coming out were those of Methodist preachers. The Bible Christians had ceased to serve the community, probably because man-power was so scarce. At union, the Methodists erected a church here.

Bethel:

Bethel Bible Christian Chapel was built in Lot 8 on three

quarters of an acre on the farm of Charles MacDougall. It was located along the O'Leary Road, and was referred to as The O'Leary Chapel. It was a neat frame chapel measuring 28 feet by 40 feet, built in 1873 and dedicated in 1874. The lot also contained a cemetery.

At the 5th Anniversary celebrations a tea was held and the public invited to attend. The event raised $130.^{00}, enough to pay off the existing debt on the chapel - $116.^{00} - and have some left over to paint the church.

In 1878, Rev. John Ball, the incumbent on the circuit wrote .... *"Financially we are doing better than last year, but we are still a long way behind with money very scarce. The financial night has been long on the Island. The want of money is the cry on every hand. It (money) was conspicuous by its absence at the Quarterly board Meeting."*

In 1844, shortly after Rev. William Harris arrived on the Island he wrote this ....

"I am sorry to say that trade is dull indeed at present. There is but little money in circulation. The business is carried on by bartering one thing for another. This will very materially make against our finances and lay us under the necessity of drawing more heavily from the missionary fund than we should other wise do."

Things had not changed much in 34 years!

From the O'Leary Pastoral Charge - photo by Wendell Cameron, PEI.
The West Devon Bible Christian Chapel later Methodist.

West Devon:

From Warren Goss we have this interesting piece of information about the date of the building of the chapel at West

Devon, also known as The Lot 10 Chapel ....

"Bible Christian Chapel records of 1855 mention a resolution to ascertain where land could be had for missionary premises in Lot 10, West Devon, and to communicate with Brother Francis Metherall as to the suitability of the site.

In the Christmas Quarterly meeting in 1860, Resolution No. 6 stated that 'each family connected with our congregation is expected to provide a seat after a given pattern, the seats to be free.' *For these reasons the members of West Devon believe their church building was erected in 1860."*

The reason I quote this, and likely the reason Warren Goss went looking for the answer, is that the Bible Christian Property Book tells us that the first church at West Devon was built in 1872. I would suggest that an existing chapel was renovated in that year.

This was a frame chapel, 24 feet by 34 feet on half an acre of land. A cemetery also located on this parcel, is the last resting place for many old Devon families.

Knutsford:

Because the Bible Christian Property Book was written about 1874, the chapel at Knutsford is not mentioned in it, being erected in 1879 and

Knutsford Bible Christian Chapel, now part of the Museum Complex at O'Leary.

dedicated in 1880. When the Methodist Union took place, and the chapel became a Methodist Church, the Methodists called it, *"a neat and comfortable church with a large congregation"*.

It seems that the Methodists moved the chapel to O'Leary at some point, so the staff at the O'Leary Community Museum have discovered. They also tell us that the chapel was eventually sold to the Catholic congregation at O'Leary and was again moved to a new location where it sat serving the community until 1990 when the last service was held in it.

In 1993 the chapel was sold to the Museum and once again it was on the move, this time to the Museum complex.

Miminegash:

This chapel, too, was constructed in 1879. At the time of Union in 1884, the congregation met the decision with disbelief, or so says Warren Goss. They did not wish to join this union with the Methodists, a feeling that many congregations held, but kept silent and joined anyway, being told that there was no way out, it had all been signed, sealed and delivered, and was for the best.

This congregation didn't believe that for a minute, but by the act of parliament that allowed the two bodies to join, the Methodists legally owned their church. The dissenters only totalled twelve families (the rest didn't mind joining the Methodists), and so these twelve raised what money they could toward buying their church back from the Methodists. They could not do it on their own and so approached the local Presbyterians for assistance. The Presbyterians agreed and gave them the balance owning. The Miminegash Bible Christian Chapel then became the Presbyterian Church.

Of this church the Presbyterians said this ... "*Miminegash has a very neat little church capable of seating about 150.*"

It was a frame church, and from the above description it was likely about 24 feet by 34 feet, or a similar measurement.

Preachers to serve this circuit over the years included:
1834-44 - Francis Metherall
1845 - William Harris
1846-52 - Francis Metherall
1853-54 - William Calloway
1855-56 - Jacob Gale
1857-58 - Francis Metherall

235

1859-61 - John Watson Butcher and Francis Metherall
1862-64 - Isaac Ashley, Thomas Short and J.T. Sencabaugh
1866-67 - J.J. Rice
1868 - Alexander Richard
1869-71 - John Chapple
1872-74 - John G. Yelland and Francis Metherall
1875 - John G. Yelland and Thomas J. Sabine
1876 - Thomas J. Sabine
1877-78 - John Ball
1879-80 - John Ferry
1881-83 - William Bryenton

Our American Cousins

When the mid-western states of the United States of America were opening up most of the immigrants entered at ports along that country's eastern seaboard, then travelled inland.

The fare to Canada was cheaper, and many came via Quebec, travelling up the St. Lawrence River, up the Great Lakes (skirting Niagara Falls) and most often crossing at Sandwich (now Windsor) and Detroit.

Most who went were settlers in search of free or cheap land, or in search of their fortunes. Among their number were Cornish miners and rock quarriers destined for many parts of the country.

Some were Bible Christian preachers. Each had a variety of experiences as they made their

A sketch of the Steamship Ontario, the first side-wheel passenger steamer on the Great Lakes. Built at Sacketts Harbour its engines were designed by Robert Fulton. It served on Lake Ontario until well into the 1840's, taking passengers as far as Niagara Falls.

way to the small communities nestled in the bush of Northern Wisconsin and the Northern Peninsula of Michigan, and each had a destiny to fulfil.

It is from the diaries of these travellers that we get a fleeting glimpse of the land and communities, as well as some of their experiences which range from easy and boring to almost beyond human endurance.

Thomas Rundell left St Eval, Cornwall, in 1848, sailing from Padstow 15th April on board *The Clio.*

According to his diary contrary winds impeded the journey two or three times, but it was fairly uneventful, everyone arriving at Quebec safe and sound on 26th May at about 1:00 p.m. in the afternoon.

"It is a fine town," he says, *"High stone houses, stone walls, roofs covered with tin.....Put our things aboard **The Queen**, a steamboat. It is the finest boat I ever saw. Paid our fare to Montreal. Left Quebec at 7 in the evening."*

Thomas Rundell's diary has been transcribed by Phil Ellery, and this transcription allows us a chance to find out what people thought of the countryside as they travelled through it.

The diary goes on to tell us ...

"May 28th: The scenery on each side of the river is beautiful. ... The cattle feeding on the rich pastures. The river and land just level and large rafts of timber carried grandly down the stream. Arrived at Montreal at 3 in the afternoon. At 4 we went ashore and found F. Turner's house. He kept an English house. Here we had 3 pints of cider, 4 basins of tea, ½ lb. butter and a large loaf of bread for 2 shillings. Six pence each for our beds, good accommodations.

"May 29th: Paid our fare for Kingston. First we were taken 9 miles by rail to Lachine. The land here is not so good as it is back further. Went on board another steamboat. Soon got into Upper Canada, good land here, large fields, fine orchards, flourishing trees.

"May 30th: Arrived at Kingston at 4. Did not see much of this town. We paid our fare to Buffalo. Went on board another steamer, started at 5 in the evening.

"May 31: Arrived at Oswego at 3 am. This city in New York State. Here we found another English House. Got a good breakfast cheap. It is a fine country here. Left at 9. We are crossing Lake Ontario. Stopped at Rochester. Arrived at Lewistown at 5 am.

"June 1st: Here we had our baggage carried up over the

hill in a wagon. Then for three miles we were drawn by horses over a railroad. Land light here. We went into the railroad carriages and started at 12 o'clock. Arrived at the Niagara Falls at 1 o'clock. Took dinner by the side of the splendid falls. Started at 2 o'clock and arrived at Buffalo at 4. Took our things to an Englishman's house, Mr. Well's Hotel. Here we paid our fare to Milwaukee. We went aboard **The Baltic**. Left Buffalo at 7 in the evening. This is a large town. Good place for business.

"June 3rd: We are now crossing Lake Erie. Stopped at Cleveland. Small town. Dirty streets.

"June 4th, Sunday: Now we are in Lake Huron. Foggy. We can hardly see land.

"June 5th: This is a large lake. The wind is blowing strong. It seems as though we are in the ocean. Now we are in Lake Michigan.

"June 6th: We are in our long looked for and much desired state, Wisconsin. It is better land here than it was farther back. It is a red soil, trees are small, so some pretty places near the lake. Arrived at 6 o'clock. This is a thriving town.

"June 7th: We are now 180 miles from Platteville. Here the wagoner charged $20 for 20 hundred weight, either passengers or luggage, to carry to Mineral Point. Engaged a teamster to take us to Mineral Point. Started a 10 o'clock. Travelled 29 miles. Stopped at a tavern. They charged us 50 cents a head for supper, bed, and breakfast.

"June 8th: Started at 6. Passed some very good land today.

"June 9th: It is tiresome to travel on a wagon. Weather hot and dry.

"June 10th: We are now crossing some beautiful prairie land. I did not expect to see so much good land free from trees.

June 11th: Arrived Platteville exactly when they were coming out of the chapel. Met with Stephen and Eliza [Carhart] here and went home with them. Glad we met with relatives and friends in a foreign land.

This account of the journey, though uneventful, gives us

a wonderful account of the places along the route, and how the countryside, in both Canada and the U.S., was developing in 1848. Even with steam ships and railroad, it still took two weeks to travel from Quebec to Platteville, Wisconsin.

John Gundry of Wendron, Cornwall sailed on the Barque *Roslyn Castle*, from Falmouth, April 6th, 1849. It was another fairly uneventful crossing, the ship arriving at Grosse Isle on May 24th.

"May 24th: About 10 o'clock the doctor came on board and examined us and about half hour afterward they took the anchor up and made for Quebeck, got in about 4 o'clock.

"May 25th: We left about 5 o'clock in the afternoon by the Quebeck for Montreal and got in the next forenoon and heaved on to The Passport for Kingston.

"Witsunday: We went through the lake of the thousand isles and got in to Kingston about 4 o'clock in the afternoon.

"Witmonday 28th: We walked about the city. It is a fine place but I think not so well as Montreal. In the afternoon about 4 o'clock we left again by the New Era for Toronto and got in the 29th about 7 or 8 o'clock and left again by the Chief Justice for Queenstown, then by railway for Chippewa about 9 miles. We saw the falls of Niagara as we were riding on, it is a grand sight, we did not stop. We got in to Chippewa and left again for Buffalo by the Emera and got in about 7 o'clock in the evening. Stopped there that night and walked about the city the next day, it is a beautiful place. In the evening we left again by the Nile for Chicago.

"May 31st: We put into Cleveland

"Friday, June 1st: We put into Detroit.

"Saturday 2nd: We put into Mackinaw and got some fresh fish and saw a great many Indians and some wigwams. We got into Milwaukee about 4 o'clock in the morning of the 4th June .

Both accounts serve to show us what the average trip across the country was like - more mundane than eventful. But the land appears to be well established with large towns and cities and prosperous countryside, even at this early date. They provide us with good accurate historical data.

But how did they know which boat to catch? Which train to take? Where to direct the teamster who hauled their goods? It is possible that most people had a letter from a friend or relative telling them how to get to their destination. But what about those who had no letter? No direction? It did happen.

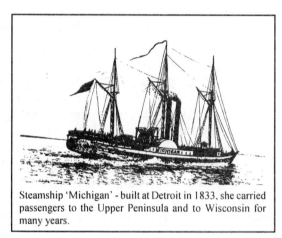
Steamship 'Michigan' - built at Detroit in 1833, she carried passengers to the Upper Peninsula and to Wisconsin for many years.

At the district meeting at Bowmanville, June 11, 1846, a request was made of those preachers gathered there for volunteers to go to Ohio and Wisconsin as missionaries. William Hooper, gives this account ....

"Every one refused to go to Wisconsin. Bro. George Rippon volunteered to go to Ohio and for a time the meeting was at a standstill. I walked outside, leaned my head on the gate post, and lifted my heart to God in prayer; and while so doing felt willing to offer myself for Wisconsin, to which all readily agreed. But I knew no more about Wisconsin than Abraham did about Canaan, and no one could tell me anything, save that I had the address of Mr. G. Ebbott, who had written to the committee in England desiring a missionary to be sent to them. However, in a true, missionary spirit, on Tuesday, the 16th of June, we, i.e. myself and wife, Br. Rippon , wife and two children, left Cobourg wharf for our destinations - he for Ohio, I for Wisconsin. [via Lewiston,

then Buffalo].

"*Before we left Buffalo, I went to a book store and purchased a book giving a description of Wisconsin, and containing a map of the country. I saw by my book and map, that I should have taken passage to Milwaukee, but I saw it too late. Off we go with about 900 passengers, like bees in a hive [for Chicago]....*"

What a way to start a journey into the unknown taking passage on the wrong boat! I doubt Brother Hooper was the only one who ever did it!

Both George Rippon and William Hooper worked on their respective missions until 1850. In that year they were relieved by two other ministers - John Chapple to work at Ohio and Joseph Hoidge to work at Wisconsin.

In 1855 the Canadian Conference was separated from the English Conference (all but Prince Edward Island) and those missions and circuits in the US were given to the Canadians to look after and administer. The English Conference had found it too expensive an operation and found it too difficult to assist the missionaries from so far away. And so, now, with most of North America under one administration, we see more and more ministers being assigned to the missions and circuits in Ohio and Wisconsin. These areas were now able to be more highly developed, and two new areas were begun - the Upper Peninsula of Michigan, and a small corner of Illinois.

The Wisconsin Mission and the Michigan Mission suffered greatly from the transient nature of the people in these areas. Much of the employment here was in mining, and as mines were opened the population was at a high, but as soon as veins started to peter out, so did the population. In other words, a congregation was flourishing one day and dissolved the next due to lack of members.

In the early days it was lack of man-power that was the real problems. The missionaries were stretched to their limits and could visit each station perhaps only once every six or eight weeks. One woman wrote saying that between the visits of the ministers the people would forget what he'd told them and " *turn wild again*" before he came back.

The late Elizabeth Ebbott and her husband Ralph Ebbott did a tremendous amount of research into the Bible Christians of the Upper Peninsula of Michigan, and I have been fortunate in that some of this research was given to me by Mr. Ebbott for this project. Some of this work included items written by the early ministers to this area and from some of these passages we get a vivid description of the conditions under which these men laboured.

For the most part, travel by boat around the shores of the Great Lakes was the easiest mode of transportation, however, this was not possible during the winter months. During these times travel on foot and by cart or dog sled over bush trails and ill-kept roads had to be accomplished. Because water travel was the means of getting from place to place the interior of many places was late in developing, and remained one of the problems of the itinerant preachers for many years.

The Steamer Niagara, prior to 1887, a passenger ship on the Great Lakes, stopping at all ports of call where Bible Christian passengers would disembark for their journey inland.

Like Francis Metherall on Prince Edward Island, the missionaries did without horses. The Mission Fund did not extend to the purchase of a horse, nor its care and feeding. Rev. Chapple was told that the Mission Committee ... "*would rather buy members than horses*". They eventually relented and allowed him to rent a horse as needed.

Like the preachers who worked in all parts of North America, those in the circuits and missions of the US in later times found an ease of travel, and far less trying conditions than during the early years. Houses were far more comfortable and improved roads, and trains where available, made it so much easier to get from place to place and visit each station on their circuits every few days rather than every few weeks.

While researching these areas, one thing is very apparent - little is known today of the Bible Christian Heritage of these areas, except by the small few who have been moved to delve into this part of their history. But then, isn't it so everywhere?

Jean Jolliffe of Wisconsin and the late Elizabeth Ebbott of Michigan laid the foundations for Bible Christian research in the US, and many thanks go to Jean and to Elizabeth's husband Ralph for their support in this leg of the research. Following, based greatly on their work, is an account of the circuits and chapels of the four States where Bible Christians were found.

Wisconsin

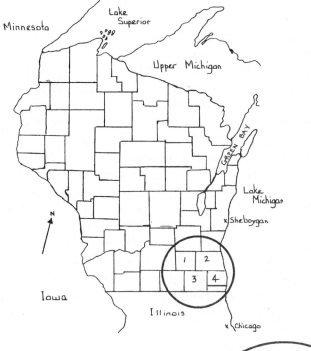

1. Jefferson County
2. Waukesha County
3. Walworth County
4. Racine County

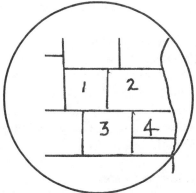

The Circuits of Wisconsin

There were five circuits in Wisconsin, and by all accounts these seem to be the busiest and most fruitful of all the endeavours in the US by the Bible Christians.

The first missionary to Wisconsin was Rev. William Hooper. Even though he laboured under difficult pioneering conditions, as did Francis Metherall on PEI and John Hicks Eynon in Ontario, he does not seem to have received the same degree of notoriety as did the other two. Perhaps this was because his missionary work did not begin until 1846, 14 years after the others, and perhaps it was because he was English, representing an English church, two qualities that would not endear him to die-hard Yankees. At one point the Rev. Paul Robins wrote to the English Conference that it was a useless endeavour to continue in the US because of the general feelings of the population. It was his suggestion that the Conference cut their losses and retire from the field as soon as possible. But despite this rather widespread feeling, Rev. Hooper persevered and laid the foundations for a successful Wisconsin District, though he was never pleased with the few good results he had. He always felt that the field was too unyielding and the results too few. This just helps to show us that we seldom see the good in our own work.

Eventually the five circuits would look like this....

In Jefferson County:
Palmyra Circuit:
Zion, Siloam Chapel at Palmyra, Pleasant Valley and Ottawa. Each of these places had, at one time, a chapel. This circuit also had a number of preaching places which included Baker's, McKeys, Rome and Johnson's - sometimes called Henry's School.

In Racine County:
Yorkville Circuit:
Yorkville, Rose Hill and Ives Grove. There were chapels

at each of these places, and at least five meeting places as well, which included: White's School, Paris Corners, Greenville, Beaumont and Bethany, and by 1878 - Kansasville. Yorkville and Ives Grove are/were in Yorkville Township while Rose Hill was in Dover Township. So, too, the various meeting places were dispersed between these two townships.

Burlington Circuit:
There were chapels at English Settlement and at Burlington Road. No further meeting places have been found.

In Waukesha County:
Lisbon Circuit:
Chapels here include Brookfield and South Lisbon with the parsonage at Sussex. There were some known meeting places which included Merton, North Lisbon and quite likely at Sussex.

In Walworth County:
Little Prairie Circuit:
It seems this circuit had only one chapel located at Little Prairie, but there were important meeting places at Round Prairie and LaGrange.

Note:
The source for the chapel locations is the Bible Christian Property Book, housed at the United Church Archives, Victoria University, Toronto, Ontario. The source for the meeting places for each circuit is the research done by the late Elizabeth Ebbott of Michigan, and articles in various issues of The Observer, the newspaper of the Canadian Bible Christians

It is difficult now to know exactly when each of these congregations started. It is a given that they were not all on William Hooper's appointment list between 1846 and 1850. Many were started by Rev. Joseph Hoidge during his tenure 1851-56, and some by those ministers who followed.

Rev. Hoidge wrote an account of his mission and it was published in the Bible Christian Magazine, September, 1853 edition, a copy of which was kindly sent to this project by Jean Jolliffe of Brookfield, Wisconsin.......

"We live and preach in the township of Palmyra. Every township or parish, is six miles square and every county 24-26 miles square, according to American rule. I preach in four different counties: Jefferson, Walworth, Dane and Waukeshaw. I do not preach in any place that can be called a village, consequently our congregations are small, from 10 to 100. Much depends on the weather. I preach at 6 places once in 4 weeks, at 3 places once in 6 weeks, and at 2 places once in 2 weeks. The places at which we hold meetings are school houses, built by districts, so we occupy them by the suffrages of the said districts. We have one tolerably neat chapel in the township of Eagle, County of Waukesha, and our friends have succeeded this winter in making it free of debt; nevertheless our congregation is small, partly in consequence of a difference of opinion at the time it was built as to the locality, there being a number of English settled all around. Some proposed that two chapels should be built; only one, however, was built and that one at the extreme point of the settlement and out of the township of Palmyra. The consequence is, that the greatest number attend a school house about 2 miles distant, which is by far the most central point. Here we get a larger congregation than at the chapel."

This letter shows us how widespread a circuit was in those days - four counties! According to old records, the first chapel in the Wisconsin District was built in 1850 at Siloam on the Palmyra Circuit. This would probably be the one discussed above by Rev. Hoidge.

In this same letter Rev. Hoidge echoes the sentiments of Rev. Paul Robins and others ....

"Where we go so seldom to preach, during our absence services are held by other ministers, with whom Yankees would rather unite, in consequence of their great pride of American Independence and greater prejudice against British rule....There

248

are ministers belonging to three or four different denominations fixed in almost every village or town, sent from the Eastern States, supported by the Home Missionary Society until the church can support them. The reason of our going into four counties to preach is because the people are so widely scattered and settlements of foreigners interspersed between. We must confine ourselves to the English settlements altogether, or go so far to those places where we have a few friends. For the establishment of the Bible Christian cause in the United States I very greatly fear, unless it be attended with much expense."

By 1850, Rev. Hooper was writing much the same in his letters....

"1 October, 1850: We have labour enough for three or four preachers ... In my opinion the idea of having only one preacher in Wisconsin is absurd A single preacher 1,300 miles from other branches of the connexion! You must send more than one preacher to Wisconsin, or abandon it altogether...."

Again, the lack of man-power came down to a lack of money, or a refusal to spend it. The English Conference and the Missionary Committee did not understand the nature of the country and therefore labelled most requests 'excessive demands' - they did not understand the difference in weather conditions and the extra costs of travel and housing it caused, nor did they understand the pioneer condition of living. It was this foreign concept and the cost of doing business in the US that was the catalyst in having the US Districts become part of the Canadian Conference in 1855, the same year that Canada broke away from the English Conference to administer her own affairs. The English solved their problem by passing it to others and washing their hands of the whole thing.

Once the Canadian Conference was in control things began to change and the missionary presence in all US Districts increased.

But what of the people who came to Wisconsin? They came to the shores of 'America' from all over the world, but the people with whom we are interested in this project are the Cornish. A few Devon folk were found in Wisconsin, but by far the most numerous of these two counties were the people of Cornwall.

The Cornwall Family History Society published an article in 2001 by Mary Paynter whose ancestors arrived in Wisconsin from the Launceston area of Cornwall. Here, in part, is what Mary said .....

"In examining the history of my father's family (especially his parents and his grandparents who emigrated from parishes in East Cornwall), I find two main reasons for this phenomenon:

1. Already established ties with family members and /or fellow villages from the Launceston area who had come to the Wisconsin farm frontier in the 1840's, 1850's or 1860's, meant they could count on being welcomed and supported until they could 'get on their feet' in the new homeland - they would not be 'strangers in a strange land'.

2. Close allegiance to their religion - most were Bible Christians - and the realization that they could count on finding other Bible Christian communities concentrated in the area of south-east Wisconsin, in Jefferson and Waukesha counties and in Palmyra and Sullivan Townships especially.

My father's parents were good examples of emigration for both reasons: Thomas Henry PAYNTER, of Week St. Mary, earlier of Jacobstow and Boyton, married Betsy Ann NORTHEY, of Causewell, Poundstock, earlier of Trespearn, Laneast, on the 8th of April, 1869 in Stratton. They left to begin a new life in the United States shortly after the wedding, travelling to Liverpool to set sail on the SS City of Paris, arriving in New York harbour on the 26th of April 1869. From there they travelled the usual route to Wisconsin - through the Erie Canal and the Great Lakes to the Port of Milwaukee, Wisconsin, and then the last miles overland to a farm home in Jefferson county where the 1870 census records them living with Annie's older sister Kitty (Catherine NORTHEY) and her husband Dan WARD who had come the year before. Other PAYNTERs and NORTHEYs came to the area: Thomas Henry PAYNTERs siblings - Joseph PAYNTER, farm labourer, blacksmith and musician; Cecilia; Elizabeth who was married to Simon UGLOW; and Annie NORTHEYs siblings: Charlotte who

had married Thomas *CONGDON before leaving Cornwall; Richard; John; Thomas and Harriet.*

In the early 1870's the older generation followed their children, with the arrival of Annie's parents, Gabriel and Harriet Hodge NORTHEY, of Laneast and later Poundstock; and Thomas Henry's parents, Richard and Jane Rice PAYNTER of Boyton and Jacobstow. These older NORTHEYs and PAYNTERs settled in the same area of south-east Wisconsin, near their children and near their former Cornish neighbours and fellow Bible Christians, and are buried in the Pleasant Valley Cemetery.

The cemeteries of these communities remain mute witness to the closeness of these emigrants of North-east Cornwall, now buried close to their family members and neighbours. Long after the Bible Christian denomination ceased to exist independently, merging with the Methodist Episcopal Conference of Wisconsin in 1884, the obituaries of the later period consistently mention the Bible Christian roots of these Cornish settlers."

Permission to re-print this portion of the article comes from Mary Paynter.

The Palmyra Circuit

As we have seen, there were four chapels eventually built on this circuit....

Zion:

This was likely the second chapel to be constructed in Wisconsin. It was a frame chapel measuring only 28 feet by 38 feet. It was built on a lot large enough to house a cemetery as well.

Members of the early congregation there included families by the names of Hooper, Jolliffe, Trewyn and Dodge. According to a letter written by Rev. William Jolliffe on the ocassion of the golden anniversary of Zion Chapel in 1907, we find that ....

251

"The site with adjoining burying ground was a gift of the district school trustee board, the school site being vacated to build on *a site more central."* However, The Palmyra Historical Society says the land was donated from the Bray farm. Perhaps the Brays donated it to the school trustees and they in turn donated it to the church trustees.

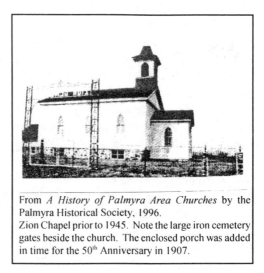

From *A History of Palmyra Area Churches* by the Palmyra Historical Society, 1996.

Zion Chapel prior to 1945. Note the large iron cemetery gates beside the church. The enclosed porch was added in time for the 50th Anniversary in 1907.

At a meeting held on January 12, 1857, it was agreed to build a chapel. Rev. William Jolliffe was the minister there at that time and he acted as part of the building committee, apparently taking an actual hand in the erection of the building. He and his wife boarded the workers on the church, and his letter to the 50th Anniversary committee mentions these things ....

"I do not regret the arduous labour of the summer 1857, nor also the strenuous exertion of my dear wife, in boarding all the mechanics engaged in building, but rather rejoice in that instrumentally we were able to perform what we did for the good of the community, and for the Glory of God."

In 1884 this congregation united with the Methodist Episcopal Church. In 1928 the church ceased to be used for regular services, and was taken down about 1945.

Siloam Chapel at Palmyra:

From 'The Dousman Index' newspaper, January 31st edition, 1963, we have this account of the history of the church....

"*At a meeting of the trustees of the Society, held at the home of Henry Stacey, the following persons were present: William Jolliffe, David Crerar, Charles Box, Richard Sleep, Henry Stacey. Voted Henry Stacey chairman, David Crerar secretary, and Richard Sleep treasurer. On motion we adjourn. Dated March 7th, 1850, Palmyra.*"

From *The History of Palmyra Area Churches*, the Palmyra Historical Society, 1996.
Siloam Chapel sometime after the 'vestibule' was added in 1904

This then was the formal beginning of this congregation. The article goes on to say....

"*After having had several meetings, and finding there was a sizeable congregation in the community, the trustees and other interested men decided to build a church in which to hold their meetings. Heretofore, meetings had been held in the homes. Some of the lumber for the new church was donated and some was purchased. On March 15th, 1850, 3,971 feet of lumber was bought at $7.00 per thousand feet. The first work on the church is credited to Richard Sleep, he having worked six days at 50 cents per day. The first actual money paid [toward the building] was a donation of ten dollars by Christopher Lean. David Crerar was the carpenter and Charles Box was the painter.*

This first church building was located diagonally across the road from the site of the present church, in a field owned by Merton Uglow, Town[ship] of Eagle."

From the Bible Christian Property Book we learn that this

first chapel was 26 feet by 36 feet. It was replaced in 1869 with a brick chapel, perhaps the one quoted as being "the present building" diagonally across the road. This second chapel was 28 feet by 40 feet. A cemetery was located near this chapel, which was erected ... *"at or as near the site of Rainous School as can be obtained."*

Early families in the Siloam congregation include Bluett, Burton, Crerar, Coad, Giles, Hanford, Longley, Lean, Noyes, Uglow, Williams, Box, Stacey and Sleep.

The records in the Bible Christian Property Book , and in the work of the Palmyra Hiostorical Society state that the parsonage at Palmyra, was built on half an acre donated by George Hooper ... *"to build a house for the use of the minister on this station."* . The parsonage was built in 1853. The parsonage, though small, just 18 feet by 24 feet, and of frame construction, was likely compared to a palace at that time. It was located on an acre of land, but whether this also housed the chapel is not known. There was certainly enough room to have a garden for the preacher. An account of living conditions prior to its construction can be found in the journal of Rev. William Hooper which, in part, says.......

(After being asked by a few 'friends' to stay among them and preach, and readily agreeing to find Rev. and Mrs. Hooper a house, Rev. Hooper returned to Racine to collect his wife and luggage. They hired transport to get them back to Palmyra).....

"There was not a friend to meet us or to greet us. There was one tavern in the village, but the old keeper had moved out and the new one had not moved in, so 'there was no room at the inn' for us. Our teamster said he must unload our things somewhere and return. I told him to put our things down in the street. There were our boxes, and the Missionary's wife sitting on one and keeping watch overall while the writer was running from house to house to hire lodgings, or rent rooms, or anything. but after fruitless efforts, he returned and sat down with his wife. Hardly knowing what to do, as we could not leave our things in the street nor find any place of safety to put them, we stood still to see

the salvation of our God. At this juncture, a village blacksmith - and by the way, a Universalist - came home to his tea, and I accosted him, told him our situation and asked him if he could direct us to any lodgings etc.

'Hang it altogether' said the stranger, 'this is too bad; something must be done'. So after a little consultation with his family he said, 'My house is small and my family large. I have no rooms to let, nor have I room for your luggage, but there is a new unfinished house which my son-in-law is building and you can put your things there, and we will board you and your wife for a few days till you can find a house to rent.' The only thing I could do was to accept the offer of Mr. John Medland. His little log house was about 3 miles north of Palmyra. This house consisted of two rooms, one on the first floor and the other on the second. The upstairs, or second floor, was unfinished, even for the finish of a rude hut in the woods. A loose floor had ben laid; at each gable end there was a kind ow window, or a little hole cut, one of which was darkened by an untanned sheep skin as a curtain, and as there was no glass to keep out wind or rain, this blind was, after all, more serviceable than elegant. At the other end, there was a sash with a few pains of glass, and others of paper and shingles; but the room was not dark, for innumerable apertures admitted more or less light. The room had only been used for Indian-corn, dried herbs, etc. Well, it was in this room that the first B.C. Missionary to Wisconsin with his wife had to take up quarters. I should say that this was our bedroom, parlour, sitting room and study. Our dining room, cook house, etc., were on the first floor with the family. Mr. Medland was a good man, and he might truthfully have said: 'Silver and gold have I none, but such as I have, give I unto thee'.

Our means of access to our bedroom was a strong ladder erected under a little hole in the second floor; it required a little practice, especially for Mrs. Hooper, before we could ascend and descend with graceful facility."

During their five years in Wisconsin they occupied six houses, one of them an unfinished log cabin in the woods, half a mile from their nearest neighbour. As the woods were full of wolves this was a very upsetting time for Mrs. Hooper while William was away on his circuit rounds.

Most of the early preachers tell much the same story, so it was good to have a 'good' house for them, finally.

Pleasant Valley:

From *A History of Palmyra Churches*, by the Palmyra Historical Society, Pleasant Valley, also called Pumpkin Hollow and '*Punck*' for short, was not a name which appeared in Bible Christian records until 1869.

From *A History of Palmyra Area Churches* by the Palmyra Historical Society, 1996. Pleasant Valley Chapel before 1910.

Early families in this congregation include the names Burton, Bogie, Beider, Coad, Campbell, Dawe, Ebbott, Edwards, Giles, Howell, Jaquith, Lean, Mules, Meracle, Northey, Paynter, Pethick, Reed and Thomas.

As early as 1860, Punck appeared on the circuit plan, but the chapel was not built until 1874. It was a frame chapel with a stone foundation, measuring 28 feet by 40 feet in size. It was built on a half acre parcel. No mention of a cemetery is made in the Bible Christian Property Book, but the Palmyra Historical Society tells us the cemetery is across the road. It may be of a later date than the chapel.

In 1884 this congregation joined with the Methodist Episcopal Church . In 1910 the church was hit by lightning and

burned to the ground. All was lost but the pulpit and the Bible, and most of the records were destroyed. The present church dates from the rebuilding at that time.

Ottawa:

This appointment on the Palmyra Circuit was also known as Sandy Island, and Sandy Island Community. Ottawa refers to the name of the Township.

The Sandy Island chapel was a late chapel, constructed in 1880. It was a brick veneered chapel, 28 feet by 40 feet.

Ministers serving the Palmyra Circuit were:
1846-50 - William Hooper
1851-56 - Joseph Hoidge
1857 - Henry Ebbott
1858 - Henry Ebbott, George Parsons, William Jolliffe
1859-60 - Henry Ebbott
1861-63 - John Williams
1864 - William Wade
1865-67 - Robert Hurley
1868-69 - Henry Kenner
1870-72 - Thomas Raynor Hull
1873-76 - Robert Davidson
1877-79 - William R. Roach
1880-81 - Robert Baker
1882-83 - William Medland

Yorkville Circuit

The Yorkville Circuit had at least three chapels and about six meeting places. These were found in the two townships of Dover and Yorkville, both found in Racine County.

Jack Rumpel, who grew up in the English Settlement

church, on the Burlington Circuit, tells us that the Beaumont meeting was held in the home of the Beaumont family.

Yorkville:
This was the main station on the circuit, and the chapel here was the first one built on the circuit. It was a frame church built in 1856 just before Rev. Joseph Hoidge left the circuit. It measured 30 feet by 40 feet, and was erected on an acre and a half of land on which the congregation started a cemetery.

The circuit parsonage was also at Yorkville. It was built during the pastorate of Rev. Henry Ebbott in 1859. It too was frame and according to the Bible Christian Property Book it stood on its own quarter acre of land. It was a good serviceable house measuring 18 feet by 30 feet.

Ives Grove:
This place is also in Yorkville Township. In 1870 a Bible Christian chapel was erected on one acre that had been donated. This was a frame chapel measuring 28 feet by 40 feet. Because it was a late chapel it was not replaced by a brick church up until union, but may have been in later years.

Rose Hill: (aka Rosehill) (aka Kansasville)
This was the last chapel erected on the Yorkville circuit, and was the only chapel built in Dover Township. It was also the smallest of the three chapels being only 18 feet by 24 feet. This frame chapel was constructed in 1875 on a lot 25 square rods in size - for the modern thinker that's about half an acre.

The reference I found for this chapel says that the same year this chapel was moved to Kansasville and re-dedicated November 7 & 8.

It is also found in the 1876 Racine County Directory as *"Rose Hill Bible Christian Church, Main Street, Kansasville, Rev. T.H. Dry."*

Lucille Sheahan who sent information to the Burlington Historical Society, found this ....

"The Rose Hill Bible Christian Church was situated in Kansasville on the east side of the street at 'number 5 south of the railroad tracks'. Sometime in the 1930's the church building was moved east and north a short distance to sit among the farm buildings on the Frank H. Cox farm."

Courtesy: Burlington Historical Society
Rose Hill Church just before it was moved to the Cox farm.

From the *Illustrated History of Racine County, 1879*, we have this short biography of one of the members of the Kansasville Bible Christian congregation...

"Mrs. Elizabeth Wilford, Section 35, P.O. Kansasville, born in Cornwall, England in November, 1800. Her maiden name was Elizabeth Bartil. She first married in 1822, John Hancock, a native of England. They had eight children - John, William, Thomas, Richard, Samuel, Mary and Ann and one unnamed who died in infancy. Mrs. Wilford and her husband came to Wisconsin in 1842. They first located in Dover Township, Racine Co., and he engaged at farming on the place where Mrs. Wilford now resides. Mr. Hancock died in 1845 and she married again Amos Wilford in 1846. They had no children. Her son Richard enlisted in the army, mustered out in 1865 when he returned to his home and died. Mary Ann and William died. Thomas enlisted in the army in 1861 and was mustered out in 1865, and is married. John enlisted in 1861, was mustered out in 1865. Mrs. Wilford owns 152 acres of good, productive land, commodious barns and comfortable home. She is a member of the Bible Christian Church."

The ministers who 'laboured' on this circuit were:
1861- Henry Ebbott
1862-63 - William Jolliffe
1864-65 - William Jolliffe with John Shortridge in 1865
1866-67 - Henry Kenner
1868-69 - Robert Hurley
1870-71 - Henry Ebbott
1872-74 - Samuel Jolliffe
1875-76 - William R. Roach
1877-80 - Robert Davidson
1881-83 - William Rollins

Burlington Circuit

From the Burlington Historical Society comes this information...

"*The 1876 Directory of Racine County, pg. 198, showed a Bible Christian Church in section 12, town of Burlington, with Rev. T.H. Dry....*" (See the map at the end of this section)

And another record for that year...

"*The 1876 Racine Advocate Directory for Rochester, Racine Co., Town of Rochester...... Town No. 3, Range 19 East....Bible Christian Church situated on section 13. Services Sundays at 2:30 pm and semi-monthly at 7pm. Prayer meetings Thursdays at 7 pm. Class meetings Sundays at 10:30 am and Sunday School at 1 pm. No. of members: 20. Rev. T.H. Dry, Pastor.*"

I can only assume that these two entries represent the two chapels known to us today - Burlington Road and English Settlement, but it would take a local person, familiar with Section and Range data to know which was which.

Burlington Road Chapel:
This chapel was located about 5 miles east of Burlington

on the Kenosha Road. From the Burlington Historical Society we have this information ......

"*This society was organized May 14, 1862, and meetings were held in the homes of members. A Warranty Deed, dated May 8th, 1867, from James Cole and wife to the Bible Christian Society of the Town of Burlington conveys part of the south-east quarter of section twelve, Town two (2) North, Range nineteen east, containing one and one half acres of land, on which a frame church was built, measuring 16 x 25 feet, 1½ stories, with a wood-shed added later.....*"

Also recorded in their information, the Historical Society has a list of members from 1873 which they have also kindly supplied to this project .....

David McDonald   Class Leader   (moved to Kansas)
Ellen McDonald
William Leach   (Died)
Sarah Leach
Agnes Leach
Thomas Wheeler   Society Steward
Walter Duckett
Mercy Duckett
Thomas Duckett
James Cole   (Died)
Henry Shepstone
Mary Ann McDonald   (Removed)
Ann Wilson
Maggie Wilson
Mary Norris
Sarah Norris
Harriet Simmons

Additions to the list at a later date included....
Jane Edwards - admitted Dec. 14, 1877
Sarah Leach - admitted April 29, 1877
Oliver Leach and wife (illegible - Ester Cox?) - adm't Apr 2, 1880
Mrs. H (R?) Ebbott - admitted July 1880

The Bible Christian Property Book lists this chapel as

being erected in 1862, and this is quite possible. Many times, the initial donation of land was a verbal agreement only. The chapel was erected, or a cemetery started, then many years later the land was officially transferred from the donors to the local society trustees. This may be the case at Burlington Road.

The parsonage was also built at this station, though no date has been found for its construction. It was a small frame house measuring 18 feet by 26 feet and was located on 3/4 acre of land next door to the chapel.

English Settlement:

Most areas had an *English Settlement,* and there are records of many places with this name, however, there was also one in the Burlington area, and a Bible Christian chapel was built there. The records in the Bible Christian Property Book say the chapel was constructed in 1847, although that is a very early date. The following has been supplied by The Burlington Historical Society. They say....

"The first mention made of what is now the English Settlement United Methodist Church was in a letter dated October 7, 1843, written by Edwin Bottomley to

Courtesy: Burlington Historical Society
A very old photo of The English Settlement Church.

his father in England. In it he says that preaching services and Sunday School were being held every Sunday afternoon in the home of Mr. Earnshaw, who lived about one-half mile east of the present church corner.

It was during the following year, 1844, that a new schoolhouse was built on the northeast corner of the intersection of what are now County Trunks A and J. The church congregation was then allowed to use the schoolhouse for their services until April of 1846. In January of 1846 they began making plans to build a new chapel. With a strong desire to build and not much money to do it, they decided to write home to England and ask for some help. The subscribers in the settlement pledged $210, most of which were $5 pledges. The money sent from England amounted to $407.30 in American money. This gave the settlers new courage to go ahead with their chapel.

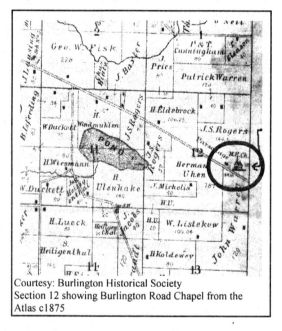

Courtesy: Burlington Historical Society
Section 12 showing Burlington Road Chapel from the Atlas c1875

Mr. Alexander Stenhouse gave them approximately an acre and a half of land in the southwest corner of the intersection of the present County Trunks A and J on which to build their chapel. The remainder was to be used for a cemetery.

The heavy timbers for the frame were given by various people in the community and a great deal of the work was done by the members. One of Mr. Bottomley's letters mentions that because of poor crops in 1847, he and his neighbours were unable to finish the building as soon as they would have liked. By

Christmas of 1848 they had the windows in and one stove, so they could have their "Love Feast" on Christmas Day. New Years Day of 1849 found the entire community gathered for the dedication Service."

Until 1865, the ministers who served this congregation were local preachers or lay preachers, then in 1865 the Bible Christian Circuit Minister took over the services. The circuit at that time included Yorkville, Rose Hill, Burlington Road and English Settlement. In 1873 Burlington Road and English Settlement were withdrawn into their own circuit. At Union in 1884, this congregation, like the others in Wisconsin, joined the Methodist Episcopal Church.

Ministers who served this circuit include:
1873-75 - Thomas Harrison Dry
1876-78 - John Dumbleton
1879 - Supply
1880 - J.S. Lean
1881-82 - R. Davidson
1883 - Supply

Lisbon Circuit

There were three chapels constructed on the Lisbon Circuit, one at Brookfield and one at South Lisbon, although this second one is now known as Lisbon. The third chapel was at Sandy Island in the Town of Ottawa.

It appears that this area was not visited until about 1859 on a regular basis, though I imagine Rev. Joseph Hoidge and Rev. Henry Ebbott both visited and sporadically conducted meetings during their respective tenure between 1851 and 1857.

In 1858 George Parsons took the circuit which at that time still included Palmyra. It was separated in 1859.

This circuit had at least two meeting places, one at Sussex and one at Merton, though no chapels were built at these places.

Brookfield:

Although the circuit had been worked by Rev. George Parsons from at least 1858, it seems that a church was not erected here until 1869. At that time a frame church was erected on half an acre of land. It was 36 feet by 42 feet.

The history of this church was searched out by George Robinson in 1927 when Bible Christian records should still have been accessible, but he found that much of what happened with that particular congregation over the past 60 years had been considered unimportant by most people and never recorded, or if recorded had not been saved. In 1927 he wrote 'a paper' he hoped would be useful to people in the future, setting out what information he could find. A debt of gratitude is owed Mr. Robinson for his diligence and forethought. In part, this is what he found.....

The congregation of the Methodist church was divided on political grounds after the Civil War. This came to a head one Sabbath when Rev. Grant, a Methodist minister, preached to them on the subject, 'The Late War.' Rev. Grant was a Republican and his sermon reflected his strong beliefs, but the congregation, for the most part were Democrats and the presentation did not sit well with them so they parted company and began their own congregation.

During 1866 and 1867 this small band of people met in the old frame school-house at Putney's Corners. They joined with the Bible Christians on the Sussex/Lisbon Circuit, where a young minister, Rev. Samuel Jolliffe was preaching. Mr. Robinson says of him ...

"This Sussex society was ministered to by Samuel Jolliffe, a young man of unwavering faith, with unbounded enthusiasm and inspired with a zeal for the furtherance of Christ's kingdom..."

At that time there was a Congregational Church sitting empty for want of a preacher. The minister who had been there had gone south with the 39th Regiment of U.S. Volunteers as its chaplain.

In 1868 the congregation purchased the old Congregational

church and moved it one and a half miles west onto a half acre of land sold to them by Mrs. Ann Eubanks for $50.^{00}

In his paper, Mr. Robinson mentions the names of some of the early members of this Bible Christian congregation ....

"Mr. Taylor, known as Father Taylor, and his good wife, their sons Charles and Samuel Taylor and their wives, Mrs. Edward Coke and her husband, Miss Jemima Taylor, Mr. and Mrs. John Dixon, Mr. and Mrs. John Spencer, Mr. and Mrs. John Eubank. The Choir consisted of Edward Coke, O.G. Philbrook, Edward Faulkner, Mr. and Mrs. Nelson Strong and Miss Mary E. Brown as Organist.

The second generation of families included Davis, Strong, Mitchell, and Bolter ..."

At Union this congregation united with the Methodist Epicscopal Church, the new board of trustees of that united congregation being mostly former Bible Christians - John Spencer, Charles W. Davis, Edward Coke and William Dixon, a son of one of the original members, John Dixon.

From a report by Lucy Thatcher, c1934, we have this list of names associated with the Brookfield Bible Christian congregation ...

Mrs. E. Barker, Miss Libby Barker, Minnie Bolter, Charles Bolter, J.M. Chambers, Mrs. J.M. Chambers, Ethan Chapin, Alice Chapin, Charles Davis, Mrs. Charles Davis, Mrs. William Dixon, Lottie Philbrook, Maude Philbrook, John Spencer, Theresa Spencer, William Turner, Mrs. William Turner, Henry Gerritt, Sarah Gerritt, Hattie Gerritt, Lucien Hull, Mrs. Lucien Hull, Alex Mitchell, John Mitchell, and Mrs. John Mitchell.

South Lisbon:

The chapel at South Lisbon was a frame chapel, measuring only 30 feet by 40 feet. It was located on a very small parcel, just 6 square rods in size. The congregation had been meeting a number of years at Lisbon, probably since about 1858-59. In 1864 they *officially incorporated as part of* the Bible Christians ....

"We the undersigned hereafter mentioned do hereby Certify that on the 4th day of August, 1864, in said County for the purposes of incorporating themselves and did then and there elect by plurality of voices, William Medhurst, C.F. Raisen, Joseph Wildish, William Jeffery, Charles Tempest, Henry Boots and William Haskin, and said persons did then and there also determine by like plurality of voices that the said trustees and their Sucessors, should forever hereafter be called and known by the name of The Lisbon Bible Christian Society."

However, the chapel dated from 1855, when it was erected as a Union Church, many

From the collection of the Waukesha County Historical Society
The old Union Church at Lisbon. It served the community until 1894 when a new church was built.

various denominations coming together to erect a place of worship, mostly Congregationalists and Methodists.

It was erected on a parcel of land in the N.W. corner of Highway 164 and Lisbon Road, donated by Levi Russell. In 1859 this congregation joined with the Bible Christian Society.

Like Brookfield, in 1884 this congregation joined with the Methodist Episcopal Church.

Sandy Island:

Although indepth records have not been located for this congregation, three newspaper clippings from the collection at the Waukesha County Museum mention this church .....

"There was a Methodist church near Sandy Island School.

It was organized prior to 1860 and dissolved circa 1932. The stone church had been razed by 1950. The congregation may have originated as a Bible Christian Society in Ottawa. It was also known as the Sandy Island Church."

Unfortunately neither the name of the newspaper nor its edition date was recorded with this clipping, but it appears to be fairly modern in origin.

From 'The Ocono Enterprise', June 28, 1962 .... *"The Ottawa Methodist [Church] which was near Sandy Island school, closed about 25 years ago...."* (This part of an article about the history of Dousman)

From the 'Dousman Index', 23rd August, 1960 (from their column '25 Years Ago today with the original date of this being 1935).... " *The Ottawa Methidist Episcopal (better known as the Sand Island) Church was transferred to School District No. 7, Ottawa and Eagle, by the Board of Trustees of the church on the 29th of July.*

The church and one half acre of land joins the school property of Dist No. 7. This will make a valuable addition to the school ground. The church building is of brick and has stood there approximately three quarters of a century and a stipulation in the deed prohibits the sale or use of the building for tavern or dance hall purposes. The Sand Island church has been dormant for a number of years and the members and the Board of Trustees predicted it would never be available as a church and therefore gave the property to the school district for the nominal sum of one dollar."

Sussex:

Even though there was no chapel at this place, there was a congregation who had held meetings likely in the local schoolhouse.

In about 1864 (or 1866 according to the Bible Christian Property Book) the congregation built their parsonage here. It was erected on 5 acres of land. In the Property Book it is listed as a frame dwelling but no size is given. At the time the entry was made, about 1874, it was noted that the parsonage was *in bad condition*, but whether this was foundation, or roof, or everything is unknown. No further details were entered.

Found on the internet on a page called *Links to the Past*, are the following biographical sketches for Sussex people who were also members of the Bible Christian congregation at Sussex...

"William Leadley, farmer, Section 36; P.O. Sussex. Born in Yorkshire England, July 15th, 1823. In 1851 he came to the US. Shortly after his arrival he came to Waukesha, Wisc., where he lived about three years, then went to the town of Delafield, where he married Alice Chambers, also a native of Yorkshire, England. They resided in Delafield about 3 years at the end of which time they moved to their present home. Their children are Thomas, Margaret A., Alice M., Elizabeth M., John R., Ruth A., and Dora E. Mr. Leadley and his wife are members of the Bible Christian Church. He owns a well improved farm of 88 acres. He is an upright man, a good citizen, and liberally supports every enterprise that he believes beneficial to the public in general. Mr. Leadley's daughter Margaret A. is the wife of Herbert Stone and his daughter Alice M. is the wife of Charles E.Tempest."

And this one ....

"James T. Weaver, farmer, Section 36; P.O. Sussex. He was born in the town of Lisbon, Waukesha County, in 1851 and is therefore a native. He is the son of Thomas and Betty Weaver of his town (Lisbon). He married Jane Haskins, daughter of William and Sarah Haskins, early settlers of this county, and now esteemed citizens of the town of Pewaukee, where they have lived a number of years. Mr. Weaver and wife attend the Bible Christian Church. They have two children - George H. and Harcourt S. Mr. Weaver is extensively engaged in farming and is a man of much energy and push."

Unfortunately, no year is associated with either of these entries, but we can assume them to be prior to Union in 1884.

Ministers to serve this circuit were ....

1859-62 - George Parsons
1863 - Walter Ayers

1864 - John Williams
1865 - Walter Ayers
1866-69 - Samuel Jolliffe
1870-71 - Garrance Tink Colwell
1872-73 - Henry Ebbott
1874-75 - John Dumbleton
1876-78 - John Greenway
1879 - T.H. Dry
1880 - William Kinley
1881-83 - J.S. Lean

Little Prairie Circuit

As far as can be ascertained, there was only one chapel built on the Little Prairie circuit, though there were meeting places, in schoolhouses and in private homes. One of those meeting places was at Round Prairie.

Little Prairie:
There had been meetings held on this circuit for many years, likely since the early days of the Bible Christians at Wisconsin, or at least since the 1850's.

The parsonage was the first building the Bible Christians erected on this circuit. Built in 1861, it was a frame house, on one and a quarter acres. It measured 25 feet by 28 feet.

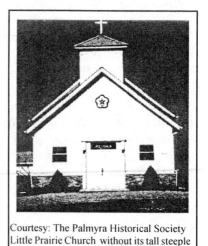

Courtesy: The Palmyra Historical Society
Little Prairie Church without its tall steeple

Eventually, in 1874, they built a chapel during the pastorate of John Greenway. It was a small frame church

270

measuring 28 feet by 40 feet. Three quarters of an acre of land was donated for its purpose. It apparently had a high steeple that could be seen for miles, but it was taken down during alterations to the building after the Union of 1884, when it became a Methodist Church.

Little Prairie was withdrawn from Palmyra Circuit about 1860 and given circuit status of its own.

LaGrange:

The chapel at LaGrange was built by the combined efforts of the Methodists and Universalists. In the 1870's there was a lapse in attendance by the ministers of these denominations, and the Ministers of the Bible Christian Church

From the Oak Creek Museum Complex, Wisconsin
The Hughes cabin, typical of the cabins constructed by and for settlers/immigrants in the 1835-40 era

at Little Prairie served the LaGrange Congregation. At the time of Union in 1884, this congregation once again joined the Methodists.

Ministers who served Little Prairie, LaGrange and the meeting places were....

1860-61 - William Jolliffe
1862-63 - Samuel Jolliffe
1864 - Walter Ayers
1865 - William Wade
1866-67 - unknown
1868-69 - Henry Ebbott
1870-71 - Samuel Jolliffe
1872 - Supply

1873-75 - John Greenway
1876 - John Dumbleton
1877-78 - Thomas Harrison Dry
1879-80 - William Willison (this is the only appointment this minister is known to have had - I believe he was a local preacher)
1881-82 - George Haycroft
1883 - Robert Davidson

Ohio

1. Cuyahoga County

Circuits of Ohio

Cleveland was the first place a mission was set up in 1846 when George Rippon arrived to build a Bible Christian presence. Eventually there would be three circuits in Ohio ....

Cleveland Circuit:
> A chapel on Orange St. at Irving St.
> At Newburg, a village just outside Cleveland, but is now part of the city.

Orange Circuit:
> At Orange, 10 miles S.E. of Cleveland
> At Warrensville 9½ miles from Cleveland

Chagrin Falls:
> At Chagrin Falls
> At Beehive, not far from Chagrin Falls.

This list shows where chapels were built, but like all circuits there were also meeting places which might include the local schoolhouse, or rented rooms in the churches of other denominations or other buildings. Where possible I'll tell you about these other places, but unfortunately, the location of many of these have been lost in the mists of time. Most of the chapels and meeting places were within 10 or 12 miles of Cleveland.

The most well known of the ministers to serve the Ohio Circuits was Rev. John Chapple, who succeeded George Rippon in 1850. Rev. Chapple's wife had recently died, as had his youngest child. His daughter was given to fits of depression for the wont of her deceased mother and his son was just five years old. He had his hands full, indeed. He decided to offer his services to go to 'America' and start afresh, and, of course, he was accepted. His daughter was left with Rev. Kinsman and his wife in Cornwall, as she seemed to be more at ease with the Kinsmans than with anyone else, and he and his small son headed off to America. His diary of the journey tells how unprepared he was for such a task - trying to look after a sea sick child while he himself was suffering, and not knowing how to cook, at least in adverse conditions such as the ship offered. In his diary is this entry ... *"I was a better preacher than sailor"*....

He and his son William travelled to Quebec and then on to their destination. The ship, **Good Intent** landed six weeks and a day after leaving Fowey, Cornwall. At Quebec the Chapples transferred to a steamer ....

"Left Quebec in a steam boat and had as much respect shown as a drove of hogs might expect from Captain and men. I will not enter into the confusion on board, and at changing from one boat to another, but it was painful the numbers of persons so great and the characters so different. I saw more Catholic Priests than I had seen for a long time. The Bishop of Toronto was on board also and seemed to be a nice old gent."

A descendant Suzanne Bailey Van Orman writes, after a trip across Lake Ontario they experienced the only land travel on their 4,000 mile journey from England to Ohio. It was a seven-mile ride in a horse-drawn vehicle that ran on rails. This took them past Niagara Falls....

"It was a beautiful day. Had a splendid view of the rainbow over the waters. Got into another boat and arrived at Buffalo in the evening. I had more to pay for a cup of tea and a beef bone than I thought was fair."

Suzanne goes on to say that they boarded their sixth and final vessel and after an overnight voyage they arrived in Cleveland where one of their new Orange parishioners met them. To become acquainted with the people of his new ministry, John started out on foot with a bundle of old copies of the Bible Christian Magazine. He called on 22 families, leaving each a copy and promising to return in two weeks with a replacement.

It had likely been nearly a year since the people of the area had seen a Bible Christian preacher, and word soon spread that one was back among them. Mrs. Bailey, at Independence, Ohio, 66 miles away, wrote and asked him to come and preach in her neighbourhood. He did, and it was likely here that he met her daughter, Sarah Ann Bailey. A few years later, on October 21, 1856, they were married.

Like most of the early missionaries in all areas, Rev. Chapple had to walk his circuit in those first few years. He suffered greatly, as did the others, through want of a horse, but like the others, he too was refused. After the first two winters tramping through the snow on foot, the Conference in England finally gave him

From the family album of Suzanne Bailey Van Orman: The parsonage built for Rev. Chapple near Chagrin Falls, Ohio in 1879

permission to hire a horse at mission expense whenever needed. I'm thinking that is why Rev. George Rippon's health failed him and he had to leave the mission.

Although transferred by the Canadian conference in 1857 to various circuits in Canada over the next 22 years, Rev. Chapple returned to Ohio in 1879. The circuit built him a parsonage that year, and he remained in it until retiring to Cleveland, after preaching for 50 years.

These two ministers, George Rippon and John Chapple were the missionaries that opened up Ohio for the Bible Christians. Their stories are the stories of most of the immigrants - the harsh conditions of pioneer times was their way of life.

Chagrin Falls Circuit:

Chagrin Falls

From, *History of Cuyahoga County, Ohio* we have this information about the congregation at Chagrin Falls....

"*The Bible Christian Church at Chagrin Falls was organized in 1846 with seventeen members. In 1851 the church had increased so that it was able to build a small, framed house of worship, which was occupied by them until 1874 when the present commodious brick edifice was erected. The church is now in a flourishing condition (1879) with sixty two members and a Sunday School of about 90 members.*"

Courtesy: Bell Street Federated Church, Chagrin Falls, Ohio.

The second Bible Christian chapel, though I would suggest it has had an addition. The parsonage may be the house on the far side of the church nestled behind the Spruce trees.

The missionary here was George Rippon, who arrived in 1846, after volunteering to come to Ohio from Ontario, Canada.

The first chapel was 24 feet by 36 feet, of frame construction, and located on a lot 60 feet by 200 feet. The second chapel was brick and considerably larger, 35 feet by 60 feet. It was located on Bell Street, now 76 Bell Street. Whether or not both chapels were at this location is not known.

The parsonage was also on Bell St., but whether or not it was erected on the same parcel is unknown. By 1870, when the parsonage was built, it was said to be located on 2 acres- perhaps the Bible Christians were able to purchase adjacent land. The parsonage was of brick construction, 20 feet by 22 feet with a back wing 20 feet by 14 feet - good size house.

In the early days of settlement, most of the people in this area were from Devon, and many had either been christened into the Bible Christian Church in Devon or had their children christened in it. It is sometimes difficult to find mention of the members of any one congregation, but in *Memorial To The Pioneer Women Of The Western Reserve*, we find this passage...

"William Hutchins and wife, Mary Downs, from Devonshire, England, both hired out to work for Dr. Vincent, Mr. Hutchins helping to build the house that afterward became their own. They received $12.⁰⁰ a month for their labour, he $8.⁰⁰ and she $4.⁰⁰...... They did much for the Bible Christian Church and by honesty and industry amassed a handsome fortune."

At the time of Union in 1884, this congregation united with the Congregational Church. In 1919 the present Federated Church was born as a result of a federation between the Congregational and Disciples of Christ churches.

Beehive

Even though this is not listed in the Bible Christian Property Book, the research of the late Elizabeth Ebbott indicates that this was at least a meeting place, where, as in other places, the people met in the schoolhouse, or rented time in the church of another denomination. Unfortunately, this place had a name change so long ago that no one now knows where this place was.

Ministers who served this Circuit included:
1846- 1850- George Rippon
1850-56 - John Chapple
1857-59 - Joseph Hoidge
1860-61 - William Roach
1862 - Henry James Colwell
1863 - William Hooper

1864-68 - George Haycraft
1865-67 - Lewis Wickett
1868-69 - Roger Allin
1869-71 - John Harris with Alexander Richards in 1871
1872-75 - John Chapple
1876-77 - George Bodle
1877 - Richard Mallett
1878-81 - Herman Moore and possibly Lewis Wickett
1882-83 - Fergus O'Connor Jones, and possibly Richard Thomas

The Orange Circuit

Orange

Known by at least three names, the settlement where the Bible Christian Chapel would be built was called English Settlement, Orange, and Lander Circle.

The first settlers at the English settlement were Almon Smith and his family, arriving about 1832. By 1833 the Abell's were in the area, and by 1835 Row Jackson from Yorkshire had taken upland. In 1836, John Stoneman and his wife Ann Newcombe had arrived from Devon. Not only did they farm but John built a steam sawmill, in operation until the close of the century. These first few families were all charter members of the Bible Christian congregation, with it's beginnings about 1839.

There were no missionaries at that early date, but these Bible Christians met in one another's homes under the leadership of a lay or local preacher.

In those early days the whole of Ohio was under the Ohio Mission. By the 'whole of Ohio' I mean that part of the state where the Bible Christians would develop congregations and build chapels. This would have been in the general vicinity of Cleveland, extending not much more than 15 miles or so from that place.

George Rippon was the first missionary to be sent to Ohio, arriving in 1846. He was responsible for the initial contact and initial development of all the Ohio Circuits. I'm sure he was extremely pleased to find a ready-made congregation waiting for him at the English Settlement. By 1848 this congregation had built their first chapel, more than likely a log chapel, erected on land donated by John and Ann Stoneman. A cemetery was started on the same parcel.

In 1864 the congregation built a new frame chapel, measuring 28 feet by 38 feet. The Abell's donated the half acre parcel for this chapel on the north side of Kinsman Road now Chagrin Boulevard.

Now called Garfield Church, this could easily be the old parsonage, remodelled to serve as a Sunday School, or rooms for other church uses. Renovations may have occurred in 1915 when the new Church was built.

The circuit parsonage was located at the English Settlement and was likely constructed about the same time as the second chapel, or perhaps 1873 when the whole of the Bible Christian District in Ohio became known as the Cleveland District.

It was a frame parsonage, 20 feet by 24 feet in size with a kitchen wing on the back measuring 12 feet by 18 feet.

In 1884, at the time of Union, the Orange Bible Christian congregation joined with the Orange Methodist Protestant Church. In 1929 the church was re-named in memory of President Garfield who had been born in the area. At that time, the President's widow donated $150 toward the inset of a new window.

Warrensville

Located 9.63 miles from Cleveland, it can be assumed that

a log chapel was erected at Warrensville not long after Brother Rippon first came to the area. In 1871 a frame chapel was erected on a third of an acre, donated for the use of the Bible Christians. It was the same size as the Orange chapel, 28 feet by 38 feet.

Ministers who served this circuit included:
1846-50 - George Rippon
1851-56 - John Chapple
1857-59 - Joseph Hoidge
1860-61 - William Roach and Joseph Dix
1862 - William Hooper and Henry James Colwell
1863 - George Parsons and Michael Pett
1864 - George Haycroft and Michael Pett
1865 - John Pinch and Lewis W. Wickett
1866-67 - Charles J. Pearce
1868 - Lewis Wickett and Roger Allin
1869 - John Harris and Roger Allin
1870 - John Harris and William Kinley
1871 - John Harris and Alexander Richards
1872 - John Chapple
1873 - supply, likely by John Chapple
1874-75 - George Johns
1876-77 - George Bodle
1878-81 - Herman Moore
1882-83 - Fergus O'Connor Jones

The Cleveland Circuit

Cleveland

Ebenezer Chapel at Cleveland was located at the corner of Orange Street and Irving Street. It was constructed in 1855 during the pastorate of John Chapple, and for that time it was likely an impressive structure. It was a large brick chapel, measuring 37 feet by 65 feet. Very little room remained on the town lot on which it was erected, that lot measuring 40 feet by 72 feet.

The parsonage was located at 20 Henry Street, but I do not know how far away from the chapel that was. It was a very small frame house, only 18 feet by 28 feet. It was on a very narrow town lot, 24½ feet by 130 feet. There seems to have been enough room behind the house for a garden for the preacher's family, or a shed in which to keep the preacher's horse. No date for the building of the parsonage is available.

In 1865 Cleveland was withdrawn from the Ohio Mission and given Circuit status.

The "Flats" at Cleveland, 1857. In the distance there are steeples visible on the hill. Perhaps this is the area where the Bible Christian Chapel was located

Ministers who served the circuit included:
1850-56 - John Chapple
1857-59 - Joseph Hoidge
1860-61 - William Roach
1862 - William Hooper, Henry James Colwell
1863 - George Parsons, Michael Pett
1864 - George Haycraft
1865-66 - John Pinch
1867-69 - J.T. Sencabaugh

1870-71 - William G. Beer
1872 - William Hodnett
1873 -74 - Richard T. Courtice
1875-76 - Samuel Jolliffe
1877-79 - Henry James Nott
1880-82 - Samuel James Allin
1883 - Francis Metherall Whitlock

The Cleveland Mission - Newburg

This station on the Cleveland Circuit was at Newburg. In the early years of the 19th century, Newburg rivalled Cleveland in population and importance, and so it was an important place in which to build a congregation. As a mission it was served until 1874 by the same ministers as served Cleveland chapel.

When the first chapel was constructed here I do not know. It may have been a log chapel, but seeing as there was plenty of industry here at an early date, that is highly unlikely. It is possible that the local congregation met in rented premises until a chapel was constructed here in 1873. Located at the corner of Home and Walnut Streets, it was a frame chapel 34 feet by 47 feet in size on a very good size town lot, likely a double lot, measuring 68 feet by 75 feet.

Courtesy: Clarington Museums, Sarah Jane Williams Heritage Centre
John Pinch was the first minister to serve the new Cleveland Circuit in 1865

From 1874 the ministers who served the Cleveland Mission included:

1874 - John Ball
1875 - George H. Copeland
1876 - James Pollard Rice

In 1877 the Newburg congregation was no longer considered a mission and was given station status. The ministers included:

1877-78 - Herman Moore
1879-83 - by supply from other Cleveland District Circuits

It appears that by 1879 the Bible Christians had spread themselves pretty thin in Ohio.

Michigan

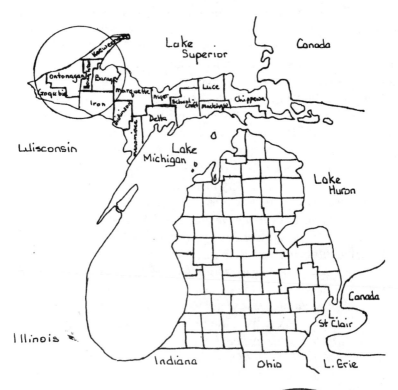

1. Houghton
2 Otonagan
3.Keweenan

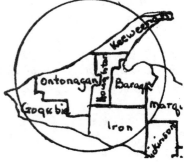

Circuits in the Upper
Peninsula of Michigan

The Upper Peninsula of Michigan was settled, to a great degree, by Cornish miners, drawn to the area by the flourishing mines. Many had Bible Christian connections and backgrounds. The mine owners offered much support once the Bible Christian missionaries began to arrive in the area. They even went so far as to advance cash wages so pledges could be paid to the preachers.

From the work of the late Elizabeth Ebbott and her husband Ralph, we have this......

"The miners, too, were interested in having the church. In the first year at Rockland, membership stood at 87...."

This is indeed a far cry from the 17 members Rev. William Hooper raised in his first year at Wisconsin.

"....This grew to a peak of 121 in 1867. Money was raised quickly and a church was built in a matter of 5-6 months. The nucleus of this group had been active in the church in England and there were many willing volunteers to serve the church as local preachers and Sunday School teachers."

But apparently this seeming prosperity was not to continue. Here is a further quote from the Ebbotts' work .....

"In the end, primarily because of the instability of employment, the church failed. As reported in 1869, 'At present there is a great depression among the mines here. A large number of our people have left and are still leaving.' In June of 1869, at the Conference Meeting, it was resolved 'to withdraw our agents [from the Lake Superior District] in view of the present position of our affairs, our state of funds, claims on our labour, etc.' A determined local group in Hancock did continue, at least for several more years, building its own small church and running it with local preachers."

Oddly, these circuits in Michigan were not recorded in the Bible Christian Property Book., so information about the location and size of chapels is not available, unless stated in someone's report. The last entries for most of the appointments in Michigan end in 1870 on Walkington's list of ministers who served the Canadian conference, and so this gives us an indication why these places were not in the property book which was written in about 1874. Michigan had long been abandon.

Both the Bible Christian Magazine in England and the Observer newspaper in Ontario carried reports from the various men who served that area, the appointments consisting of: Rockland (aka Rosendale), Portage Lake, Hancock, and a handful of meeting places where chapels were never built.

The Ebbotts collected many of these and I have chosen a few here to show you what conditions were like in Michigan at various times......

The dock at Hancock. Notice the steamer by the wharf. It would have taken passengers and Bible Christian ministers up and down the coast when the roads were bad.

In 1861, Ebenezer Thorne wrote to the Bible Christian Magazine in England (this was just before he returned to England from Orono, Ontario where he published a number of Bible Christian periodicals and broadsheets, among them The Day Dawn, the first Canadian Bible Christian newspaper). He says ....

"*I have a letter from a member of our connexion at the Ontonagon Copper Mines in Michigan. There is in that place a population of 1800- 700 of whom are Cornishmen, numbers of whom were members of the Bible Christian Church in England. There is a Roman Catholic and an Episcopal Methodist church and this is all. The people are very eager to have a preacher sent and have offered to support a married man and his family. They can meet at first at the good Templars Hall which will*"

*accommodate 200 people .... and they will as soon as possible
erect a place of worship.*"

And so began the 10 year mission in Michigan, in what
was called the Lake Superior Mission, which would eventually
consist of two circuits:
Rockland - also called Rosendale
Portage Lake - referred to often as Hancock Circuit.

Rockland or Rosendale Circuit

In work compiled in the past, there has been some
confusion as to whether or not Rockland and Rosendale were
separate places. They are often mentioned in reports together
which indicates to most of us they were separate places, and well
there may have been separate meetings - one at Rockland and one
at Rosendale, however, Joanne Olson from the Rockland Historical
Museum tells us this ...

"*Rosendale is part of Rockland, not a separate place as
you mentioned. Rockland was first platted as three villages in the
late 1850's - Rosendale, Webster and Williamsburg. Even today
our property tax descriptions still use these names though the three
separate villages no longer exist as such.*"

Knowing this it seems that Rockland is the name given to
the amalgamation of the three smaller places. So in those early
days there may well have been a meeting place in all three
locations, with the church at Rockland being built in that section
called Rosendale.

The missionary sent to open this area was Henry James
Nott. In 1862 he wrote ...

"*A new church was built by July, measuring 70 feet by 40
feet. Brother J. Chappel, President of the Bible Christian
Canadian Conference, went to speak the last Sunday in June to
open the new church, about 2000 miles there and back.*"

288

The ministers who toiled on the Wisconsin Circuit must have been quite hurt, for they never received the courtesy of a visit from the President of the Conference, or anyone else for that matter.

Various reports tell us this...

1862 - 63 members
1863 - 87 members
1864 - 94 members

These are full members, which means they not only have paid their dues/subscriptions but they have served their trial and been accepted. These numbers do not reflect those in the overall congregation each Sabbath.

In 1864, William Hooper wrote to the Observer,

Courtesy: Clarington Museums, Sarah Jane Williams Heritage Centre
Henry James Nott, 1865, Missionary to Michigan

his statistics for the Michigan mission appearing in the March 12th edition of 1873 ....

1 itinerant preacher,
6 local preachers,
17 Sunday School teachers,
113 Sunday School Scholars,
1 church building,
4 other meeting places,
4 members on trial.

It looks as if the Mission in Michigan is building well, however in 1867, although the membership that year had risen to 121, 62 of these left the area. The debt had been retired at Rockland that year making the circuit self sufficient, however failure of mining interests in the area lead to many people leaving in search of employment...... so reports Rev. Walter Ayers in his report published in the Observer, December 24th edition, 1867.

Those who served the Rockland/Rosendale Circuit included.....

1861-63 - Henry James Nott
1864-65 - Samuel Jolliffe with assistants John Edwards and George Dunkley
1866 - Michael Pett
1867-69 - Walter Ayers
1870 - abandon

Portage Lake Circuit

In January, 1869, the Observer ran an announcement that a preacher was needed for Portage Lake, Michigan. Nothing happened until the Conference in June when Garrance Tink Colwell was appointed to go. Until his arrival, the Mission at Portage Lake had been 'by supply' from Rockland as and when possible. In a statistical report from John Harris in December of 1869, there was 1 local preacher, 7 Sunday School Teachers, 25 Sunday School students, 1 chapel and 3 other preaching places.

From the Old Victoria Restoration Society, Rockland
A restored miner's cabin.

Besides doing the job of minister at this mission, Garrance Tink Colwell was sent ...

"to explore the future possibilities for the denomination. He was designated 'Superintendent of the District', the first and

290

only time this title was used in Michigan. There were two stations, Rockland and Portage Lake. Colwell was able to build a church at Hancock, 30 feet by 35 feet. It was opened November 13-14, 1869." So says a report in the Observer December 1, 1869.

Again, there was a visit from the Canadian President, William Pascoe, ... *"to create a greater interest on the part of our friends and the public generally in extending our cause in that region."*

The statistical report above mentions 3 other preaching places, and from what I can gather these would have been at Hancock, Marquette and Calumet, though these places were well spaced out, with many miles of horrid roads between.

In 1868 John Harris wrote to the Observer from Hancock....

"When I first came here we intended to occupy four places, Hancock, Houghton, South Pewabic and Calumet. Houghton and South Pewabic are for the time given up. Our principal interest is in this place.

We encountered much opposition in getting a place to preach in but the Lord has made the wrath of man to praise him, and the remainder thereof he hath restrained. A room has been rented for $10 per month; we have preached in it every Sunday evening and intend to have service in the morning also. At present there are 23 members, a congregation of 200, a choir with a melodeon and a Bible class.

On Dec. 26th we had a Christmas Festival to aid in paying for the furnishing of the Minister's residence. The choir did us good service on the occasion. Short addresses were given by Messers Ladu, Gerry, Carter and Harris, profits $80. We ought to have had a man on this ground before now, but still there is a prospect of doing much good and of building up a thriving church.

Calumet is a newly-opened mining district and is growing in population rapidly; it is 12 miles from here on the Eagle River Road. I have organized a small society there and I think that we shall succeed if we can get a place convenient in which to preach the word. The people here gladly welcome one of their own

291

ministers."

John Harris wrote again to the Observer in January, 1869.....

"At present there is a great depression among the mines here. A large number of our people have left and are still leaving. But not withstanding this depression, Bro. Ayers and the friends have exerted themselves nobly. The Sabbath School celebration on Dec. 20th is reported as being the most successful ever held. On Christmas Eve our friends had a Christmas Tree and Father Christmas was very beneficent in his gifts to Bro. Ayers. Among other things he received a whole sheep, two geese, one turkey, fowls and a fur; nor was Sr. Ayers forgotten. Yesterday the butcher, not to be behind, presented the preacher a rump of his Christmas beef."

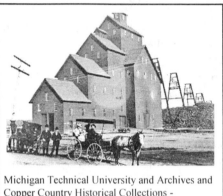

Michigan Technical University and Archives and Copper Country Historical Collections - Neg.#01306
Shaft #6, Quincy Mine, Hancock, Michigan, c1880

The report goes on to describe a trip to Rockland on December 30th that same month ....

"Early on December 30th I started for Rockland by mail stage, the roads were very heavy and progress was comparatively slow. We soon entered the bush and after a ride of six hours, we were refreshed with the sight of a small clearing and the half-way house, a small log building half way between Portage and Rockland. 45 minutes for dinner and to get warm, then a fresh team proceeded with us through the woods. The country here is very romantic; the road wound around steep precipices, deep ravines and high rocky hills. Rockland was reached at 9:30 a.m.

and I was gladly welcomed by Br. Ayers. This is the same road over which Br. Nott travelled some seven yeas ago on snowshoes and had to stay all night in the open air by a fire; and though I should not like such a journey as I have had, I was certainly in better circumstance than Bro. Nott."

The reports of travels to various places around any circuit tell us a lot about life at that time. Garrance Tink Colwell visited the mines at Calumet shortly after his arrival in July of 1869 and reported what he saw.......

"I took the stage at Hancock last Friday morning at eight o'clock a.m. We reached our destination at 12 noon. I enquired for and found the residence of the Class Leader, Brother Fregans, where I was warmly received. As my host was engaged in the day shift, as it is termed, I accompanied him to the mouth of the shaft and felt considerably amused to see the men descend the ladder with a lighted candle stuck on top of their hats to enable them to see their way down. In the afternoon I found out and had a lengthy conversation with a young man, formerly a local preacher with us on the Gwennap Circuit. I was

Michigan Technical University and Archives and Copper Country Collections, Neg#01271B Centennial Mine, Calumet, c1880. Note the candle in each hat as described by Rev. G.T. Colwell

kindly invited to tea by the lady of the house who, with her husband, are both from the Mother land. In fact, the great majority of people here are natives of old Cornwall.".

It was in September of 1869, that William Pascoe, president of the Canadian Conference made his tour of the Michigan area. In a report to Cephas Barker, editor of the

Observer, he says .....

"*Bro. Colwell and myself girded our loins for a rough and tumble journey over a horrid road of twelve miles to Calumet by stage. Was successful in getting through without our necks being broken and found kind entertainment at the house of Bro. Fregans. On Sunday, Sept. 5th preached in the Calumet Schoolhouse in the morning, rode over the detestable road aforesaid in the afternoon, and preached to a large and crowded house at Hancock in the evening.*

Sept. 7th, I had designed to start for Rockland by stage, but upon hearing the state of the road described, thought it most prudent to go round to Ontonagon by steamer which, however, did not arrive."

Even though we see these ministers getting from place to place with some regularity, we also see that travel anywhere, at any time of the year was a difficult task - especially when they miss the stage!

Rev. William Pascoe, in his report about his visit to the area in 1869, says this ....

"*Arrived at Ontonagon at two p.m.. On landing I found that I was 12 miles from Rockland, the stage was gone and no other conveyance save 'Mr. Trot's ponies' available. I was in a quandary, called a council of war in which I was chairman and all the members too. Subject of discussion being the following: 'Being ignorant of the road, having a heavy bag and coat to carry, and the sun being hot, shall I proceed? Yea or Nay' The 'yeas' had it. Was an English travelling preacher to stick just before a twelve-mile difficulty? Manhood forbade it,*

From: A Century of Service, The History of Crediton Church
Rev. William Samuel Pascoe

and I pushed on. Mercy, how hot it was! Got over three miles, found that my white 'duster' was getting black in spots with sweat and the dye from the back of my vest. At this juncture a buggy dashed up, one of its occupants informed me that our kind friend Mr. W. Harris, Esq. was looking for me up in Ontonagon and having ascertained that I was gone, would be along in a short time, sure I had better wait. I did wait and in the meantime, toiletted, my wash basin being a ditch and my towel my pocket handkerchief. After a while my friend drove up and the journey which began so unpropitiously was finished with comfort."

Besides the dangers and discomforts of travel were the dangers of everyday life. On April 11, 1869 a fire burned down most of Hancock. In an unsigned report to the Observer we learn this about that day's events.....

"Sunday, April 11 was a sad day for Hancock, Michigan. Many who awoke in the morning in possession of earthly comforts, at night scarcely knew where to lay their heads. About breakfast time the 'Mine Whistles' blew the fire alarm. It was quickly ascertained that a house standing close to the business part of the town was on fire with the wind blowing directly over the town. The houses being all of wood, the flames leaped from house to house and from street to street until, at last three quarters of the place was destroyed. There is not a single Provision, or Dry Goods store remaining.

I want, Mr Editor, to call your attention to the following facts. You and your readers can draw from them what inferences you please.

1st: The origin of the fire was connected with a dancing party.

2nd: There were burnt down about 30 Saloons, Taverns, etc, while four or five remain.

3rd: Before the fire there were 5 preaching rooms and churches. Only one, the Congregational, was destroyed. The Roman Catholic and Methodist Episcopal churches, and the Bible Christian preaching room were in great danger.

4th: There are eight resident Ministers of religion, none of whom is burnt out."

Although the Bible Christians stopped sending ministers to Michigan in 1870, the congregation at Hancock continued to meet with local preachers. In fact, in 1872 they even managed to build a church. In a report from Portage Lake, Brother Vincent wrote....

"On Dec. 24th 1871 we opened our new church. You will be glad to know that we are doing well and also that the Lord has given us souls for our hire. Our little church (we have plenty of room to enlarge when necessary) is regularly deeded and

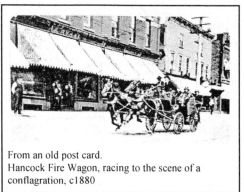

From an old post card.
Hancock Fire Wagon, racing to the scene of a conflagration, c1880

recorded as a Bible Christian Church. Dear brother, do send us a minister not later than the spring."

The Editor of the Observer published these remarks following the above report ....

"What say some of our good readers to the above? A people, from whom we withdrew the missionary and left them to unite with some other section of the church, keep together, have their private means of grace, erect a small sanctuary and dedicate it to the service of God, and already the Master has poured them down showers of blessing. Still the work goes on."

...And, sadly, that much needed preacher never arrived.

Ministers to serve Portage Lake and Hancock area included.....

1868 - John Harris
1869 - Garrance Tink Colwell
1870 - withdrew

Illinois

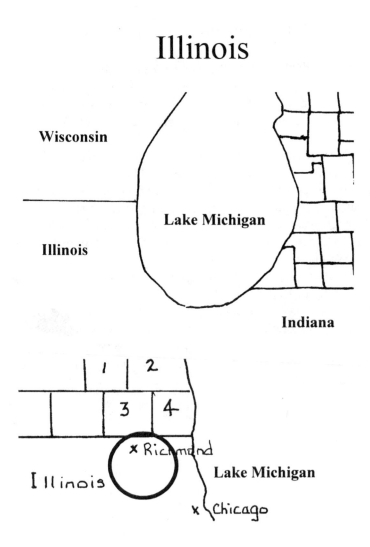

Bible Christians in Illinois

It is doubtful whether there were ever any chapels constructed at Illinois. You can see by the location of Richmond that both Richmond and Bunker Hill were likely served by the preachers on the circuits in either Racine County or Walworth County in Wisconsin.

The people in this area had heard about the Bible Christians just a few miles away, and had likely gone to hear the preachers, for they had asked that a preacher be sent to their area. In about 1860 I believe that Michael Pett, a young man of about 21 years of age, was asked to serve at Richmond as a lay preacher. In another two years he was taken on probation as a minister and went on to serve many circuits.

To date, I have not located Bunker Hill, but I believe it was in the vicinity of Richmond.

I have not been able to find out how long the Bible Christians held meetings at these places, nor have I been able to find out if meetings had ever been held in nearby places. One thing is certain, the Bible Christians did not have a strong or long-lasting foothold in Illinois.

Addendum

Further Information

 Elim Cemetery

Centralia Cemetery

 Columbus Cemetery

Further Information

Inevitably, when a work of this nature is being compiled there are a few items which slip through the cracks, and indeed there was a very important item which slipped through the cracks in this project.

The Circuit of **Manvers and Cartwright** was just such an item! The chapels on this circuit were attached to two different circuits at various times. In the beginning, when the Bible Christians had not yet reached all the towns and rural communities of later years, only Cartwright Township, located in Durham County, had any chapels. These were connected to the Prince Albert Circuit in Ontario County, seeing as they were all fairly close to Prince Albert and Port Perry where that circuit had its central membership.

As Prince Albert Circuit grew, so did the number of meeting places, and eventually chapels, in the Durham County portion of the circuit. These were spreading over into Manvers Township, east of Cartwright. It was a cumbersome circuit that could not be looked after by a preacher and his probationer. With the circuit and chapels under so many varied jurisdictions, is it any wonder it was forgotten?

Cartwright and Manvers Circuit

In the early days there were so few people in the 'back' townships of Durham county, that they were served by the preachers who worked the Prince Albert Circuit near Port Perry on Lake Scugog in Reach Township, Ontario County. Cartwright was just across the Shirley Road south of Port Perry and Manvers just east of that again.

In later years the care of Manvers and Cartwright was given to Victoria County, and the ministers of the itinerancy who worked in Mariposa and Ops Townships looked after these congregations too.

300

Eventually however, there was enough membership to warrant full time ministers and a circuit of their own, this withdrawal taking place in about 1874. The chapels on this circuit were village and hamlet chapels, except for two that were 'town' chapels - Blackstock in Cartwright and Janetville in Manvers.

In the Cartwright portion there were Caesarea, Bethel, Carmel, and Blackstock (aka Williamsburg and Cartwright), and in the Manvers portion there were Newry, Janetville, Fleetwood (aka The Brick Corners), and Franklin.

Caesarea:

The chapel at Caesarea was in Lot 12, Concession 9, right out near the lakeshore. Caesarea was a port town receiving lumber and grain from the towns of Victoria County and sending back imported items such as English wallpaper, French wine and the latest fashions from Montreal. It was a busy little place and the population fluctuated with the prosperity of the village. It is very probable that early meetings were held in the home of Thomas Werry, for there is mention of 'Werry's Meeting' in old records. A 26 foot by 36 foot frame chapel was constructed in 1874 on 333 square feet of land. Who the trustees were, or who the congregation included is not known. Thomas Werry acted as a circuit trustee and his name appears on the Blackstock deed as such.

Blackstock:

The chapel at Blackstock was built at the south end of the village, the land, one quarter acre, being bought from William Axworthy for one hundred dollars. The date of the deed is April 19, 1871, and a 34 foot by 48 foot brick chapel was built upon the parcel and dedicated in 1872. An article in the Bowmanville newspaper, The Canadian Statesman, dated October 19, 1883 describes this chapel.......

"A modest, but neat brick structure, erected in 1871, is a credit to the denomination...."

At its dedication, congregation member Aaron Butler donated a clock. It is interesting to note that in 1937 this timepiece was still being used in the United Church and was still keeping good time after 66 years!

At the time of Union the Bible Christian Chapel was found to be too small to hold the combined congregation and was taken down.

Bethel:

Located on Lot 1 in the 3rd Concession this congregation is perhaps the oldest one in the township, maybe the oldest in the circuit. By 1857 the congregation found themselves in financial difficulties and wrote a letter to the Bible Christian Conference (at Belleville that year) asking for the sum of £10. It is not known if they received the money, but they must have for they continued to flourish. In 1860 it was discovered that the half acre of land on which the chapel stood, at the south-west corner of Lot 1, Concession 3

Photo by Roger Leetooze
One of three surviving stones in the little Bethel Cemetery. This one is for pioneer Charles Hambley, a Bible Christian.

had never been officially transferred to them or deeded. It was suggested that this be done as quickly as possible for the adjoining land was soon to be disposed of. With no deed to their plot the Bible Christians could find themselves without a chapel. According to records at the Scugog Shores Museum, this transaction did not take place immediately. It was finally registered at the Registry Office at Bowmanville, on September

20th, 1861. It tells us that the land was sold to the congregation by Henry Elliott for one hundred dollars.

But long before official congregations and the bulding of chapels, we know there were Bible Christian families living in the area. One story handed down in the township is that of the Hambley family. In 1837 a baby of that house died. Charles Hambley walked all the way to Hampton to give the child a Christian burial in the old Bible Christian cemetery there. Though most of the congregation seems to have come from Reach Township in Ontario County, other Cartwright families who attended this chapel were Charles Trick and family, and the Ward family. Early records that actually mention names are hard to find.

Carmel:

This was a difficult chapel to find. The Bible Christian Property Book simply lists it as a late addition to the list ....

"Carmel, Cartwright, 26 x 36 frame, 1874 on 1/4 acre."

During the first attempt at Union in 1874, there was quite a lot of heated encounters between the various sects as they fought to keep their identity. Shortly, I will tell you about some of the events in Manvers Township, but for now I want to say that Carmel was mentioned along with Newry (Yelverton) as not wishing to join with the Methodists. If they were very far apart they would not have been tied together in that statement. The closest community at that time to Newry was on the Cartwright Manvers boundary road, a little place called Burton or Burtonville by some. Sadly, Burton burned to the ground in the late 1890's and everything was lost - except for a few yards of cloth from the general store. There is no sign of the community today, and the history of the place was never written down. I can only assume that Carmel Chapel was likely at Burton.

Janetville:

Janetville Chapel was another late chapel. It was constructed in 1874, of frame, 26 feet by 36 feet in size on one quarter acre of land. It was also called 'The Frame Church in the

Hollow' and sometimes "The Church by the Cemetery", to distinguish it from the other churches in the village.

The parsonage for the circuit was at Janetville. It was a neat 24 foot by 30 foot frame house on one quarter acre of land in the village. The deed for the parsonage was held by Mr. L. Grandy. The assistant ministers and the probationers stayed at the parsonage at Blackstock, and often at the Philp farm near Nestleton on what is now Highway 7a. In 1881 we find Rev. James Hoskin at the home of Thomas Werry at Ball's Point near Caesarea, but whether he is visiting or boarding there is not known.

From the book, 'Spirit of the Hills' by Isabelle Challice and Grant Curtis, we learn that the organist at the time of union was Annie Whitlock (Mrs. Annie K. Ashton). Rev. Jesse Whitlock served this circuit 1879-82, and this is likely a daughter of his.

At Union, the frame church by the cemetery was no longer needed and was taken down, the congregation now meeting at the Brick Church in the Hollow that had been constructed by the New Connexions Methodists. The Methodists continued to use the Bible Christian parsonage at Janetville.

Yelverton:

Yelverton was at one time called Newry by the first settlers in the area, after their home in Ireland. The Bible Christian congregation at Yelverton did not have their own chapel. They rented one hour from the New Connexions Methodists, in their chapel, every Sabbath.

It was at Yelverton that things got a little 'down and dirty' during the first attempt at Union of the various Methodist denominations. In fact, two years later there were still letters going back and forth in The Globe newspaper, each side still calling names to the other. One of these articles, dated January 19, 1876, pretty well sums up what had happened at that time.

"*At Newry and Carmel the people were a unit in rejecting the terms of Union...*"

The article goes on to tell about the chain of events that took place ....

"On the very first Sabbath the Methodist Pastor sent one of his colleagues to preach in Newry, at the New Connexions regular hour of worship. The people assembled as was their wont and found the Methodist preacher had taken possession of the pulpit during the Sabbath School session. After a short time Mr. Grandy, accompanied by the Bible Christian Preacher, arrived. Mr. G. went to the pulpit and informed the Methodist preacher that it was their hour, and that he could not be allowed to preach and therefore he had better come down.

The Preacher objected, stating that he was there in the name of the Methodist Church of Canada. He was then told that he would not be allowed to preach in their hour. He asked how they would prevent it? 'We shall see', was the reply. He came down and the Bible Christian Preacher went up and conducted the service.

On the following Sabbath, the Methodist Pastor put in an appearance with the view of making sundry explanations, when some altercation ensued...."

'Some altercation' is an understatement. In another letter, a rebuttal from the 'other side', spelled it out. Apparently, there was a discussion between the Methodist Preacher, Mr. Hart, and Mr. Grandy, the class leader of the Newry Society. Again, apparently the Methodist preacher refused to give up the pulpit, and the Bible Christians, Mr. Grandy included I would assume, took the Methodist minister outside and bloodied his nose.

At one point in all this flurry of letter writing, the Newry congregation had been referred to as 'the mob', and in this case the person was probably right.

On two subsequent occasions the Methodist preacher left an appointment at Newry and the residents of the place showed their mind on the matter by staying home. The only congregation that the Methodist Minister had was the people he had brought with him and one young man from 'the swamp' (did the newspaper article mean 'the marsh'? If so, this is an area on the boundary of Manvers and Cavan near Glamorgan.)

Fleetwood:

The community of Fleetwood was also known as The Brick Corners because the school across the road was also brick, making all the buildings at that crossroads brick. Sometimes it was referred to as The Brick.

Up until 1874 the Bible Christian congregation rented space from the Wesleyan Methodists. Because feelings ran pretty high during that first attempt at Union,

From the collection of Grant Curtis
Fleetwood, or The Brick Corner, with the church in the foreground and the schoolhouse behind on the other corner.

they erected their own chapel. It stood on one quarter acre and measured 28 feet by 38 feet. The parcel of land was purchased from Alexander Cairns, and the builder who put up the chapel was Thomas Staples. The minister who was in charge at the time was Rev. John Harris, according to Isabelle Challice in her book, Spirit of the Hills.

At the time the chapel was built the trustees and members of the congregation included Henry Nugent (lay preacher), Robert Staples, John Hart, Christopher Chittick, James Dean, David Hart, George S. Staples, and Jacob Hart.

Fleetwood did not escape conflict during that first attempt at Union. That same newspaper article that told the story of Newry, went on to tell about the happenings at Fleetwood's new Bible Christian Chapel ...

"*At the Brick, parties from a distance, under the leadership of a J.P., said to have been appointed as Trustees by the Quarterly*

306

meeting of the Methodist Church, forcibly entered the church, removed the lock from the door, put on another of their own selecting, locked the door, and went their way. The next day, (Saturday) the legal Trustees removed the newly fixed lock, and put another of their own preference."

Franklin:

Franklin used to be located at the top of the hill in Lot 25, Concession 11, Manvers Township. It was a pretty windy and cold place to be, as it was right atop what is today The Bethany Ski Hills. The settlement was moved down the hill to a more sheltered spot - blacksmith shop, church, school, everything! That early church was a Bible Christian chapel, possibly a log cabin, but likely a frame church.

In 1874 a new brick chapel was erected, measuring only 18 feet by 38 feet. This little country chapel sat on one quarter acre.

At the time of the first attempt at Union, few people were in favour. An article in The Globe early in 1874 had this to say ....

"At Franklin not one contributor toward the erection of the church has accepted the Union. The congregation stands about 100 against Union and about 10 in favour of it."

You will notice that most of the Bible Christian Chapels in Manvers Township were constructed in 1874. It was a year when the Bible Christians decided to show they existed, that they were strong and would not be forced into a Union with which they did not agree. They built chapels to prove it!! This was alsos the year that the Manvers and Cartwright were withdrawn from Victoria District and given circuit status.

Unfortunately, Union was inevitable, and over the next ten years negotiations were carried out all across the country. New tactics were used to bring everyone together.

About 2 years after that first attempt at Union, Mr. Willoughby, the district president for the Methodist's of the Peterborough District, announced that most of the people of the area were now 'loyal Methodists'.

This statement after the congregations at Newry, Franklin, Janetville and Carmel were threatened with legal action if they did not join *quietly*. I think it was just a threat. I have not been able to find evidence of actual legal action being taken against them. They did not, however, join with the Methodists at that time, but stayed home week after week. Soon, most tired of the *fight* and slowly drifted back to church, though I would not go so far as to say they were 'loyal Methodists'.

Preachers to serve this circuit after it split from Victoria District were:

1874 - William Kinley and George Fulcher
1875- 77 - John Harris and Richard Thomas
1878 - John Harris and Moses Metherall
1879 - Jesse Whitlock and Moses Metherall
1880 - Jesse Whitlock and James Hoskin
1881 - Jesse Whitlock
1882 - Jesse Whitlock and Thomas Brown
1883 - Edwin A. Tonkin and J. Wesley Down

Index

Campbell, ... 256
Campbell, Andrew 167
Campbell, Robert 167
Cann, Edward 55
Cannom, G.F. 172
Cannom, J. W. 58, 66, 92, 111,
Cantlon, David 57, 66, 92, 113,
116, 165, 172, 174,
Carhart, Eliza 239
Carhart, Stephen 239
Carscallen, George 12
Cairns, Alexander 306
Carter, ... 291
Challice, Isabelle 304, 306
Chambers, Henry 82
Chambers, Mrs. J.M. 266
Chambers, J.M. 266
Chapin, Alice 266
Chapin, Ethan 266
Chapple, John 28, 52, 66, 133,
217, 222, 236, 242, 243, 274,
276, 278, 279, 281, 282, 288,
Chapple, William 275,
Chastre, Arthur 93
Chidley (Chitley), William 90,
190,
Chittick, Christopher 306
Ciphery, G. Jr. 103
Clark, Archibald 20, 22, 28, 38,
52, 74, 92, 99, 104, 116, 190,
Clark, J. 103
Clark, John 19, 20
Clark, John W. 227
Clark, Thomas 167
Clarke, A. 167
Clarke, J. 82
Clarke, Mrs. O. 103
Clarke, Thomas 168
Clatworthy, Joseph 55
Clemens, Joseph 46

Clemens, Mrs. M.A. 47
Cleverdon, Miss M. 45
Coad, ... 254, 256
Cobbledick, ... 51
Coke, Mrs. Edward 266
Coke, Edward 266
Cole, Mrs. James 261
Cole, James 261
Cole, Jean Murray 72
Cole, John Roger 48
Cole, Matthew 49
Cole, Miss P. 49
Cole, Roger 48
Cole, Thomas 27
Coles, Jonas O. 186
Collacott, Robert 48
Collins, James 6, 43, 58, 83,
94, 140, 165, 171, 198,
Collins, James H. 126, 206,
227, 229, 230,
Colwell, Garrance Tink 5, 12,
66, 167, 171, 270, 290, 293,
294, 296
Colwell, Henry James 66, 92,
108, 165, 190, 278, 281, 282,
Congdon, Thomas 251
Connell, ... 51
Cook, David 227
Cook, George 170
Coombe C. 45
Coombe, William 28, 45, 172,
Cooper, Jeanette 71
Cooper, Jonathon 167
Copeland, George H. 33, 120,
126, 140, 284,
Coppin, Thomas 188
Cotton, Richard 205, 219, 220,
222, 223, 224, 229,
Courtice, Andrew Cory 28, 116,
140,

312

Jackson, James 115
Jackson, Row 279
Jacobs, Mrs. J. 45
Jacobs, James 27
Jago, Martha 202
James, Phillip 27, 28, 57, 66, 108, 128, 178, 184, 185, 186, 205, 209, 219, 220, 223, 228,
James, William 86
Jaquith, ... 256
Jarvis, Mrs. ... 89
Jeffery, ... 103
Jeffery, William 267
Jennings, R. 45
Johns, Miss S.J. 47
Johns, George 281
Johnson, Leo A. 98
Johnston, Justin 37
Johnston, Thomas 62
Johnston, William 184
Jolliffe, ... 251
Jolliffe, Jean 244, 248
Jolliffe, Samuel 94, 260, 265, 270, 271, 283, 290,
Jolliffe, William 28, 45, 52, 66, 120, 138, 140, 142, 251, 252, 253, 257, 260, 271,
Jones, ... 137, 183
Jones, Ann 159
Jones, Fergus O. 92, 203, 278, 281,
Jones, John 159
Jones, Lewis 148
Julian, Richard 90

Katerson, Richard 55
Keeler, Charles 86
Kelly, Arthur 122
Kemeys, John 66, 83, 92, 112,
Kemlo, David 80

Kenner, Henry 52, 57, 58, 92, 165, 257, 260,
Kenner, John 28, 52, 99,
Kenner, William 92, 99, 116, 125, 140,
Kernick, Jim 170
Kernick, William 169
Kestle, ... 164
Kestle, James D. 26, 33, 92, 189, 220, 222,
King, ... 8
King, George 89
King, Martha 89
Kinley, James 231
Kinley, Samuel 231
Kinley, William 13, 38, 116, 140, 213, 270, 281, 308
Kinsey, John 6, 7, 8, 13, 92, 131, 152, 165, 178, 180,
Kinsman, Rev. 274
Kirby, ... 101
Knight, ... 161
Knight, D. 168
Knight, J. 45
Knight, John 168
Knight, Miss E.A. 45
Knight, Miss M.J. 45
Kopp, Rita Bone 101,
Krause, ... 163

Lacey, Albert J. 25, 26
Ladu, ... 291
Laird, James 218,
Lambert, Nancy 47
Lambert, Robert 47
Lamont, ... 179
Langdon, John 43,
Langlois, Mary 219
Lavis, J.R. 55
Lawry, Julio(?) 93

318

319

320

Wedge, E. 103
Wedge, T. 103
Weese, George 187
Weir, F.W. Rev. 113
Wellington, Peter 27
Wells, Mr. 239
Welsh, Ann 159
Welsh, Richard 159
Werry, Agnes M. 48
Werry, B. 46
Werry, John H. 48
Werry, H. 49
Werry, P. 49
Werry, Peter 55
Werry, Thomas 301, 304
Werry, William 47, 48
Westaway, William 198
Westcott, E. 45
Westcott, Elizabeth 159
Westcott, Henry 159
Westcott, Mrs. Isaac G. 168
Westcott, J. 45
Weyler, ... 143
Wheeler, Thomas 261
White, ... 103, 163
White, W. 45
Whitlock, Annie 304
Whitlock, Francis M. 66, 140,
150, 154, 173, 283,
Whitlock, James 129
Whitlock, Jesse 6, 57, 58, 92,
103, 144, 165, 166, 204, 205,
206, 216, 220, 304, 308
Whitlock, Silas 171
Wickett, Lewis, W. 16, 33, 115,
140, 165, 279, 281,
Wight, G. 47
Wight, R. 47
Wight, W. 49
Wilcox, Jane 159

Wilcox, Paul 159
Wildish, Joseph 267
Wilford, Amos 259
Wilford, Elizabeth Bartil 259
Williams, ... 254
Williams, Daniel 16, 122, 147,
150, 153, 172,
Williams, Miss H. 45
Williams, Jesse 88
Williams, John 5, 12, 15, 89,
108, 111, 114, 116, 171, 190,
257, 270,
Williams, John J. 86
Williams, Richard 129
Williams, Samuel 27
Williams, T. 49
Willison, William 272
Wiloughby, ... 307
Wills, James 158
Willwood, William 115
Wilson, Ann 261
Wilson, John 176
Wilson, George 91
Wilson, Maggie 261
Wilson, Robert 168
Windatt, W. 46
Wingrove, William 94
Wood, Samuel Casey 87
Woodger, Frederick 92,
Woodley, ... Sr. 49
Woodley, John 184
Woodley, R. 49
Woodley, T. 45
Woodman, William 12, 74, 111,
198, 206, 217,
Worsley, Edwin 81
Wright, J. 47

Yelland, John Gibbs 45, 144,
220, 222, 236

List of Contributors

Alves, Helen
Bourgault, Diane
Boyce, Gerry
Cameron, Wendell
Chellow, Gail
Collings, Donna
Cook, Karen
Cooke, William
Cooper, Jeanette
Curnoe, W. Glen
Curry, Erica
Ebbott, Ralph
Forjan, Janet
Furness, Gordon
Goode, Mabel
Hicks, Ann
Jackson, Wes
James, Wendy
Jolliffe, Jean
Kerslake, Shirley
Kopp, Rita Bone
Mair, Nathan
Martindale, Bob
McCallum, James
McClelland, Bonnie
Page, Jill
Paynter, Mary
Rosen, Marg
Rowe, Ann
Rumbles, Shirley
Rumpel, Jack W.
Schmid, Helen Lewis
Temple, Pat
Thomas, Morley
Thompson, Roberta

Thompson, Reg
Wilson, Audrey Kent
Young, Gord
Anglican Church Niagara
    Diocese
Burlington Historical Society
Cobourg Historical Society
Federated Church, Chagrin
    Falls
Georgina Historical Society
Hamilton Public Library
Hastings County Historical
    Society
Ingersoll Heritage
National Historic Sites - Parks
    Canada
Ohio Wesleyan University
Oxford County Library and
    Archives
Oxford Historical Society
Pickering Library & Archives
Scugog Shores Historical Mus.
Seventh Town Historical Soc
Stratford-Perth Archives
Trent Valley Archives
Tweed Heritage Society
Twist, William - Christ Church
    Community Museum
Uxbridge Township Museum
Uxbridge-Scott Museum &
    Archives
Western Reserve Historical Soc
Windsor Community Museum